# Working Up a Storm

JEANNE M. PLAS, Ph.D.

KATHLEEN V. HOOVER-DEMPSEY, Ph.D.

# Working Up a Storm

*Anger, Anxiety, Joy, and Tears on the Job*

W · W · NORTON & COMPANY · NEW YORK · LONDON

*First Edition*

The text of this book is composed in Times Roman, with display type set in Typositor Windsor.
Composition and manufacturing by the Haddon Craftsmen. Book design by Marjorie J. Flock.

Library of Congress Cataloging-in-Publication Data

Plas, Jeanne M.
  Working up a storm/Jeanne M. Plas, Kathleen V.
  Hoover-Dempsey.—1st ed.
    p.   cm.
  Includes index.
    1. Work—Psychological aspects.  2. Emotions.  I. Hoover-Dempsey,
Kathleen V.  II. Title.
HF5548.8.P49  1988
158.7—dc19              88-4840

ISBN 0-393-02612-4

W. W. Norton & Company, Inc., 500 Fifth Avenue, New York, N.Y. 10110
W. W. Norton & Company, Ltd., 37 Great Russell Street, London WC1B 3NU

1 2 3 4 5 6 7 8 9 0

*Dedicated to
Barbara Strudler Wallston
with feelings of
love, respect, and loss*

# Contents

# Introduction

WHETHER CONSCIOUSLY OR UNCONSCIOUSLY, most people believe that emotions are messy, are almost never productive, and will always interfere with clear thought. Many think that emotions are personal and have few legitimate functions at work because the workplace is for getting the job done, for the cool application of reason in the service of production. The workplace is not for the boisterous, the giddy, the sad, the anxious, or the tearful. Those who are emotional do not belong in the office, the laboratory, the factory, or wherever serious "grown-up" people are trying to earn a living.

But in fact, emotions do pervade the workplace. They always have and always will.

Feelings—the pleasant ones and the uncomfortable ones—have always served positive productive work goals. They are often responsible for personal commitment and corporate excellence. They fuel the energy that ensures the creation and completion of projects that matter. They signal the emergence of critical problems, like project derailments, compromised values, or goals under fire. When people are most committed, most involved, and most concerned about outcomes, emotions are very definitely present and very often expressed.

Beliefs which downplay the presence and function of emotions on the job, which declare that emotions and emotional employees belong elsewhere until control returns are suspect at best and destructive at worst. They mask and subvert the reality that emotions are vital to personal commitment and productivity on the job.

The real issue is not whether emotions belong on the job but how people can make emotions work for them rather than against them.

Perhaps in no other aspect of work life today have the variety of expectations and the press to do it well, do it fast, and do it in a way that reflects personal credit on one's own ability emerged more strongly than they have with the issue of emotions in the workplace. As pace and pressure to produce have increased, so, too, have opportunities for frustration, disagreement, misunderstanding, and poor communication.

For example, everyone worries about burnout on the job these days. Countless words have been written about the subject, but the bottom line is that people burn out at work because their emotions burn out. How well people deal with feelings at work—their own and other people's—constitutes the critical difference between those who burn out in stressful situations and those who do not.

Emotions are as important for successful work as they are for successful marriage or successful parenting. The work setting requires that emotions be expressed and received from others in different ways from the manner in which they typically are in personal lives. But deal with emotions people must. Whether individuals are conscious of them and channeling them or unaware of them yet controlled by them, feelings make a big difference in what gets done and how it gets done at work.

But emotions function differently at work than they do at home and require different responses there than in more private settings. Most of us have heard countless words of advice from family and friends on how to deal with feelings in personal relationships. Hundreds of books emphasize the role of emotions in successful marriage, child rearing, friendships, dating, health, and a host of other personal issues. There are few suggestions out there, however, for developing effective ways to handle anger, anxiety, joy, or tears on the job.

In fact, people have characteristic ways of experiencing and expressing feelings and of receiving the emotions of others while on the job. But most people aren't aware of that. Sometimes they recognize that certain co-workers (or bosses) have unique ways of dealing with personal feelings or others' emotions at work. However, most people have trouble identifying their own patterns of emotional response and action in the workplace.

Our interest and work in this area began about twelve years ago, as we explored a question raised by some preprofessional people in one of our doctoral training programs. Deeply, almost secretly, these women had been privately wondering if it really could be true that they were as successful and competent as many supervisors and observers had testified, given that they had "broken down" in tears over work-related issues and, perhaps worst of all, had occasionally felt tears threaten to flow while they were actually on the job. The results of our investigations into weeping by professional women at work led us to broaden our studies to include the work-related tears of men.

Over the years we have come to identify many differences and similarities between women and men in the experience of workplace tears. We have also collected information on the frequencies and reasons for choking up or crying at work for both sexes and have identified the most common styles that people have for dealing with their own tears at work as well as those shed by others. One of the most striking findings to emerge from this project has been an awareness that crying on the job has been a "closet" experience for the vast majority of the many people who have dealt with their own tears at work. Those who have choked up or cried (both men and women) tend to believe that they are among the few people who have ever done so. And those who have experienced great discomfort at not knowing what to do when someone has cried in front of them at work tend to assume that the incompetence they feel at those moments is uniquely their own. Neither assumption is correct.

Early in our work it became clear that, for both men and women, when tears appear at work, they are a manifestation of a wide variety of emotions that might range from joy to frustration. Therefore, our interest quickly broadened to include emotions in general at work. As we began to explore a broad range of emotions on the job, we turned to people in workplaces across the country. Our interviews with them focused on the emotions they experienced most often at work and those they considered the most problematic or important within work settings: anger, anxiety, and feelings of joy, appreciation, and caring.

Most of the working population has felt anger, anxiety, and joy at some time during their work lives. But people differ widely in how they feel these emotions and what they do with them. Human beings show great individuality in their styles of expressing emotions and in their patterns of responding to the feelings of others. While many styles may "work" in the same job setting, the unique ways in which people express and respond to emotions on the job, and the fit between personal style and workplace culture, can be critical for job success.

As a result of our interviews with many people in a variety of settings and occupations, we have identified the most common styles that people have developed for coping with emotions at work. Each style is described in the chapters that follow; the composite descriptions are based on the real situations and experiences of the many people we interviewed. Styles of experiencing and expressing anger, for example, include *slow burners*, *tinderbox* people, and the *I don't get mad, I just get even* type of response. Among typical anxiety styles we found those who *deny their emotions* and those who can *make it useful*. Crying styles also differ and include *submergers*, *deniers*, and those who get the *surprise of a lifetime* when they realize that tears have formed in their eyes at work.

Styles of expressing joy and caring are similarly varied and include people with very different approaches, like the *I run a business, not a charity*! and *I just don't know how to handle all that*! groups. Styles of responding to emotions in the workplace tend to be equally diverse, ranging from those who leave the scene when someone gets angry at them to the *I just want to help* reactors who swing into action when someone cries in front of them.

The importance of the varied styles of expressing and responding to workplace emotions lies not in the fact that some styles are "right" and some "wrong" but rather in the reality that each style has its advantages and disadvantages. Each may be effective, in light of personal characteristics and workplace expectations. Ultimately the effectiveness is dependent on the individual, the demands of the job, and the culture of the workplace.

The power of a specific work culture to elicit some emotional styles and stifle others cannot be overstated. For example, *I run a business, not a charity*! people cannot survive in some work environments, notably those that require teamwork and allegiance to group-developed values. And people who always keep the lid on their emotions—those who are unable or don't want to express strong feelings like anger—may not be well suited to work in environments that rely on high energy and emotional exchange in order to produce and market the creative product.

As we talked with people about their work-related experiences with emotions, we heard countless stories of the various problems that people have found to be associated with the styles they employ for dealing with emotions at work. We have responded to these issues by developing step-by-step strategies that can be used to create style changes. Throughout, however, it is important to recognize that no single style or set of change strategies can possibly be appropriate or useful for everyone. Each person is unique. And each holds dear a personal set of values and attitudes. Personalities and styles reflect these realities. In fact, the most effective and satisfied people at work usually have developed styles for feeling, expressing, and receiving emotions that are compatible extensions of personal values.

Creative and competent work results when working people retain individuality and commitment to personal values while on the job. Equally important, good work requires that people recognize the influences of the specific work cultures that surround them. Ultimately, however, results at work—the failures and the successes—are dependent upon personal styles of experiencing, expressing, and receiving emotions. Changing styles that are ineffective can transform the energy trapped in "working up a storm" into exciting opportunities rather than uncomfortable scenes and wasted time. Emotions are as important at work as they are at home or anywhere else. Effort devoted to understanding one's own emotional styles and those of co-workers can pay off—in increased personal satisfaction and greater corporate output.

# Acknowledgments

MANY PEOPLE have directly and indirectly contributed to the work on which this book is based and to the writing project itself. We are especially grateful to the hundreds of men and women who took the time to talk to us about their experiences with emotions at work. Without their honesty and openness we could not have developed our understanding of the dynamics of emotions in the workplace. The spirit of these contributors can be found throughout these pages.

Special thanks go to the chairperson of our Department of Psychology and Human Development at Peabody College of Vanderbilt University, Howard M. Sandler, who provided instrumental support and encouragement just when we needed it. Barb Carroll, Sandy Chauvin, Linda McClure, Kathy Adams, and Corinne Bickman were part of a great office team that made many contributions that made a difference. Marcie Pospichal, Mike Miernicki, Matt Ebeling, and Karen Byrne provided very helpful research assistance.

Ruby M. Saks supplied background material, editorial comment, technical assistance, and some much appreciated emotional support during the important initial months of the project's life. We are very appreciative of her contributions.

Our thanks go also to Gary Gore, Vanderbilt University designer, who connected us with the right person at W.W.Norton, who connected us with our editor, Linda Healey. Linda's immediate enthusiasm for the project and her expert assistance in the development of the book meant a great deal. When Linda moved to another publishing house, Carol Houck Smith, with insight, competence and effectiveness, shepherded the project through its final stages. We are deeply grateful for our association with Carol.

We both have special lists of supporters whom we are delighted to acknowledge. Jeanne Plas (with smiles and applause) thanks Augie Hermann, Susan Underwood, Judith Davis, Midge Ross . . . and most especially Michael Raymond. Each gave support, a bit of magic at times, and many precious feelings. In his or her own way each communicated something very important about faith, trust, and the things that truly matter in life. Kathleen Hoover-Dempsey offers special thanks to her family: Randy Hoover-Dempsey, most especially for faith and commitment, and her children—Joshua, Jesse, and Jordan—who, with Randy, have given countless gifts of energy, interest, humor, and perspective. Her thanks also go to Kristin, for enthusiasm; to Jacquelyn Reher and Jane Stranch, for very helpful advice; and to Kay and Burt Hoover, for abiding support.

Acknowledging the importance of the contributions of our late colleague Barbara Strudler Wallston is difficult because there are too many contributions to list and because she is gone. Barbara's role in our professional and personal lives was unique and important. She was special—and we miss her.

# Working Up a Storm

# 1

# Anger in the Workplace

It is easy to fly into a passion—anyone can do that—but to
be angry with the right person to the right extent and at the
right time and with the right object and in the right
way—that is not easy, and it is not everyone who can do it.

— ARISTOTLE

You want to know how story go, wait till quarrel come.

— CARIBBEAN PROVERB

THERE WERE FOUR PEOPLE involved in the huffing and shouting
match that started at eight twenty-five that morning and didn't
really end until almost three weeks later. Some of the observers
thought that Laura, if not at fault, was at least at the center of
it somehow. Others thought Gary had started the whole thing. At least
three people ended up blaming it on someone who had been out of town
for three days and wasn't even there at the time.

One of the surest truths about anger at work is that when it happens,
people will automatically try to figure out who was at fault. Sometimes
observers will shrug their shoulders and declare that all parties were to
blame; rarely will people locate the problem in situations rather than
people.

Laura, the thirty-six-year-old life-styles editor of a large metropolitan newspaper, had held that job exactly fourteen months on the day
in question. She liked her job. She was good at it. She was well paid.
As she left the house that morning, she was vaguely aware that she was
anxious over something. She tried to figure out what the anxiety was
all about as she sat in downtown traffic for twenty minutes, waiting for
a single lane of rush-hour traffic to ease on by a jackhammer crew. She
finally passed her mood and the day off as just a bad Wednesday
morning.

Most often Laura was a no-nonsense kind of person at work. She
limited her emotions on the job to the positive ones. She smiled a lot
and was particularly respected for her energy level, and colorful writing

style. Laura believed that the best way to get good work from people in her department was to be aware of everything that was going on at all times and to be instrumentally and emotionally supportive of her staff. She kept her own problems—personal and professional—to herself.

As soon as Laura arrived at work that morning, the state editor caught her arm and offered congratulations on a particularly gutsy story on AIDS that she had run the previous Sunday. When she got to her desk, she saw that her computer terminal actually *had* been fixed and that the long-overdue in-house repairman had left a daisy on top of it along with a note soliciting forgiveness. Thus, the day was off to a better start than she'd anticipated when the managing editor hollered across the newsroom to her semipartitioned corner. "Meet me at the coffeepot," he yelled. "We've got a problem."

Gary had been the managing editor of that newspaper for eleven years. He was the career managing editor type, not likely to move up, but well respected in the tough frontline position that he occupied. He wielded a lot of power at the paper. He wasn't necessarily known for his tact, but people at the paper always said that he had good instincts, that he knew what was worth sending a reporter out to cover and which tips weren't worth answering the phone for. On that particular morning he was feeling quite a bit younger than his fifty-one years. Before work, his son had called to tell Gary that he was going to stick it out at college after all. The night before, he had successfully made a spaghetti dinner for a new woman in his life who seemed more important to him than any woman he had met since his divorce four years before. This morning, like most mornings at the paper, he was on automatic pilot.

Gary was the kind of person that people make room for, and he held the kind of job title that often elicits deference. When he wanted people to get things done faster, he yelled a little louder. When he saw something that deserved praise, he gave praise where it was due. He respected people's personal lives and personal business. He prided himself on being fair. Beyond these efforts, Gary paid little attention to his effect on other people's emotions or productivity. But he got the job done.

About five minutes before all the shouting started that morning, Cynthia had been called to the coffeepot area by Laura. And Hank had wandered into the conversation as well.

Cynthia was twenty-eight, bright, efficient, and emotionally expressive. She ran six miles every morning just for the sheer joy of it. Cynthia came from a long line of newspaper people and was one of Laura's very best writers.

Hank was ten years older than Cynthia. He was quick-witted and humorous, known for teasing all the women at the paper and for being able to drink everyone under the table at the annual picnic. He had been attracted to Cynthia for months but had kept his distance, knowing he would take advantage of the first real opportunity he could find to ask her out without getting "shot down." Hank was one of the best city hall reporters that the newspaper had ever had, but he was a little worried lately about where he was going in the newspaper business.

When Laura had joined Gary at the coffeepot, she began the conversation by complimenting him on an investigative series he had instigated on road contracting corruption at the state level. Gary said, "Yeah, thanks," and without inhaling a second time continued: "You're going to have to kill this thing I hear your people are doing on the quality of life in the west suburbs. You've got the water issue in that thing, and we're not ready to do anything on the water until we get more facts. I've got Hank working on an investigative piece, and until we're ready to go with that, I don't want water even mentioned in this paper. Tell your person—is it Cindy?—to give all she's got on the water to Hank."

He turned abruptly to walk away, and Laura touched his arm to detain him, saying, "Wait a minute, Gary. Cynthia's the one who dug up the stuff that got you people interested in this story in the first place. It's her story, and it's definitely a life-styles issue. This water business is a big part of the quality of life over there. We're going to have to work something out on this."

Laura called to Cynthia just as Hank was within hearing distance. He ambled on over as he heard the words *water* and *Cynthia,* figuring that the conversation was going to be of some interest. After a few sentences passed among the four of them, Gary was irritated. He didn't know what Laura's problem was, and he didn't have time to find out. He also wasn't all that interested. Underneath those particular responses, there was a strong desire not to have anyone rob him of his exceptionally good mood that morning.

Laura was angry. She and Cynthia had been working on this story for weeks, and it was going to be a good one. She privately granted Gary the point that there was a thin line here between a life-styles interest and a hard-news story, but she held firmly to the value that in this business the one who gets the story first gets to use it. Her anger was well controlled, but her words were just a little clipped.

Cynthia was just reacting. Basically she was afraid that the best story she had produced in a year was about to be yanked away from her. The part of the story on the water was her favorite part. She believed that this kind of journalism was what the life-styles section needed. It was stories like this that would stimulate thought and community interest. Comments about the water belonged in her story, especially since she was the one who had dug up the most startling facts about the issue. Cynthia wasn't aware that she was afraid, and some other emotion was threatening to display itself.

Hank was somewhat puzzled but mostly hurt. Cynthia kept glaring at him. Laura wouldn't take her attention off Gary and kept ignoring Hank's comments. And Hank couldn't figure out why his boss had let this happen when just yesterday Gary had given him the definite impression that this switch of story and information from Cynthia to him was just fine with the life-styles people. Hank felt innocent, attacked, and somewhat betrayed.

At a point when there was an awkward pause in the debate, Hank took advantage of the momentary silence to snap that the editor in chief, who was out of town at the time, could get out a heck of a better paper if he'd just establish some clear territorial boundaries for a change. Gary commented that there wasn't any boundary problem to worry about. "Society page girls like Cindy here," he snapped, "just need to write about what they're supposed to write about." Cynthia was halfway through an angry threat to the effect that people had better stop calling her Cindy when a couple of tears formed in her eyes. Somebody told somebody else to "stuff it," as Hank curtly commented that when Laura got her priorities straight, he'd be happy to work this out with Cynthia. Then somebody knocked over a coffee cup, and someone else grabbed a newspaper and threw it down on the coffee. Within ten seconds the coffee area was empty, and the noise level in the newsroom had dropped by over half as people stopped what they were doing to take it all in.

## What Is Anger?

The people around the coffeepot that morning were angry. That's obvious. But just what is anger anyway? Psychologists and other social scientists can't agree. There is no way to measure anger, so our quantification-oriented culture has found it difficult to assess and even harder to understand. Surprisingly, most social scientists today are not engaged in a direct study of human emotions in general, let alone anger in particular.

During the last half of the nineteenth century, when the science of psychology was brand-new, a large number of psychologists did devote their scientific careers to the goal of describing and understanding human emotions. However, controversy and confusion quickly arose, and the young science of psychology abandoned close attention to human emotion in favor of studying issues that seemed to require prior attention, such as how learning occurs.

Despite the current profusion of confusions and disagreements about anger in the world of social science, it is possible, at least, to get substantial agreement these days on some of the most basic ideas. For example, many philosophers and psychologists agree that rage is something that animals typically experience while only human beings can experience anger. No matter where in the sequence of events our knowledge of our own anger occurs, it cannot be experienced independent of our personal interpretation of the situation, something animals cannot do. It is our reasoning faculties that make it possible for us to understand an event and to react to it with anger. Cynthia's angry statement that people had better stop calling her Cindy reflects a multitude of attitudes, both personal and cultural. It would be impossible for your dog, *Spot,* to react with anger if Gary had referred to him as *Spotty.* Anger is a distinctly human experience, the result of our ability to invest life with meaning.

Knowing this, we can begin to see that emotion and rationality are not opposites. Indeed, a major part of successful parenting lies in the ability to help the child learn to use reason and feeling harmoniously. Feelings such as desire, anger, and affection are the most useful tools children have for understanding their needs. The parent's task is to help the child attend to these important messages and to learn ways of allowing reason to temper and guide feelings so as to get needs met. When you were a child, one of your major learning tasks was to develop the ability to express your anger without hurting others or yourself.

There is a continual interplay between anger and reason in the adult. The interpretations of our world that reason provides are necessary for the creation of important feelings. When someone violates our sense of the way things ought to be, we tend to blame, and anger is the natural result. This is why some theoreticians today are convinced that anger is a peculiarly moral emotion. Our anger is based on our sense of values, a reasoned understanding of what is right and what is wrong.

The term *moral,* as used here, refers to an individual's unique set of attitudes, standards, and values growing from a sense of what is right and wrong. We do not mean to say that the moral aspect of anger is related to a single standard of right and wrong and that everyone who gets angry is doing so in the service of what is *truly* right. A boss who gets angry at the newest employee because all the office rules have not been learned within the first hour of work is not angry in support of a commonly agreed-upon set of standards. Nonetheless, the boss's anger may be "moral," in light of what we mean by the term here. In this context, the sentence "He has bad morals" makes sense. That thought reflects that his moral judgments are based on attitudes and values that most of us do not endorse. Often we use the idea that a person's anger is not *justified* to convey that same thought.

As we will see in the next chapter, some people have trouble getting angry and expressing it because they need to believe that their anger is fully justified before they will permit it. Since we all are unique in our understanding of what life is all about and how it should be lived on a daily basis, it's usually impossible to be quickly sure that almost everyone else in the world would agree that a specific moment of anger is justified. In most cases everyone else probably wouldn't. Within the American judicial system there is a sentence that expresses this same idea, revealing our belief that law is necessary: "Reasonable men differ." The harmonious interplay of feelings and reason within healthy adult human beings does not guarantee agreement among people. What is guaranteed is uniqueness, different sets of interpretations about what is right and wrong in any situation.

Gary's lack of understanding of Laura's "problem" occurred in part because he was unaware of how she was interpreting the situation. He did not know that Laura was asserting for herself at that moment the conventional newspaper business value that the person who gets the story gets the by-line. She also might have been cuing into a common social value that interprets brusqueness as lack of respect, and therefore, her anger might have been increased because of her understanding that Gary had violated a second norm she held dear. For his part, Gary's irritation was motivated by his own interpretations of what was right and wrong in that situation. His primary valuing just then was connected to the importance of efficiently using his time, the deeply rooted belief that "hard news is hard news" and thus easily recognizable, and his emphasis on the personal importance of maintaining his own good mood that morning.

Angry feelings, like those experienced by these four newspaper people, are among those emotions that emerge from communication glitches and value clashes at work. Most often the angry feelings are tightly managed. Often they are controlled so quickly and effectively that we fail to notice the possibilities for seriously angry feelings. We simply move on through our busy days, perhaps feeling a little ill at ease or out of sorts. When we consider the prevalence of this kind of work-related episode, it's easier to see that controlled anger is indeed more common at work than many have previously assumed.

### Rage, Anger, and Irritation

For purposes of the discussion that follows it will be useful to distinguish rage from anger and irritation. We think of rage in human beings as an experience similar to that of rage in an animal. Someone is caught in an event, is suffused with feelings, and is driven by those feelings. For a time the personality is beyond all rational control. This experience is sometimes successfully interpreted as "temporary insanity" in American litigation. Given this definition, many of us have never seen an adult who is truly enraged.

In contrast, anger involves an interchange between rationality and feeling. Seneca, an early Roman philosopher and social commentator was right on target some two thousand years ago when he said, "Wild beasts and all animals, except man, are not subject to anger for while anger is the foe of reason, it is nevertheless born only where reason dwells." He was one of the first Western thinkers to become aware that when your intellect interprets a situation as offensive, demeaning, unjust, and the like, it is natural to have a physical reaction to that information. The visceral experience is unpleasant, usually involving a tightening of various muscle groups and a change in the flow of blood through the circulatory system. We may clench our teeth, grit our teeth, stiffen up, clench our hands, purse our lips, or have trouble breathing. Statements like "I got so angry I couldn't see straight" illustrate the loss of muscle flexibility that accompanies the feeling of anger.

Irritation is akin to anger; however, it is a much milder version of anger. When you are irritated, you are provoked, but the experience involves more hassle than intensity. For some people, irritation is a precursor of anger. They do not suddenly get angry over anything; countless irritations build up, and the feeling changes from annoyance to the stronger emotion of anger.

## Our Denial of Anger

Laura and Gary and Hank and Cynthia were pretty angry in the coffee area that morning. And while each of them experienced the anger in a different way and acted very differently, each also believed that angry outbursts don't occur very often where they work and that they aren't the kind of people who get involved in angry episodes on the job.

There are two reasons for this apparent denial of the rather universal phenomenon of anger in the workplace: a confusion of the *feeling* of anger with anger-generated *behaviors* and the strong messages within our culture that it is childish to be angry in public places, especially at work.

Most Americans equate anger with aggression. For most of us, to *be* angry means to *act* angry. Therefore, along with Laura, we're likely to say that we do not get angry at work. Most of us rarely yell, hit, scream, slam, snarl, or huff off when we're out there earning our livings. We don't tell people off, put them in their place, or pound some sense into them. Nonetheless, we do get angry.

### Anger and Aggression

We do not necessarily react with directed behavior when we are angry. The automatic equation of anger and aggression in our society is unnecessary and unfortunate. An animal must act on its feeling of rage unless a competing feeling, such as fear, is stronger. Very young children act out aggressively when enraged, but adult human beings are capable of simply seething. Jake, an articulate young Washington attorney, tells of the time his senior partners called a rare staff meeting for all of the firm's legal associates. After an hour or so of plodding through a simple accounting of all the cases the firm was working on at the time, Benson, the most senior partner, launched into a description of a case that Jake had won the previous month. He explored Jake's handling of the case from several different angles, concluding every few sentences or so that an approach such as Jake had used was destined to fail nine times out of ten. Benson wondered what the law schools were teaching these days. He wondered why young attorneys didn't ask as many questions as they did in "his day." He wondered if everybody appreciated the important lesson that could be learned from the discussion. Needless to say, sitting there in front of twelve of his peers, Jake was not one of those who could appreciate the lesson. During the twenty-five minutes that the focus remained on his case, Jake said nothing. He reported that at first he was sure he had turned "beet red" from embarrassment. Pretty quickly, though, the embarrassment turned to another emotion as he found himself with clenched fists at his sides. He then (literally) bit his lip in order to hold back a sharp retort or a sarcastic comment. In telling the story, he remarked that he would have "decked the guy" if he had been a senior partner. "But," he said, "I'm proud to say I didn't get angry!" What Jake meant was that he was proud that he had not given in to his desire to strike back—with a word or a fist. Surely he had been very angry indeed. But as long as he had not acted on his anger in an aggressive manner, he felt justified in reporting that he had not become angry.

A lot of anger exists at work. We simply don't often express it with an aggressive act, word, or tone of voice. Most often we do what we once were taught that adults do: We control our tempers. And then, like Jake, we proudly report that despite incredible provocation, we "didn't get angry."

The difference between feeling anger and expressing anger cannot be overstressed. The consequences of a lifetime of experiencing unexpressed anger have been much discussed in the medical and psychiatric literature. People who habitually "swallow" their anger have been warned that any number of dire consequences might befall them, ranging from ulcers to clinical depression. On the other hand, the consequences of habitually losing one's temper have been well documented as well. Marriages have been broken, children have been hurt, and jobs have been lost.

Most mental health experts maintain that you should not habitually restrain anger or habitually express it. They say that consistently doing one or the other is what causes the personal and social ills associated with either of these emotional styles. At first glance the reasonableness of that position is obvious. Extremes in anything usually aren't good for us. But how do you know when a bit of anger should be expressed and when it should be stifled? For that matter, how is it possible in the midst of today's very stressful work situations to be quickly and certainly and consistently sure that you *are* angry? When should you take a stand, and when should you wait for just the right moment to come along? And if you wait, do you lose something important—like spontaneity? Is anger that is planned and controlled really anger? Perhaps of ultimate importance is the multitude of issues surrounding the effects of anger. What do you gain and lose when you express anger? What do you gain and lose when you don't express it? What positive and negative effects do those around you experience when you make a decision either to reveal your anger or to withhold it?

The answer to those questions must be: "It depends." At work, as in other places, dealing with anger effectively—yours or someone else's—depends on who you are and what situation you are involved in. No single answer can fit for each of us because we have different

values, histories, and goals. Yet we fall into fairly recognizable categories when it comes to anger and its expressions in the workplace.
Therefore, it's possible for you to discover which styles of anger and
anger expression tend to be yours. And it's possible to work toward
style improvements that feel comfortable to you and are useful.

However, before we look at anger styles, it's important to take a
look at the second reason why many people deny that anger is commonplace in our work settings: our shared belief that expressions of anger
in adulthood are childish, the result of an inability to control oneself
as an adult should.

## Anger and Our Cultural History

Chances are great that you—as we did—grew up with the belief that
anger was something you possessed; you had it or didn't have it at any
given moment. Furthermore, most of us were taught that having it or
not was largely determined by personal temperament. As twentieth-
century children grew up, comments such as "Nothing riles that boy"
and "She's got her father's temper" were commonplace and well understood by adults and children alike. A tendency toward anger or
equanimity was believed to reside exclusively within a person.

Most of us who are adults today have grown up without an appreciation of the historical and cultural significance of anger. We have
tended to accept that throughout history all people have experienced
anger as we do in the twentieth century. We think that contemporary
attitudes and struggles with anger are as old as humanity itself. Anger,
however, is an experience, not a "thing." It is conditioned by the
characteristics of a situation and the values and norms of a culture
every bit as much as it is influenced by a given person's temperament,
a term that refers here to one's customary set of dispositions resulting
from personal history and physiological makeup.

To a large extent an individual's culture makes it possible for him
or her to feel angry in any given situation. Consider the ancient South
American Indian cultures—and many others—that offered human beings as sacrifice to the gods in supplication or thanksgiving. Indeed, the
Old Testament tells of Abraham's obedience to God's command to take
his son Isaac to the appointed spot for sacrifice. While the ancient
Indian priests and the Hebrew Abraham no doubt felt a great many
emotions, such as sorrow and anxiety, it is probably unlikely that anger
was prominent among those feelings since in those situations the sac-

rificial act was culturally sanctioned. In contrast, if you were to hear of a contemporary religious ceremony of human sacrifice occurring in this country—or even of one that occurred long ago—you would be capable of feeling extremely strong anger, no matter what your religious persuasion.

In a comparable way our personal histories condition our emotional capabilities. The moral instructions we are heir to have a lot to do with our current understanding of right and wrong as well as with our emotional responses to such issues as injustice, waste, and human insensitivity.

Margie, a research associate who was employed some years ago in a corporation where one of us used to work often returned to her desk out of sorts after a trip to the nearest women's room. Not always, but often enough to be noticeable, she would mumble to herself after these trips in an inaudible but definitely grouchy way. She was also likely to be uncharacteristically sensitive to petty annoyances for a half hour or so following a rest room break. Except for these moments of being strangely in ill humor, she was direct, skilled, efficient, cooperative, and spontaneously witty. What was going on? When the connection between the break and the subsequent attacks of irritation became obvious, Margie was asked that very question, and she readily supplied an answer.

It seems that she had grown up in a neighborhood where disorder was the norm. Both her own parents, however, were adamant in their faith that "Cleanliness is next to godliness." Before taking her research associate position, she had been employed at a place where the rest rooms were always a mess because the company was underfunded and could not afford to hire good maintenance people. In addition, the morale of the total staff was low, contributing to an attitude of indifference toward the work and the surroundings. She said that the rest rooms there always seemed to have dirty paper and water on the floor, smudges on the mirrors, and dirt of unknown origin in the sinks. Margie appreciated some of the reasons for her former co-workers' lethargy in the matter, but she didn't know of any good social excuses for that kind of behavior in her current building. Yet from time to time the rest room was in disorder. That fact challenged Margie's faith in a decent citizenry—and it made her mad. But there was no one handy to blame and thus to get angry at. So, Margie said, while she hadn't really realized it, she was apparently taking her irritation out on whatever little things captured her attention after her rest room trips.

Anger is cultural as well as personal. It is always the product of a transaction between an individual and a particular situation that contains social understandings and expectations. In *Anger, the Misunderstood Emotion* Carol Tavris underscores that idea and exhorts us to push toward a greater understanding of what anger is and how it functions since "anger, like love, has such a potent capacity for good and evil."[1] Tavris complains about what she sees as the contemporary desire to release controls on anger, "letting it all hang out." She says that everywhere we turn, people are telling us to experience our anger and to express it. She implies that the general public thinks a "ventilationist" approach is best, that there is great personal and social good to be realized if we will just get "in touch" with our feelings—especially anger—and then discharge them. Having identified such a general cultural attitude, she then observes that this kind of approach can cause much personal and social harm.

We have reached a different conclusion: that the contemporary general public doesn't believe in ventilating anger. In fact, one of the difficulties with anger at work is that most people assume they should deny its existence when they feel it or see it there. Most mental and physical health professionals believe that attention to repressed and suppressed anger is important for individual development and social growth. However, it is not the case that most working men or women believe that anger and its expression are useful for helping individuals feel good and for getting the job done. When was the last time your boss said, "Go ahead, get angry, we both know it'll be good for both of us"? Occasionally a good neighbor, friend, or relative will suggest that your physician, therapist, or spouse has been right in pointing out that you've been under a lot of stress lately and that keeping some strong feelings to yourself might be contributing to problems you're experiencing. However, these moments are rare in the lives of most people.

During the Middle Ages in Europe anger was legitimized both inside and outside the home. And unequivocally it was an anger that traveled down the hierarchy of status, rather than up. Whoever possessed the greatest social power was in a position to wield that power with as much anger and physical aggression as he saw fit. (And usually it was a he, not a she.) Displays of emotion were the norm. Physical aggression was routinely accepted in many settings. Laws protecting the rights of the worker did not exist even in the minds of most social visionaries of the times. All the rights resided in the employer since it was he who provided the money that kept a man's family alive.

Centuries later things had not changed very much in Europe, and the colonies, of course, such as those in North and South America, reflected the Old World standards and values. Charles Dickens shows us the lives of mid-nineteenth-century people who trudged off to work routinely expecting to receive only a few shillings' pay and to absorb whatever outbursts of anger their employers cared to give. Boys apprenticed to a skilled master or commercial employer were especially vulnerable to angry outbursts. A thorough boxing about the head and shoulders was not uncommon. Indeed, cultural norms for the workplace led employers to expect that physical aggression directed toward young workers would encourage them to work more quickly and with better results. Stories of the personal and livelihood-related plights of such characters as David Copperfield, Oliver Twist, Nicholas Nickleby, and Bob Cratchit reveal a set of social norms that the Western world was beginning to react against, even as Dickens put pen to paper in service of their display. Victorian England was beginning to become a reality that was to have an effect on the personal and social development of people all over the world for years to come. And its influence persists. In fact, an understanding of contemporary attitudes toward angry expressions at work cannot be complete without consideration of Victorian standards and demands.

### Anger and the Victorians

By 1860 or so, when the Victorian age really began to come alive, society had apparently had enough of its own aggressive emotionality. Among the many things that the culture strained to have more control over were anger and aggression, both public and private. As society began to require conservative sexual mores and more stringent social standards in general, domestic violence and the value of the worker came under scrutiny. Change was slow, uneven, and perhaps not always in the long-run best interests of developing human beings. Nonetheless, things changed. For example, the diary of Samuel Pepys, an adoring husband and wealthy, respectable representative of British society, contains this entry for December 19, 1664: "Going to bed betimes last night we waked betimes, and from our people's being forced to take the key to go out to light a candle, I was very angry and begun to find fault with my wife for not commanding her servants as she ought. Thereupon, she giving me some cross answer, I did strike her over her left eye such a blow as the poor wretch did cry out and was in great pain. . . ."[2] In contrast, by the mid-nineteenth century it was becoming very improper among the middle and upper classes for the man of the house to be so aggressive with his wife. However, it was still considered important to be physically aggressive with children "for their own good." Still, the plight of some members of the household was getting better as Europeans and Americans took a closer look at what they were doing in the name of passion and feeling.

At work a new climate was emerging. Charles Dickens's sensitive portrayal of the value, dignity, and plight of his characters reflected an increasing awareness and respect for common lives. While the liberal efforts of such intellectuals as John Stuart Mill began to effect change in the political realm, Dickens's caricatures helped stimulate the new social conscience through literature. Visualize for a moment the abuse that Scrooge heaped upon Bob Cratchit for requesting an extra lump of coal for the fire or an extra hour off at Christmas. Recall the good Cratchit's denial to his wife that Scrooge was beyond the limits of decency as he pointed out to her that his family owed everything to Scrooge, who had a right to expect what he wished from those in his employ. Equally revealing of the emerging sensitivity of the times are the scenes at the beginning and end of *A Christmas Carol* that show Scrooge in conversation with other employers who solicit contributions for the sick and other needy souls. Initially in the story Scrooge reflects the value that those who cannot help themselves deserve nothing from their betters—those who *can* help themselves to a satisfactory standard of living. Scrooge's turnabout by the story's end provides a metaphor for the social conscience of the Victorian age. Even as Dickens wrote, the mood of the marketplace was changing.

As we turned the corner into the twentieth century, the world of work became a different one. Often in response to employer violence, labor unions also became violent in the service of worker goals. And labor eventually managed to dictate to the industrial and commercial world what the financial issues of importance were to be for decades to come. The major item on the agenda was the rights of the worker not only to a more substantial share of the profits but also to better working conditions that included a cessation of social and physical abuse from those higher up the corporate ladder. The boss's anger was no longer an inevitability. An employee's lack of response to that anger was no longer a matter of necessity.

Anger control was far more successful at work than at home in the early days of this century as well as now. One of the strategies that the new personnel specialists advocated involved programs designed to help bosses understand that a worker's annoyance and anger on the job might well be the result of stresses from some problematic situations at home. Those in charge were asked to take that kind of thing into consideration as they attempted to work with an employee's irritability on the job.

By 1920 the art of "management" had been born. This was the beginning of the golden age of management, when all were told, and most believed, that anything at all could get "better" if it were properly managed—your money, career, and anger as well as corporate profits and personnel problems.

Carol Zisowitz Stearns and Peter Stearns have shown that after World War I we believed that our anger at work could be channeled productively into such things as competitive behavior and creative endeavors of every sort. While the overall success of these channeling strategies is unknown, it is indisputable that by 1930 the workplace had changed dramatically from what it had been for the several hundred years prior to the dawn of the Victorian age. While many of the Victorian values gave way to twentieth-century norms, the emphasis on control of feelings and their expression at work was not among the Victorian values that receded to the background. Indeed, the need to "control oneself" in the marketplace was an idea that not so surprisingly found its way to the center of one of the most widely read books of all time, Dale Carnegie's *How to Win Friends and Influence People.*[3] Since its first printing in 1936 over five million copies of this enormously influential work have been sold.

With the publication of his seminal self-help book Dale Carnegie set the standards for work behavior in the United States. Until only very recently these standards have controlled the workplace. While most people who are active in today's American work force have probably never read this book, most of their parents and many of their older bosses have.

For the reasons outlined above, the times were right for Carnegie to design his version of the American dream; nonetheless, he was as much a creator of the corporate future as he was a recipient of the Victorian past. Therefore, if we intend to understand the place at work of emotions in general, and anger in particular, we must understand the Dale Carnegie message.

One of the pioneers of the traveling corporate workshop, Carnegie tells the "rules" for getting along with others, indeed for "winning them over" to you in order to further your goals. The book indirectly conveys several messages. Among them are the beliefs that all people can benefit from and should learn the *same* set of strategies, that appearances are crucial, and that the other person needs to believe that you are more interested in him or her than you are in your own needs and opinions.

Throughout the book Carnegie's efforts to help people be genuinely interested in others turn out to contain lots of advice on impression management—how to make someone *think* you are genuinely interested. For example, in one section Carnegie tells how for years he engaged people he met in conversations about astrology (though he hadn't the "foggiest bit of faith in astrology") in order to encourage them to reveal their birth dates casually. He would then repeat the month and the day to himself over and over and later would write it in his date book. Then, on the person's birthday, he would send a card or telegram. "What a hit it made!" he wrote. "I was frequently the only person on Earth who remembered." The point that needs careful attention here is that strategies like this were designed to make the other person feel special. They were designed to make the individual think that Carnegie considered him or her particularly important—enough so that he would remember a casual mention of a birth date.

The book focuses almost exclusively on encouraging people to develop friendly and interested demeanors at work. Unpleasant feelings are largely ignored, just as if capable people simply didn't have them while on the job. As a result, the concept of anger is hardly mentioned throughout the book! Carnegie had no *use* for anger. He didn't seem to know what to do with it. There is no room in his approach for the feelings of the reader—the person he is attempting to train. In the section telling his readers how to win people to their way of thinking, he presents his only formal comment on anger: *"Control your temper. Remember, you can measure the size of a person by what makes him or her angry."* (Italics added.)[4]

That's all the advice the book has to offer on the subject of this important human emotion. In a way the absence is not so surprising actually since Carnegie has no serious interest in his reader's unique feelings or needs. His struggle is to help his reader learn strategies for managing people. He was interested in indirect influence, as were so many people in those days.

In the United States many people had become uncomfortable with total commitment to individualism as people in various places began simply wanting to get "better," to become more moral, to achieve happier lives through an appreciation of *all* lives. The Second World War contributed to the shift. As it ended, the idea of moving in a more indirect fashion toward the achievement of personal and corporate goals seemed an attractive one. War—the ultimate attempt at direct influence—had a profound influence on most of the Western world. Subsequently the idea of *indirect* influence in international and local affairs became very seductive. It succeeded in capturing the imagination of the times, for it suggested that we might be able to achieve our goals without hurting others, without getting angry, or having them get angry at us.

At its worst this commitment to indirectness resulted in manipulation and the corporate yes-man, who began to show up in the 1950s. The yes-man knows what he wants but takes special care to keep his real attitudes and feelings to himself. If someone higher up—or in a lateral but useful position—states an opinion, yes-men are likely to nod, smile, and remark on the dazzling brilliance that it takes to produce such a powerful thought. While this kind of personality is viewed very negatively by many in our culture, we still have a lot of them around. In fact, it's probably true that each one of us acts like the yes-man occasionally. As Carnegie suggests throughout his book, developing genuine interest and respect for others is almost always satisfying and productive. However, many people have learned that concentrating on creating the *impression* that the other person is important to us in order to further our own goals is bound to become troublesome sooner or later.

Emotions at work are beginning to come of age. We are on the verge of accepting them, understanding their value, and learning effective ways of communicating them on the job. Totally direct and totally indirect approaches are no longer the only options. It's becoming apparent that many people, situations, and goals are best served by a combination of strategies. Spontaneity, emotion, respect, and restraint *can* be part of the same experience at work. Authenticity and dignity are *not* polar opposites.

## With Whom Are We Getting Angry These Days, Where, and Why?

With whom are we getting angry? James Averill, a research psychologist, has reported[5] that over half the angry episodes his subjects have described involved a loved one or some other person who is well known and liked. His subjects reported getting angry with a well known and disliked person only 8 percent of the time. Averill's work and our own interview data strongly suggest that the common belief that we tend to get angry only at our enemies is simply not true. We get angry most often with the people we know and care about.

Averill has further related that targets of angry expressions overwhelmingly report that the angry episodes have helped them realize their own faults. Approximately 75 percent of his several hundred research subjects reported such an outcome. Importantly, 35 percent of the time the men and women in his studies revealed that the relationship in question became weaker after the angry episode. However, more angry episodes seemed to result in a strengthened relationship between the parties involved. People indicated that the relationship improved almost half the time.

Obviously some crucial factors must account for the differences in outcomes here. If an overwhelming majority of us do get important information about our weaknesses from the anger of others that is directed toward us, and if half the time our relationships get better after anger, but often they do not, we must ask ourselves, What are the variables that seem to promote good outcomes? Our discussions with both men and women have shown us that at least two or three of the major factors can be identified with some certainty. For example, when the person who is receiving the anger is permitted to express a wide range of responses in return, things seem to go better. That is, if the target of the anger is encouraged to state another side of the issue in whatever way works best for him or her, it's more likely to be a positive interchange. Also, if angry individuals do not kid themselves about the issues, a strengthened relationship is more likely to result. For example, emotional distance will probably occur when the angry person gives in to the temptation to pretend that his or her anger results from an obviously justifiable reason, rather than disclose what the more authentic reasons might be. It takes a lot of energy to try to convince someone that your anger is logical, justified, and "appropriate" when it truly emerges from feelings of anxiety or jealousy. Often, emotional honesty brings people together while pretense drives them apart—even when the emotion involved is anger.

Huffing off in the midst of discussion is almost always disastrous for both parties concerned. Our interviewees have told us that when an angry person leaves them in the middle of an upsetting episode, they tend to feel abandoned and defensive and suspect that the other is angrier than he or she often really is. Those who abruptly end conversations also usually feel worse than before. In the stalking off there is apparently a moment of exhilaration for some, but it tends not to last. These people remember points they wish they had made and find it doubly difficult to reconnect because of the awkwardness in the last parting.

How often do we feel angry? Many researchers have reported that angry feelings occur with a fair amount of regularity for most people. That is, most of us will feel anger anywhere from two or three times per day to two or three times per month. This does not, of course, mean that we express that anger. Reliable data on the number of times a typical person is likely to *express* anger either at work or in his or her personal life have been almost impossible to discover. Of primary importance is the fact that the "typical person" really doesn't exist. Frequency of expressions of anger vary for each person from year to year, job to job, relationship to relationship. In addition, there is disagreement in the literature on what constitutes expression of anger. For example, if I say nothing in response to your offensive behavior but do indeed stage a work slowdown, does that constitute an expression of my anger? Certainly it is not a direct one.

Many people habitually withdraw and withhold when they are angry. When your child refuses to kiss you good-night because of an imagined or real offense, you are witnessing a very indirect response. Yet there is a message there. Unfortunately some of these indirect messages are so subtle that the intended receiver does not understand what is meant. It is also the case that many people are unaware of their angry feelings and thus unaware of their indirect responses. A spouse may take a little longer than usual coming home from work. Such a behavior might constitute an indirect expression of anger, but if the angry individual is unaware of the feeling and thus has little insight with regard to the behavior of arriving late, should we count it as an expression of anger? If so, how can social scientists possibly collect data concerning these events since in this situation we obviously are not working with a person who has the ability to report on the feeling? He or she really is quite unaware. Whether the person has knowledge of his or her own feeling or not, psychologists sometimes refer to these indirect expressions as passive aggression.

The question of *why* people get angry has been addressed many times during this chapter. Averill has put it this way: "In short, anger is a response to some misdeed. . . . More than anything else, anger is an attribution of blame."[5]

## *Anger: New Understanding*

It is not anger and aggression that are bound together. It is anger and blame. When we are angry, we believe that the other person's behavior was not justified and that the offense could have been avoided if he or she had tried. Rarely do people get angry when they understand that another did what seemed necessary and that any unfortunate consequences were simply unavoidable. This seems to hold true even in situations that involve considerable damage, either emotional or material.

Jerry, an optometrist, overslept by about forty-five minutes one morning a year or so ago. His wife, who was in the habit of reminding him several times each morning that he needed to "get up and get going," was distracted that particular Tuesday by a minor injury that their seven-year-old son had sustained. Because of all the confusion, time slipped by, and Jerry rolled out of bed late, irritable, and hungry. He took the time to stuff a sweet roll down and to drink a cup of coffee. Then, assuring himself that his son was really OK, he headed for the garage and out into the morning traffic. He didn't keep his own schedule at work, his receptionist did, and therefore, he didn't know if he was going to be late for his first appointment that morning or not. He hated the idea of keeping a patient waiting. Bad style, he believed.

As he rounded the corner at Second and Broadway, he realized that if he stepped it up a bit, he could probably make the next light a block away. He stepped it up.

The car he hit was somebody's brand-new station wagon. It still had the pricing information on the rear window. Jerry hadn't even seen the car. But apparently the driver had been pulling into the traffic lane from a parallel parking spot. Responsibility was quite clear. As the driver and her passengers quickly began pointing out, she had already taken possession of the lane when Jerry's car came around the corner like "a bat out of hell." In the first moments of their interaction she asked Jerry what his "problem" was, and he mumbled that he was late for work. She was angry, and she made no effort to conceal that fact. She clenched her fists and snapped that the major problem with the whole city was "drivers like you." She swung her own car door shut forcefully (a failed attempt, however, since there had been some damage to the hinges). What followed after that was fairly typical. We see these scenes all over America every day as we drive on by: Damaged cars, angry drivers, businesslike traffic cops, pacing passengers.

That same month in the same city a hardware department clerk named Tony was getting ready for work, when his pregnant wife, Sally, began screaming in the kitchen. Instantly he had a feeling in his stomach that he had rarely felt—gripping fear.

As he ran downstairs, the only thing on his mind was fear for Sally's pregnancy. Her screaming for him hadn't stopped by the time he hit the first floor, and it was then that he heard the cries of his four-year-old daughter as well. When he swung around the kitchen door frame he saw that his daughter's clothes were on fire and that his wife was frantically trying to throw kitchen towels over her and to press her own body into the flames. He grabbed the child and went crashing through the back door, rolling with her on the ground until the last flame was out. Sally had grabbed a blanket and headed for the car. As she started the motor, Tony slid his daughter onto the blanket in the back seat and got in the rear with her.

Sally was going too fast when she rounded the corner onto the main street in their neighborhood. She sideswiped a car (later she could remember only that it was red), and her car's rear end then slid again into the back of the car she had hit. The violated driver leaped out of her car and began yelling as she realized that the "crazy woman" who had just run into her was not going to stop, that she was going to "leave the scene." She had managed to reach Sally's car and was in the middle of a typical "Look, lady!" sentence when Tony yelled out the back window that his child had just been badly burned and they couldn't stop. As Sally pulled their car back into the traffic lane, the wrathful motorist caught a glimpse of the child's badly burned body. Her anger instantly turned to fear and empathic concern. As she told a friend later, she was sure she would remember the picture of that child lying there for the rest of her life. Later she never felt a moment's anger over that event even though her insurance company's efforts to cite the unfortunate couple failed, and she had to pay the deductible portion of the substantial bill for her automobile's repair.

When there is no possible object of blame, we don't get angry. When our values aren't violated, there is no object of blame. The car that Sally hit was driven by a woman who shared the value that a little girl was far more important than her car. The one that Jerry hit was owned by a woman who did not think that oversleeping was a justifiable reason for ruining her car and her morning. Anger emerges from blame, and blame flows from values.

Fixing responsibility and deciding that you are at least partially justified in doing so constitute two necessary and interwoven components of feeling anger. The more mature we become, and thus better able to listen and to empathize, the less likely it is that we are able to assign unequivocal responsibility for an uncomfortable event. This is especially true for everyday situations such as those we encounter at work.

The better we get at seeing all sides of an issue and appreciating the stresses that affect the behavior of others, the more likely that we will not be comfortably able to blame someone who lets us down. When we can't easily blame, we have trouble permitting ourselves to feel angry. We can't justify it.

It is not uncommon that people find themselves in such a bind. In these situations the most likely target for anger seems to have a good "excuse." When the innocence of another is even partially accepted, some people will direct the blame and anger for pain they have suffered—or seen others suffer—toward a group of people, a type of person, or life itself and its perceived "unfairness." Eventually some even turn the blame and the anger toward their idea of God, the entity they hold ultimately responsible for having created all this.

One Sunday afternoon a woman named Theresa heard people shouting and dogs whining insistently in the backyard of a house near the one she was visiting. She discovered that two men were allowing some hunting dogs to nip and tear at a live rabbit with a broken foot in order to give the dogs their first "taste" of rabbit, thus preparing them for hunting trips that would follow. Theresa was sickened and furious. But she was a bit afraid of those men, and she did not want her blaming to result in confrontation in that situation.

She also felt that she could not fully blame those particular men because she believed they themselves were victims of a set of cultural values that looked upon hunting for sport as a good thing and training exercises such as that one as legitimate. Despite her unsuccessful efforts to understand the motives of these men, she was still angry, feeling that somebody, or something, was responsible for hurting the defenseless rabbit. Eventually, she said, she settled for blaming "stupid human ignorance"—and the dogs. She found herself seeing pictures of those dogs in her mind's eye for several days after the event. Each time the image recurred, she felt anger toward the dogs that bordered on fury. She did not feel angry toward the adults.

Theresa's story provides a good illustration of one of the important points to remember about this complicated emotion. That point is that the objects of our anger, the ones we eventually settle our blame upon, are sometimes strangely chosen. We have to satisfy a host of values as we choose them, and the process is not always a thoughtful one. When anger is present, we are aroused. Unfortunately, when we identify the object of our blame in these situations, we do not always stop to clarify our values or the situation in as reasonable a manner as our ability allows. Even over time we do not always settle upon an object of anger that makes sense to others or often even to ourselves.

Freud used the term *displacement* to describe this phenomenon. He believed that on some occasions you become understandably too threatened to allow yourself to fix the blame for an anger-producing event exactly where it belongs. In these situations you fear that you will lose something important if you get angry at the appropriate person. If you blame the boss, for example, you may get fired. If you blame your spouse, he or she may stop caring for you. If you blame your neighbors, they may write you off. Nonetheless, you are angry. Freud claimed that it is common at such times to turn your anger toward a "safe" object. At work you may become livid at the boss's secretary, truly believing that she, not the boss, was the real culprit in an offensive event. At home you may turn your anger toward the very next family member who enters your line of vision. For example, you may suddenly remember that your son promised to mow the grass two days ago and you abruptly get angry at his irresponsibility. Whether at work or at home, dealing with your anger by kicking the nearest dog has become the classic example of displacement.

Another way in which discomfort with the idea of blaming occurs these days is connected to the heightened awareness we have of the effects of "circumstances" on people's behavior. A couple of hundred years ago everybody assumed that if you did something wrong, you did it because you were bad, or evil, or at best a fool. Those were the days when you could get locked up for stealing a loaf of bread to feed your hungry family, and the incarceration was destined to continue until you paid for the bread—as, of course, you couldn't do when you were behind bars and had no hope of earning any money. Today all codes of justice in Western countries contain the important idea of mitigating circumstances. Most religions also acknowledge the relevance of the circumstances surrounding misbehavior and sin. Contemporary fiction and nonfiction alike are full of references to the idea that a person's behavior, while not at all necessarily determined, is nonetheless often understandable and forgivable as some of the influences in the individual's personal history and the circumstances surrounding the offensive event come to light.

Sometimes a recognition of the stresses a person is under makes it difficult for us to assign enough blame to that person to make it possible even to *feel* angry, much less to do something about it. As we will see later on, some people become habitually unable to deal effectively with anger because they rarely feel justified in blaming another for anything. Most people have been in this position from time to time. This phenomenon is one that sems to have increased in frequency during this century as we have become better at appreciating the difficulties others experience in their lives. Some American Indian groups have passed down an adage that conveys this thought perfectly: "Do not criticize a man until you have walked two moons in his moccasins."

Most of the time, however, it is pretty difficult to achieve that level of understanding of another person's life. Appreciating a situation thoroughly from two different perspectives, as if within two lives, is usually impossible for most people. Yet we seem to be trying to learn that it is useful and fair to view responsibility as a characteristic that is located in a situation. At the close of the twentieth century emerging cultural standards suggest that locating responsibility in an individual results from adopting a very narrow view of what is going on. This developing set of common values concerning responsibility is creating a problem for some of us some of the time. For example, it's not uncommon these days to find ourselves in conversations with co-workers and friends who acknowledge that they are angry with someone and then admit that they are ashamed of themselves for that because the person "probably isn't *really* to blame anyway."

Now and then an inability to cope effectively with our own anger seems to result from all this. Of course, many people have difficulty with anger in adulthood simply because they have learned well the lesson that adults control their emotions, especially in public places such as the workplace. However, the cause of this inhibition is more subtle than that—a shift in cultural values toward greater emphasis on the reduction of blame targeted at the individual. Call it sophisticated blaming, if you will. Sophisticated blaming involves locating the responsibility in a situation rather than in a single person. This shift causes disturbing problems for many who are trying to work more effectively with the angers and irritations they experience in daily living. Anger and blame are strongly related, and putting the blame on something as nebulous as a situation simply doesn't provide the intellectual or emotional satisfaction that justified anger at an individual does. A situation cannot cause itself to change. We believe individuals *can* do that. In addition to carrying a statement of blame, anger carries a call for change.

### Individual Differences

In any given anger episode each of us will have a different reason for blaming and calling for change. In addition to our unique ways of feeling and expressing anger, each of us has a distinctive set of attitudes and values that influence our interpretations of uncomfortable work-related situations. Through our inquiry into the value of emotions at work, we have heard of countless events in which everyone involved was in an agitated and angry state—and each for a different reason.

There is an important "therefore" that flows from these facts. The reality is that *there can be no single set of behaviors or rules for anger and its expression at work that can possibly be valid for every person.* Since anger is controlled in large part by a person's values as well as by a person's reasonableness, we cannot expect each person to have similar ways of expressing him- or herself while at work. Any set of ideas and strategies that is designed to help individuals cope with anger at work must recognize, first and most important, that the place of individuality in the discussion must be primary.

Some have trouble experiencing the feeling of anger anywhere, not just at work. Others can experience anger at home but not at work, or conversely. There are some people who know they're angry but choose never to express it at work or at home. Then again, others would simply prefer to express anger only within intimate relationships. A sizable number of people feel a lot of anger but just don't know how to express it in a satisfactory way. Others feel justified in trusting their judgments about expressing anger in whatever way they see fit at the moment. A large number of people feel guilty if they merely experience the angry feeling itself.

Some people know how to absorb easily someone's anger on the job. Others can respond to anger positively once in a while, depending on their state of mind that day. Still other workers can deal with anger from certain people they work with, but not others, and some people don't ever want to experience anyone's anger at work.

Dealing positively with angry outbursts means, to some, that an angry retort must be delivered. Others feel required to "turn the other cheek."

Whether one is the "owner" of anger or the "recipient," there are major differences in timing from person to person. Some burn slowly. Others fly off the handle. Some stew in their own juices.

Further, anger is a problem for some people all the time. They are conflicted over it wherever they find it—in themselves or within others. For some of us anger is an important issue on a few occasions or for a year or two, and then, as situations change or we change, other emotions and issues of personal style become more pressing. Recognizing and respecting these differences are important. Anger really isn't a childish emotion, as so many of us have believed. It also isn't a weapon that is OK for powerful people to wield at their whim—as our forebears in the Middle Ages often seemed to think. Anger isn't even something that we all should learn to be comfortable with in our own particular ways. Anger is too powerful to befriend. It must be accommodated, however, since it is an extension of a moral and principled life. It is capable of creating much pain, but it can create possibilities for a better world, a better company, and a better "you."

# 2

# Styles of Anger
## The Differences Among Us

If a way to the Better there be,
It exacts a full look at the Worst.

—THOMAS HARDY

Anger as soon as fed is dead—
'Tis starving makes it fat.

—EMILY DICKINSON

JUDITH HAD BEEN ON Bill Traub's staff ever since he first ran for mayor, two terms ago. As the mayor's adviser on public utilities and services issues, she believed she was in the perfect political job since she had quite a bit of influence but didn't have to deal directly with the mayor's constituency or the media people—components of political life she didn't relish and wasn't particularly skilled at handling. Two of Judith's counterparts on the mayor's staff, Kelly Ross and Brad Dictal, shared her enthusiasm for the influential aspects of the role. Unlike Judith, however, they yearned to run for office themselves someday.

The three of them were talking with Bill in his office one Monday morning when Betsy, Bill's administrative secretary, preempted the remainder of a discussion of the latest round of City Council battles by striding into the office and approaching Bill with a somewhat muffled but firm declaration to the effect that the two of them "needed to talk—immediately."

The unwritten rules in that work culture required all staff members at all times to defer to a request from Betsy for the mayor's attention. It was simply understood, then, that the three advisers would depart quickly, checking with Betsy later in the morning to reschedule the aborted strategy meeting. Therefore, everyone involved was a little startled to notice that Judith hadn't left the couch to join the others as they briskly moved toward the office door.

Judith turned toward the mayor slowly, saying, "Sorry, Bill, this time this one isn't going to fly." The others stopped with looks of shock, confusion, or anxiety on their faces as she moved quickly to the telephone, hit the intercom button, and told the receptionist to hold all calls until further notice.

The rest of the staff and representatives of the media attached to the mayor's office never found out what went on in Bill's office over the course of the next hour and twenty minutes. But because of the occasional bursts of shouting that could be heard all the way over in the budget office, almost everyone *tried* to find out—to no avail. There was speculation that one of the staff members involved had been accused by the others of lying, or accepting bribes, or worse. At the other extreme, some thought the whole thing couldn't have been caused by anything more important than short tempers over the budget allowance for the upcoming office remodeling since no obvious budgetary or policy consequences emerged from that meeting. Except for the way some of these people behaved with one another for a few days after the event, everything seemed to return to business as usual.

When the heated discussion ended, the first person through the door was Brad. He slammed it. When Kelly came out a few minutes later, her fists were clenched, she didn't speak, and there were unmistakable signs of tears in her eyes. Bill was yelling something about process, product, and "doing what a man has to do" as he followed Judith through the door. She huffed off, hurling behind her the only remark that was clearly possible for the rest of the staff and two reporters to hear: "Let's just do it directly, or let's just not do it!" As everyone turned to watch them disperse toward ambiguous destinations, Betsy came out of the mayor's office and quietly moved to her desk. A secretary asked, "What happened in there? Are you angry, too?"

Betsy replied, "I don't *get* angry." To herself she privately added, "I just get even. And I *will* get even over this one."

All five of the people involved in that discussion that morning were very angry indeed. Some of them got over it pretty quickly; a couple of them stayed mad for weeks. Only two of them dealt with their anger directly in the days that followed. The others used indirect approaches in an effort to deal with their anger over the precipitating issues. One of them refused to acknowledge that the event had ever occurred. The mayor talked the event through with his wife that night, and they were at it until well past three in the morning before Bill's anger was sufficiently reduced that he could get some sleep.

## Taking a Look at Yourself: A Beginning

The major variations in the styles people adopt for dealing with the important characteristics of an anger episode largely result from differing attitudes toward personal values, blame, responsibility, empathy, understanding, calls for change, and the feeling and expression of anger. In this chapter we have included the most common approaches that we have identified as a result of talking with working men and women across the United States. We have presented several descriptions that reflect the differences among people when it actually comes to *feeling* (i.e., experiencing) the emotion of anger. We have also identified several different styles with respect to anger *expression.* It is unlikely that any person's characteristic habits will be confined to just one style in either category. Each of us is unique. Though it is likely that one of the ways of experiencing anger, as well as one type of expressive style, will provide an apt description of your general tendencies on most occasions at work, you may also recognize some parts of your emotional and behavioral repertoire with respect to anger in other descriptions as well. All the characterizations we have produced are work-related. Many people respond much differently in their private lives.

Some people feel anger slowly, some quickly, and some never feel it at all. We speak here only of the feeling itself. Descriptions of styles of expressing anger occur later.

### Daniel, Elizabeth, and Mark: Running Slowly, Privately, and Sometimes Guiltily

There are three basic styles within the group of people who are slow to come to the feeling of anger. Differences with respect to focusing, guilt, and self-control tend to distinguish them. There are no apparent gender differences across these styles; both men and women seem to adopt each of them in equal numbers.

Elizabeth and Mark, coincidentally a married couple, are representative of two types of *slow burners* in the workplace. Both of them begin to feel angry long after an offensive event has occurred. For example, a couple of months ago Elizabeth, a real estate broker, was representing the purchaser in a series of contract negotiations concerning the sale of a restored historic home. Her clients had made an offer; the owner of the house had submitted a counteroffer; then the whole thing started all over again. After three rounds of tense negotiating, the owner's real estate agent presented Elizabeth and her clients with an offer that "they couldn't refuse." The proposed contract stated that both the agents would give up 1 percent of their commissions in order to expedite the sales agreement. The other agent had written this concession into the contract without consulting Elizabeth, who quickly reasoned that she needed to appear happily supportive of this clause so as not to seem less "generous" than the agent representing the other side. However, real estate traditions had been somewhat broken because she had not been forewarned, and in addition, the contract had been presented to Elizabeth for the first time while she was in the presence of her clients. The contract was accepted and signed, and Elizabeth headed home to tell Mark the good news. When he remarked, "It's a shame to lose that eighteen hundred dollars," Elizabeth agreed but said that "some money" was better than "no money." Elizabeth felt happy. The contract had been signed, and the stressful negotiations were finally over. She could turn her attention to other houses and other clients.

A few days later, as she was inspecting a new housing development she recalled the issue of the 1 percent and became irritated. It didn't last long; but after another few days the situation again came to mind, and Elizabeth felt an irritation that bordered on anger. This time the uncomfortableness increased and lasted for about an hour, and this time her feeling was clearly directed toward the other agent.

Elizabeth slowly came to the conclusion that she had been taken advantage of. After all, she reasoned, she could have found another house for her clients and been able to collect the entire commission due her. She had worked long and hard on that transaction, and she deserved her rightful pay. *What a sneaky trick,* she thought. Later that evening, when her anger changed to annoyance, she mentioned it to Mark, who sympathized for a while. Within three days she had ceased being angry but knew it would take a bit of extra self-control on her part if she found herself working with the offending agent again in the future. What are the factors that contribute to the development of this kind of approach?

During the first year of her first job Elizabeth began to believe that negative emotions at work cause trouble. She witnessed some uncomfortable "scenes" at work and didn't like what she saw. Furthermore, as a child she had been taught that adults should be in control of their emotions, that it is childish to allow a person with less style and compassion than yourself to get the "better" of you. Elizabeth has decided that getting angry at the offenses of others at work allows them to control her in an important sense. Her feelings belong to her, she reasons, and she refuses to permit mere acquaintances to have influence over something so intimate and important as those feelings.

Because she has great control over her emotions, she is very slow to recognize that she has been in a situation that might well have provoked her anger if she were a different kind of person. She doesn't see certain behaviors as worthy of her blame. "People are the way they are," she reasons. Some people are "not very nice," but getting along with them anyway is necessary in the workaday world.

So, when Elizabeth does get angry at work, it's a very uncomfortable and anxiety-provoking time for her. When the feeling does erupt, Elizabeth's self-control skills are at times taxed to their limits. Some people who have adopted this style find their self-control skills strained as they fight the desire to *express* the anger. Once the anger does come, theirs is a battle to control its consequences, to prevent it from getting beyond the feeling stage. Not so for Elizabeth. Her struggle is over the elimination of the feeling itself. In order to honor her values, she works at keeping the angry feelings from taking shape.

Mark, her husband, presents an excellent example of the second major type of slow burner, the person who feels guilt over angry feelings. Like Elizabeth, he comes to anger very slowly. Unlike her, however, once he feels angry, he immediately feels culpable because of it. As a child Mark learned the lesson well that angry feelings are childish in an adult. In fact, he probably learned that they were also "childish" in a child, and no doubt he was unable at the time to claim his right to act like a juvenile when he was a juvenile. Be that as it may, the situation for Mark now is that the anger comes slowly, but the guilt comes quickly. And the guilt is more of a problem for him.

In order to understand Mark's style, we need only consider an event that happened last fall, as he was beginning his second year as director of advertising for a mid-size plasticware manufacturer. Mark had "inherited" the advertising firm that handles most of his company's business. Some of the people in the hierarchy above him liked the way the advertising firm managed their account, and Mark was aware that he would have to live with the arrangement for at least a few years. Mostly that was OK with him since the firm usually produced high-quality, creative work. The most troublesome aspect of the arrangement had to do with one of the advertising agency's account executives, a man Mark found to be too loud, too proprietary, and too disorganized.

One Monday morning, when the account executive arrived ten days late, bearing an ill-designed set of promotional materials for a new line

Mark's company was developing, Mark took the violation in his stride. An hour later, when his immediate boss blamed *him* for the poor quality of the promotional materials that lay before him, saying that he thought Mark had more control of his accounts than that, Mark *still* took it in his stride. *Bad days have one thing in common,* he thought. *They're bad.* He still felt essentially nothing once again when the account executive, at the end of the same day, shoved an addendum to the proposal at Mark's secretary, along with a particularly sexist remark that she obviously did not appreciate.

About forty-eight hours later Mark began wondering why he had to put up with that kind of thing. He further wondered why the guy thought he could get away with "this kind of stuff" with Mark and still expect to maintain the account. It did not take him long to get angry once a few of these thoughts emerged; however, it had taken at least two days before Mark came to the point of thinking the situation through in this particular way.

Immediately Mark felt guilty for being angry. He felt particularly bad for blaming the account executive when he believed that he himself was blameworthy since it was true that he should have gained better control over the material that was presented to his bosses. *I should be able to handle someone like this guy,* he said to himself with irritation. More important, he felt bad for letting himself get angry; he believed he should be spending that energy on solving the problems in a rational way.

Mark gets angry slowly, but he definitely gets there. He experiences this emotion fairly strongly about once a month, always hours or days after the precipitating event has come and gone. He tends to remain angry for a time. However, most of his anger is quickly turned toward himself. Sometimes he struggles with keeping his anger to himself; sometimes he doesn't. When he does struggle, he wins at times, and he loses at others.

Both Elizabeth and Mark are slow burners who need some time before they can experience anger. Like both of them, most people in these two groups tend to need privacy before they can feel anger. When the anger does come, these slow burners are usually off somewhere by themselves, doing something like taking a walk, mowing the grass, or driving alone in the car. However, this is not necessarily the case for Daniel and others in the third group within this category.

Dan, a production foreman in a large appliance manufacturing plant, has trouble focusing on specific provocations for his anger at work. Throughout the course of a typical week he feels mild irritations from time to time, but not anger. Part of his strategy for controlling anger at work, an important value as far as he's concerned, involves ignoring much of what is going on in an event that includes potentially anger-provoking circumstances. If the situation contains signals that suggest his standards may be compromised by others, he blocks out as many of the signals as he can. As a result, he feels something like annoyance, but certainly not anger. What happens for Dan and many others like him, however, is that over time these offenses "build up." The realization that others have been letting him down or undermining his standards tends to dawn on him slowly. *Then* he gets angry. For example, after one of his bosses had dumped extra quotas on his section several times in one month and had failed to give his people credit on two public occasions, Dan "suddenly" felt furious when the man came to his office one morning to tell him his car was parked in the wrong spot.

On the surface, it might appear to people like Daniel that their anger comes quickly. In fact, that's what Dan usually thinks. He is a little startled by his own feelings at times, wondering how he can feel so intensely about something like a minor remark over a parking space. Usually he will decide something to the effect that "the guy just irritates me in general, and I'm probably in a bad mood or something this morning." In actuality Dan is not quick to feel anger at all. He is a slow burner who moves through many anger-provoking experiences controlling his feelings. Eventually, however, his awareness of repeated transgressions reaches a certain threshold, and he then experiences anger even though the precipitating violation is one that might be much less serious than many he has previously absorbed from a given person. What distinguishes Dan's style, then, from Elizabeth's and Mark's is that he lets things build up, and when he does react, he is *reacting to the past more than he is reacting to the present situation.*

All three groups of slow burners contain people who are certainly capable of moderate to strong feelings but are well controlled by both external events and internal pressures. Slow burners are not "cold fish." Rather, it is important to them to have strict control over where and with whom they share feelings such as anger.

In reading about Elizabeth, Mark, and Daniel, you may have noticed similarities between your style and theirs. We urge you to read carefully through the rest of the descriptions before making a decision about your general tendencies where the feeling of anger at work is concerned. You may discover that one of the slow burner styles typifies your experience of anger in some specific kinds of situations, while one of the other styles is more similar to the approach you use most often.

### Matthew, Joe, and Barbara:
### Lightning Comes in Several Colors

Some people's anger reaches them in about as much time as it takes to flip a light switch. We think of them as having a *tinderbox* style, as coming to anger "quick as a flash." Once again, be reminded that we speak here only of the *feeling* of anger; we are not thinking yet about those who display or express their anger quickly.

We have identified three basic styles among people who feel anger almost immediately after an offense has occurred. There are more tinderbox people than some may have imagined. Since many of these people do not *express* that anger, many of us have assumed it doesn't exist. Not so. There is quite a bit of *felt* anger in many work situations, but we don't see much of it because many people keep it to themselves.

Matthew, Joe, and Barbara provide good illustrations of the kinds of tinderbox people you are likely to encounter on the job. We have noticed no differences between men and women across the styles we describe here. Both gender groups seem to contain a fairly equal number of people who feel anger rapidly.

Matthew has a fairly good sense of his own values and needs, and he has rarely ever had much trouble knowing what his feelings are at any given moment. Matthew knows when he's angry, and sad, and in love. While he doesn't necessarily always know what "to do" with these feelings when he becomes aware of their presence, he's almost always quickly able to make a connection between what he's feeling and the event that precipitated the feelings. As a section director of a large metropolitan zoo he doesn't interact with people as often as many of the rest of us do at work. He has administrative responsibilities, but a good deal of his daily routine finds him spending time around the animals rather than people. Even though he has fewer opportunities to feel anger toward other people, Matthew gets angry fairly often at the humans who inhabit his work world. He also gets angry at the animals from time to time.

Matthew's anger experiences at work are relatively easy for him to identify. He has a few clear-cut standards that are violated by others from time to time, and he can quickly determine who was at fault as far as he's concerned. Usually his anger emerges immediately when he realizes that an animal has been neglected or inadvertently abused.

While Matthew is able to pinpoint the problem quickly and to acknowledge his furious feeling rapidly, he's also likely to deny himself the *right* to feel that anger. As quickly as he feels the anger he tells himself he *shouldn't* be feeling it. There tend to be two reasons for his inability to allow righteous indignation. While they both are important to Matthew, these dynamics are rarely of equal relevance in any given situation.

Since he is the director of his section of the zoo, he knows immediately whether someone above or below him in the hierarchy is responsible for an animal's neglect. The first reason why Matthew finds it difficult to sustain his blaming, and thus his anger, is that he understands the circumstances surrounding his co-workers' failures to get the job done. The zoo is underfunded. Experienced help is hard to find. Too often people are required to work double shifts. The people in the front office have to spend too much time justifying the budget to various funding groups. Since he understands these circumstances, his anger never seems fully justified.

The second explanation for Matthew's occasional difficulty with his feelings of anger involves his belief that he shouldn't be getting angry at work, no matter what the reason. Like slow-burning Mark, he believes that adults should control themselves. Further, he believes that he should be competent enough to handle situations in such a way that neglect of the animals does not occur, and thus, if he did this, his anger wouldn't occur either. Like Mark, he expects himself to control many more of the circumstances in his daily life than he is often able to control.

Matthew represents a certain kind of tinderbox person who gets angry quickly over specific violations of his values, knows whom he blames and why, and then feels guilty for the anger. The guilt arises from his understanding of the reasons why the offense occurred and from his self-recrimination for not being able to prevent his anger or to prevent the unfortunate situations from occurring in the first place.

Complicating life further for Matthew at these times is his tendency to be conflicted over the expression of his anger. Sometimes he directs his fury outward. Other times he doesn't. Those who have a tinderbox style like Matthew's do not easily fall into a single style category when it comes to expression of anger. Each has a different way of dealing with the issues that anger creates in his or her life. Some express it, some don't, and some are inconsistent.

Joe's style is less common. Joe gets angry quickly, knows he's angry, knows why and who's to blame, and feels justified in having the feeling.

Joe is the director of production for a television network adventure show. He has lots of responsibility and many tensions, and he earns a sizable salary. Sometimes, as far as he's concerned, the rewards of the

job don't outweigh the hassles. He routinely has thoughts to that effect
when he gets angry—as he does in a significant way at least once each
week.

Joe's experience of anger is straightforward, and he is not particularly troubled by it. He does wish that he didn't have to feel angry quite
so often because he worries that he "might get ulcers or something."
Nonetheless, he believes that feeling angry is simply a consequence of
his job. In fact, Joe cannot imagine anyone *not* feeling angry in his
position. When we asked him if he ever felt guilty for feeling angry at
work, he smiled with genuine puzzlement.

The week we talked with Joe the first season's filming was drawing
to a close and tensions had peaked because it was unclear if his program
would capture a decent portion of the viewing audience. That morning
he had arrived on the set and was greeted by "big-time confusion," as
he put it. The major props had not arrived, and neither had the guest
star. There were two substitute cameramen who didn't seem to know
"which end of the camera the lens was in," and there were rumors flying
that the lunch caterers had gone bankrupt and there wouldn't be any
food at noontime.

As he sees it, Joe's major responsibility is to guarantee that "production happens." He makes sure that people and props get to the right
place at the right time. Joe felt a lot of anger several times that morning.
He was particularly angry at the camera chief for sending over rookies.
And he felt furious with the props director for failing to deliver the two
specially equipped automobiles he had been promised.

Joe reported that he had called the "right people" and let them
know what he felt and what they had better do to get things back on
track. Before 11:00 A.M. he had raised his voice several times, thrown
a clipboard to the ground in angry frustration, and successfully stifled
an unknown number of his own angry retorts. Joe told of these feelings
and behaviors in an automatic way, as he might have reported the
details of a day's production schedule.

As was the case that morning, when Joe gets angry, he has no doubt
that it is a justified anger. He expects people to do their jobs and to do
them well. He also knows that people "mess up" from time to time.
When they do, he has a right to get angry, he believes. When his anger
comes, it usually rises quickly.

Most people who share Joe's style either consistently express their
anger or deal with it as Joe does, occasionally directing it toward
offenders while keeping it private at other times. Rarely do tinderbox
persons such as Joe *habitually* restrain the expression of their anger.

For them, the unequivocal decision that the anger is justified provides the opportunity to choose whether or not they will direct the anger toward its perceived source. In an important sense that decision becomes the only relevant decision. These people need not use time during tense moments to question the validity of their anger, its source, and so forth.

In contrast with Joe, Barbara's tinderbox style is often a burden to her. Barbara is a professional dancer who gets intensely inflamed from time to time while at work, but her anger is without focus. For example, in a situation that turned out to be particularly problematic for her last winter, Barbara felt her anger quickly rising but had "no earthly knowledge why." She had been putting in long rehearsal hours for a show that looked as if it would not be ready for opening night. A very professional troupe had been assembled, and Barbara was among those who believed that despite appearances to the contrary, they just might pull it all together. About a week before opening night, after a strenuous twelve-hour day, Barbara walked over to a group that included the director and a producer as well as some of the other performers. After about fifteen minutes of conversation that ranged across various topics, Barbara felt herself rapidly becoming furious. She did not know at whom and she did not know why.

This kind of moment happens fairly frequently in Barbara's life. She knows when she's angry but can't quite pinpoint the reason. In that particular conversation she later guessed that the cause might have been either a critical remark from another dancer directed toward a scene that she was in or the producer's continual interruptions of the director, a man she deeply respected. She also remembered that one of her friends had been acting during that conversation as if she were mad at Barbara. "It's possible," Barbara said later, "that Meg's hostility is what really made me feel that furious."

Tinderbox persons such as Barbara may or may not get angry frequently even though the feeling flares quickly in response to some trigger. The important part of their anger experience involves the inability to understand what caused the feeling. Like Barbara, they may still be speculating on the source of the provocation days later. Sometimes they cannot recall anything that might be responsible for such intense feelings. Usually, however, they are able to nominate several plausible causes for the anger. It may be that people like Barbara get angry quite quickly in situations where there are indeed multiple causes. However, it has been our experience that when they are offered the suggestion that the anger probably resulted from several offenses that may have occurred during the same episode, they tend not to agree. They continue to search for a single cause, apparently believing that they are less aware of their motivations than they would like to be (and that surely a single "cause" *must* exist). We suspect that they *are* largely unaware of their own motivations. We also think that in many circumstances more knowledge of their own priorities and values might make a big difference in their ability to understand why they feel angry.

Like Matthew and Joe, Barbara occasionally directs her anger outward and occasionally she stifles it. For her, the discriminating variable seems to be whether she has a relatively good idea of what the offense was and who committed it. Again, the major difficulty for Barbara is not centered on conflicts over expressing her anger. Her problems with her own anger emerge from her puzzlements concerning its sources. Since her anger seems to arrive so rapidly, she reasons that its sources ought to be obvious. But long after her anger has dissipated, Barbara often remains frustrated.

### Ruby and Meredith: When the Fire Won't Start

Some people rarely or never feel anger at work. We think of this as the *cool customer* category and have found that it seems to contain two distinctive groups. While we have chosen stories of two women to illustrate these groups, there seem to be no differences between men and women within this category.

Ruby is an attorney. She has had a successful civil practice for some years now, but before going to law school, she worked for a few years as a high school history teacher. Ruby reports that she has never, in all her working years, felt anger at work. Ruby does not take pride in this characteristic as she speaks; rather, she relates the information in the same manner she would any point of fact. Anger control is not something she had to work to acquire, and therefore, she doesn't necessarily think she should be given credit for it as an accomplishment.

Ruby really could not recall any time when she might have felt angry. When pressed, she lamely told of a group of teenagers who tried to embarrass her during her first year of teaching by walking out in the middle of one of her lectures. However, while she was irritated that day, she believes that the major emotion she felt was probably embarrassment rather than anger. Both her professional work experiences have been in occupations that many consider stressful and sometimes anger-provoking, and she admitted that "it's a wonder" she has never felt anger at work over the years. Ruby had no opinion concerning the source of her emotional control. She simply said, "I don't know. I just don't get angry."

It's useful to note that Ruby doesn't get angry in her personal life either. She gets annoyed sometimes but angry never. Thus, as we will shortly see, the characteristic that distinguishes her from Meredith is that she just does not feel intense negative emotions. Her physiological makeup in combination with her socialization history results in an absence of intense feelings in the majority of situations.

Many people like Ruby do indeed have sets of strong values. They are also quite capable of assigning blame and believing that their views are justified. Unlike others, however, depth of negative feeling just isn't something they experience.

Meredith is also a cool customer, but in contrast with Ruby, she must exercise control over her angry impulses in order to maintain her cool customer image. She is the manager of a store that sells computer equipment, and although she believes that there are many opportunities each month to experience anger in her line of work, she doesn't.

Meredith can remember being angry at work only once or twice during the past ten years. In the most memorable of these instances she found herself the victim of an irresponsible distributing company. Her store had managed to offer the most acceptable bid to the local high school when the school board authorized the first purchase of computer equipment for the public schools in her town. It was the biggest order the store had ever had, and it meant that they were "going to make it." The order went to the distributor in the spring. In August the equipment still had not arrived, and the school people were threatening to break the contract. When the equipment did arrive in mid-September, the distributor pointed out that the price had gone up and that Meredith's company was going to have to pay the new price since a small clause in the contract bound the store to absorb a certain kind of price increase prior to delivery. Meredith lost most of the profit as well as a lot of goodwill in town as a result of this event. She recalls having been very angry the day she got the bad billing news from the distributor. She didn't express that anger, however. She simply accepted the information with a response that most would have thought represented annoyance rather than fury. Like Meredith, most cool customers don't *express* anger on those rare occasions when they do feel it at work.

Meredith believes that she is quite capable of feeling anger, but on the job she finds herself exercising strong control over such feelings. She talks about frequently feeling irritated while at work. She thinks of irritations as "little pieces of anger." These "little pieces" are all she will allow herself to feel since she has a sense that dangerous consequences flow from angry outbursts.

Like many people, Meredith equates anger and aggression. She cannot imagine really feeling anger without expressing it. She is clearly unable to make the distinction between the two, and she thinks that it would be too risky to feel anger at work—whether or not it is directed toward someone.

As is the case with many cool customers, from time to time Meredith wishes that she had freer access to feelings such as anger. Occasionally she thinks that people take advantage of her because they have learned she will not get angry. She sometimes suspects that those who express their angry feelings get better treatment than she does, and she resents that. She wishes that she could get proper attention without needing to "raise a ruckus." Since she holds these views, every now and then she attempts to permit her anger to emerge. But it doesn't seem to "work." She values having control over her negative feelings at the store more strongly than she values spontaneous access to them. She is quite committed to reserving her anger for more private moments.

People who adopt a style such as Ruby's and Meredith's are aptly labeled "cool customers" since they do not allow themselves to be inflamed by offenses. We do not mean to suggest through use of this label, however, that cool customers do not have or express emotions at work at all. Often they are very upbeat people while at work. They may freely share such positive feelings as happiness and satisfaction. Cool customers like Ruby, for example, can be quite easygoing and relaxed most of the time.

## The Expression of Anger: Personal Styles

In adults the feeling of anger does not necessarily compel its assertion. That's one of the hallmarks of maturity. As we noted in earlier chapters, young children cannot make this distinction. One important parental task is helping children learn to respect and value their own feelings as they learn to use behaviors that result from these emotions in ways that meet their needs but do not harm themselves or others in the process. Even if parents do not specifically set for themselves the task of teaching children how to value and control their emotions, good parenting practices usually result in the acquisition of these skills.

All the anger expression styles described below fit with any of the styles of experiencing anger that you have just considered. Each of us puts it all together in a distinctive way. As you read through the following expression style descriptions, you will probably find that one of them represents your own tendencies, but it is also quite likely that you will see elements of your style in some of the other descriptions. For example, if you are like most people, you have a different way of expressing anger toward your boss from the way you typically deal with it when a colleague is involved. And your habits of anger expression in your personal life may be very different from those you adopt in your work role.

While there seem to be few important differences between men and women in the various styles of experiencing the emotion of anger at work, the differences between the sexes in the styles of expression are pronounced. In some cases it is rare to find women who express their anger in a given way while it is not uncommon at all for men to express themselves in that way. Conversely some expression styles are much more commonly associated with women than with men.

### "But How Long Is It Going to Last?"

Before we consider the following anger expression styles, it's important to comment on an aspect of anger that we have scarcely touched upon to this point: the duration of an anger episode. Some angry feelings come and go quickly, but at other times anger stays with us for quite a while. What controls the duration of angry feelings? Why do some people habitually feel angry for a long time while others tend to get over anger quickly?

The style of expression that an individual adopts usually affects the duration of the anger, while what you do with your anger can make a big difference when it comes to how long you find yourself having to "live with it." Unfortunately there is *not* a simple formula that reads: "Express your anger and it goes away; keep it to yourself and you keep it forever." You'll find several suggestions for coping with this very puzzling aspect of anger in Chapter Ten, where we describe strategies for changing anger habits.

The various ways of *experiencing* angry feelings discussed earlier are distinguished most basically by the amount of time it takes for people to sense the presence of this emotion in themselves. As we have seen, some people realize their own anger slowly while others come to anger more quickly.

In contrast, the various styles of anger *expression* tend to be most importantly distinguished by habits concerning the choice of object(s) toward which anger is expressed. If you do express anger, do you do so with the person or persons who are responsible for the offense? Or do you share your anger with friends or with other colleagues who may not have been involved? In any case, is your anger message direct or indirect?

### Stan, Kevin, and Kirsten: Aiming for the Bull's-eye

When they decide to express anger rather than keep it to themselves, a lot of people aim it directly toward the source of the trouble. Within this group of *straight shooters* there are several distinct styles. Three of these are the most common and are well represented by Stan, Kevin, and Kirsten, people who direct their anger toward the objects of their blame but do so in very different ways.

For ten years now Stan has been successfully involved in importing fine clothing materials from Europe. When Stan allows himself to express angry feelings, he tends to be obvious about it. A good example of this occurred when he was in the midst of arranging a particularly sensitive deal that included quickly bringing some top-quality men's suit material from Italy to New York so that a major department store chain could use it in the development of a new upscale line that had been, as things developed, somewhat prematurely promoted. Stan's overseas supplier had run into some trouble, and delivery was delayed. The department store buyer accepted the bad news gracefully, offering Stan a six weeks' contractual extension. On the basis of that verbal assurance, Stan altered—in writing—parts of his own deal with the Italian suppliers, then became involved in some other pressing issues in his business. He did not go over to the department store offices to change the contract officially until about ten days later. And then, for reasons that were unclear, the buyer, in the presence of his own boss, denied giving the verbal extension to Stan and made a further remark about the importance of "being responsible" in this kind of deal. Stan "gave him a piece of his mind." At least that's what Stan called it. Observers might have thought that phrase was far too gentle, given what they heard, since Stan made several references to the man's character and his ancestors.

Stan is the kind of person who does not concern himself with the other person's feelings when he has been wronged. He gets right to the point, often speaks loudly and fast, and indicates to his offender just what kind of person he thinks would be capable of such a misdeed. Thus, Stan doesn't confine his anger to what the transgressor has *done;* he also directs his anger toward what he thinks the person *is.* And his angry comments are not complimentary. Stan deals with his anger in the "your mother wears army boots" style. He reasons that anybody who would do something as bad as the offender has done does not deserve courtesy or sensitivity.

Stan is unafraid of the other person's responses in these situations. If somebody were to poke a fist at him, he suspects that he would be more than willing, and able, to handle it. He is not concerned that his anger might cost him the relationship. He cares about the violation of his values, and for him the "right" thing to do is to let the reprobate know clearly what Stan thinks and where he stands. He would consider it cowardly if he did not deal with his anger in this way on such occasions as this.

These particular attitudes are part of a set of perspectives that tend to distinguish male and female approaches to this kind of anger expression. Most often it is a man who tends to deal with his anger in the way Stan does. Standing up for rights—that is, verbally expressing and defending them—and doing so without fear of the consequences are actions that have been most often associated with men in our culture. Small boys are encouraged to fight physically for their rights far more often than girls are. In contrast, women are more strongly encouraged to develop and express the values of sensitivity, understanding, and demureness. Given these differences, not many women respond to their offenders at work in the way Stan does.

It's important to note that Stan does not *often* express his anger as he did with the department store buyer. Generally he comes to anger slowly and has once or twice worried about the appropriateness of feeling anger on the job at all. He tends to believe that he "shouldn't let work get to" him. Therefore, he rarely expresses his anger. However, when he does, it is direct, loud, and often offensive. Stan responds this way infrequently because like many people in this category, he controls his anger most of the time. Many people like Stan prefer to keep their anger to themselves, but when they do express it, they choose to "let the other guy truly have it." And it usually is a guy. Most of the time anger at work that is directly expressed in this bombastic style is directed toward a man. It is not that women provoke anger less often in someone like Stan. Rather, Stan and many others like him are simply not accustomed to letting women "have it" in this way. Since this style represents the one he is most comfortable with, overall Stan tends to express anger toward women at work only infrequently. If he were to direct that kind of verbal assault toward a female, he believes that it would not "work" to relieve his anger. Further, he doesn't imagine that he could handle a woman's response to him in this situation. He has a good idea how a man might react; a woman's responses would be "totally unpredictable" for him and would probably put him "off-balance," as he phrased it.

Like Stan, Kevin directs his anger toward the person or persons whom he considers to be its source. Unlike Stan, however, he limits his angry comments to issues surrounding the abuse and never addresses issues outside it. It is not always easy for Kevin to limit himself at work to the exclusive use of this strategy. He told us that he has sometimes been so mad that he wanted to "tell the person off" or, "better yet, hit somebody." Nonetheless, he focuses his anger when he feels it. He says that this strategy represents an important compromise in his life. He doesn't think it's very useful to express anger in relationships that aren't personal. On the other hand, sometimes he gets "darn angry" in his job as the manager of a large food store. At times he knows that his anger is "righteous"—that is, he believes that the other person deserves, and maybe needs to hear, how the offense has affected him, others, and what he has been trying to accomplish at the store. He may or may not speak loudly when he is sending his anger in someone's direction. He may or may not have felt his anger quickly. What is consistent, he reports, is that he gets tense, his facial and hand muscles tighten up, and he limits his "outbursts" to comments on just *exactly* what the other person has done wrong as far as he is concerned.

For example, he told about a recent episode in which his produce manager had allowed a shipment of lettuce to deteriorate before it went on display. Apparently this had happened on at least two other occasions during the previous three months. Kevin had become generally dissatisfied with the carelessness of the man's work and had decided that the situation was related to the amount of time the man was spending "trying to get to first base" with a woman working in the deli department. On the day in question, when Kevin spotted the spoiled lettuce, he walked all the way around the parking lot once, then called the produce manager into his office. Kevin was angry. His voice was raised as he told the man where he had seen the lettuce, the condition it was in, the company's fresh produce standards, the number of times the situation had occurred recently, the amount of time he had observed the man spending over in deli, and exactly what he expected in the future from him. He then asked the man if he had anything to say in return.

Kevin said that he has expressed his anger in this way with bosses as well as those directly under his supervision. He did note, however, that when a boss was involved, he would be more likely to allow the other person to terminate the conversation, rather than reserve that right for himself. "Other than that, I'd act pretty much the same way," he said.

Kevin is a good representative of a group of people who believe that their anger is important and that it should be put in the "right" place—in the hands of the person who seemed to cause it. What is most important for them in the situation is that they clearly articulate what has gone wrong and why they view the incident as negatively as they do. They carefully limit all comments to the episode that has occasioned the anger and tend to make very few references to personal characteristics of the transgressor. For example, they do not tell people that they are "irresponsible" or "careless." Rather, they describe what has happened, how the event violated expectations, and why they are angry.

These people may speak loudly or softly as they express their anger. They may come to that anger slowly or quickly. Sometimes they respond a little differently, depending upon the other person's position in the company. Despite these differences, however, people like Kevin are distinguishable as a group because of the very specific way they proceed when they are delivering their anger to its target. Importantly, they tend to "get over" their anger relatively quickly.

Women as well as men adopt this kind of style in the workplace. However, the number of men who respond this way probably is twice as great as the number of women. Since direct confrontation is involved in this style, many women—whose socialization has not often included experiences in direct confrontation—simply do not feel comfortable with it.

Kirsten is a bank officer in a mid-size midwestern city. For some time now her bank has had fewer officers than it needs. As a result, tensions are created on an almost weekly basis as the popular bank tries to meet its customers' demands. Kirsten is one of those who work long hours and take up slack for others whenever they can. When we asked about the ways she tends to express anger at work, she immediately replied with a firm comment to the effect that she does *not* express anger at work. She sees herself as a slow burner who lets things build up before she even notices that she feels angry. Once she does notice, however, she "keeps it to herself."

Kirsten expresses her anger indirectly. Since she believes that only active displays of anger "count" where the expression of that feeling is concerned, she does not believe that she delivers angry messages at work. But she does.

One morning, at the end of a particularly hectic week that involved many mortgage refinance applications, Kirsten and some of her colleagues were taking a much needed coffee break when a vice-president approached them with a stack of paper work that needed processing before an important set of planning meetings that were to begin on the next Monday afternoon. He commented that he was arbitrarily putting the load on this particular group of three officers. The group just "happened to be handy" at the time he was seeking the assistance that he needed, he said. He apologized for the extra stress this work would cause and promised that each of them would get a day or two off sometime in the future when things calmed down a bit. He did not solicit discussion of the work assignment; rather, he asked only for questions about the work itself.

Kirsten reported that about three hours later she began to get angry. In her view the vice-president had not randomly chosen that group to do this extra work. He chose them because they were the three who tended to put in extra hours without complaint and had often volunteered to do critical tasks that had been left undone during the past few hectic weeks at the bank. In other words, Kirsten believed that she had been chosen because she had already demonstrated a strong level of commitment to her job and was well known for being able to accomplish more in a shorter period of time than it took most others. She grew to believe that the request meant that the boss was taking advantage of her loyalty and good nature. She calculated that she would have to give up some of her weekend time in order "to pay the price for being such a good employee," and she resented that.

In this situation—as in other situations she encounters at work—Kirsten had no trouble in clearly identifying the person who was to blame for the offense that generated her feelings of anger. However, unlike Stan and Kevin, she has not developed strategies for directly indicating to someone that she is angry. Instead, she sends her anger messages in an indirect way. In this instance she slowed her work pace and put in only half the amount of time she knew the job required if her portion of the work load was to be ready by Monday afternoon.

Kirsten did not fear that this "work slowdown" would seriously jeopardize her position at the bank. She was confident of her value in the position she held. She hoped that her boss would "get the message" (as she put it) that he could not expect superhuman performance from her all the time. She "wanted him to learn" that she needed ultimate control over the extra time and effort she devoted to her work. She did not want someone else to take her extraordinary commitment and efficiency for granted.

When Kirsten delivered the work she had done to the vice-president's office on Monday, she did so at a time she knew he was elsewhere in the bank, and she simply left the material with his secretary with explanatory notes attached. She suspected that he would not directly address with her the issue of the amount of work she had finished. Thus, she was spared the difficulty of telling him more directly how angry she had been.

Kirsten said that she has additional ways of indirectly getting across the message that she is angry. She limits casual contact with an offender. She makes decisions that do not take that person's interests into consideration, as she typically would if she were not angry. In general, she reported, she "withholds" things that could be considered extras. She never shirks work that is rightfully hers to do; she doesn't "slow down" in those areas at all. Rather, she withholds her attention to tasks that she considers of minor importance for someone in her role but are of importance to the person who has occasioned her anger.

Kirsten said that she is likely to feel anger for quite some time over transgressions such as the one we have described. Ordinarily she does not do anything to "get rid" of the angry feelings; eventually they "just go away." Kirsten does not think of her indirect responses to an offense as "actions" that are designed to assist her in reducing the impact on herself of her angry feelings. They are more like "messages" that she sends out to warn others that they should not repeat the offensive behavior.

She imagines that most of her angry messages are interpreted quickly by others. She also strongly believes that the people she gets angry with during work hours would much rather have her proceed in this way than to "yell at them," or "lose her temper," or use some other method of direct expression that, to her, would feel very inappropriate for the workplace. Kirsten could not imagine any way of dealing with her anger other than through indirect messages, on the one hand, or yelling, on the other.

Kirsten thinks that the indirect-message approach works fairly well. Her only concern is that this style of hers probably contributes to the length of time she "has to carry anger around." She reports that sometimes she stays angry for days.

Both men and women adopt this indirect style. However, it is used more often by women. There seems to be a strong relationship between this style and many women's expectations that they operate calmly and "professionally" in the work environment. Kirsten expressed this idea well when she confided during the third interview that she "knew" that women at work "who tell others just how angry they really are" are considered by most people, men and women alike, "to be bitchy." Kirsten refuses to risk such a possibility. She believes that she avoids the "unnecessary strain" that would inevitably result if she stopped "keeping her anger" to herself. She said that she believes that the wisest and most successful people at the bank are the ones who keep their feelings to themselves, making sure that important messages are delivered in the most indirect ways possible.

### Farley, Hazel, and Marianne: Missing the Mark

There is a group of people we think of as the *deflectors*, who express their anger at work but divert it so that people involved in causing the feeling do not know of the anger. From time to time almost everyone has diverted his or her anger toward an object that does not necessarily deserve it. However, the people within these groups distinguish themselves in that they only rarely deliver their anger directly to the person they blame.

Farley provides an excellent example of one of the three major types of deflector, the person who displaces anger onto another object that seems "safer." A veteran stockbroker with one of the country's major firms, Farley has adopted this approach on more than one occasion at work. One of his experiences with a job-related accident he suffered clearly illustrates Farley's somewhat problematic approach to dealing with his anger. One day, while he was briskly walking up the stairs in his office building in order to provide himself with some exercise on the way to his office, Farley tripped over something and fell down approximately fifteen steps before he could break his descent. He cracked his tailbone, dislocated a vertebra in the lower back, and was in considerable pain for some weeks.

He had tripped over the briefcase belonging to the director of his branch of the firm. On several previous occasions he had noticed the large briefcase sitting precariously on a step in the stairwell, had been annoyed over the possibilities for dangerous outcomes, but had said nothing, assuming that his boss was making a quick stop in an office on another floor of the building and for some reason was not bothering to carry the case all the way down the hall and back. He remembers that on each of those occasions he had remarked to himself that the kind of carelessness represented by that behavior was typical of his boss. He thought no more of the incidents until the morning he was bounding up the stairs, lost in thought, and tripped over the briefcase.

Farley got mad at physical fitness proponents, not at his boss. And he expressed that anger. For weeks after the event, whenever someone praised the virtues of exercise, he would retort angrily that America is "going to hell in Reeboks." He would heatedly cite the seemingly countless numbers of people he knew who had suffered exercise-related injuries and would insist that the emphasis placed on physical fitness was providing one of the major stresses in contemporary society.

Farley was genuinely startled by the discovery he made while talking with us. Normally a confident and articulate conversationalist, he paused in the dialogue for almost ten minutes before he could collect his thoughts enough to continue. He was *surprised* to discover that he was really angry with his boss, not with physical fitness advocates. He described himself, then, as furious that his boss's "carelessness" had caused him so much pain. He guessed that he had been too angry at the boss even to consider telling the man how he felt, believing that the consequences would be disastrous. He said that apparently he couldn't risk being angry with the person who rightly deserved the blame.

When displacement is operating, the person genuinely does not know that the anger arises from a source other than the one that is being blamed. Displacement works only when we are fooling ourselves.

Fortunately, relatively few people adopt this mechanism as a style for dealing with anger at work. The consequences for the person who is wrongly blamed are certainly unfair. Another drawback is that *displacers* tend to maintain their anger for a long time. Aiming it in the wrong direction usually means that anger's going to stick with a person for a while.

Hazel well represents a group of people briefly mentioned in the previous chapter—those we have called sophisticated blamers. People such as Hazel are able to see a situation from a variety of points of view, and the result often is that they do not really identify an appropriate object of blame. Like Hazel, those in this group tend to be empathic people who have the ability to identify with the struggles and pains of others. When confronted with an offense, they are able to understand *why* a person did what was done, and they are able to appreciate the person's needs and motivations. Hazel often says, "I can understand how such a thing could happen," when trying to comfort herself or someone else who has been wronged.

Hazel told a story about an event connected with the dress shop she used to own that reveals quite a bit about the thought processes that sophisticated blamers use as they try to understand harm and its meaning in their lives. Hazel had trusted (and been quite fond of) Margaret, her shop manager of twelve years. The two of them had worried together through the early lean years, enjoyed several years of prosperity, then problem-solved and commiserated with each other as the business began to fail seriously about four years ago. When Hazel finally had to close the doors a few months ago, one of her most serious concerns involved having to put Margaret in the position of job hunting at a financially unstable point for her family. When the final auditing for bank foreclosure occurred, it was discovered that Margaret had been stealing systematically from the business for years. In fact, she had taken so much that a thriving business had been catapulted into bankruptcy.

While Hazel was very angry at what had happened, she was not angry at Margaret. She spent a long time explaining the circumstances of Margaret's early life and current situation. She talked about the pressures that human beings inevitably face as they try to do the right thing even though their personal needs may be incredibly great at certain times. Hazel was sure that Margaret was not really to blame. It was some of Margaret's family members perhaps or maybe the unfortunate way that society is organized in general. Or, she reasoned, maybe even she herself was to blame since she might have recognized what was happening earlier and could have prevented the foreclosure. Interspersed with these remarks was a genuine anger. Hazel wasn't taking this turn of events unemotionally. She felt *very* angry. She simply couldn't blame anyone in the situation. Too many mitigating circumstances in Margaret's life were understood and appreciated by Hazel, and her general sensitivity toward the struggles inherent in human living is great.

As a result, Hazel's anger has been directed toward *no one in particular.* It seems to bounce from one object to another—the bank, Margaret, Margaret's family, the system, the "incredible pain that is an inevitable part of life"—never stopping to settle anywhere. Hazel talks about how she will sometimes feel anger at a particular object for a few minutes or so and then realize that the person probably could have done no differently and that if she, Hazel, were in that position, she might well have done the same. She starts to express anger to someone, then stops, directing the rest of her remarks toward a bystander or even toward heaven. "Who's to blame?" she asks. "There are probably mean, vicious people in this world who do terrible things to others. I don't know them. The people I know are very human, struggle a lot, and sometimes make mistakes. I can't get angry at them. It wouldn't be fair."

Hazel does experience and express anger. However, when she finds herself feeling this negative emotion, she moves from one object to another, discovering that no single person can satisfy her criteria for "righteous anger." People may be culpable, but they are not to blame. Unfortunately Hazel and those like her often continue to feel angry after a precipitating event, sometimes for a very long time.

At times people like Hazel may blame others who are less directly involved than the identified transgressor, or they may blame society, or circumstances, or some other abstraction that seems to fit for a short time. Like Hazel, though, they cannot sustain the expression of anger because they reason through to the conclusion that blame is unjustified.

Hazel and others in this group provide excellent examples of the fact that anger and aggression need not be linked in adult human beings. It is quite possible to feel angry and do nothing about it. Most of us experience that combination rather frequently. People like Hazel have fashioned such a combination into a rational approach to life.

Marianne also turns her anger in directions that are far afield from its source. As a technical editor for a large publishing house she works with many people in several departments throughout the course of a day. She occasionally becomes angry but reports that she has expressed that anger on only two occasions over the course of her five-year history of employment with the company. As we heard more details of Marianne's typical coping style when her own anger is involved, it became apparent that she had meant that she expressed her anger *directly toward its source* only twice. Actually Marianne often expresses her anger when she feels it. But she expresses it to co-workers who haven't been involved in the anger-producing incident.

During a recent push to bring a trade publication out earlier than planned, tensions were obvious at the publishing house, with everyone trying to get the job done and maintain some semblance of personal stability at the same time. Marianne's immediate boss overruled one of her decisions without telling her, and that fact cost Marianne some additional time since she had gone ahead with the task under the assumption that her own decision in the matter was guiding the process. When she discovered the change, she quickly deduced the amount of additional time she would need to redo a portion of the book, and she became quite angry. Marianne shared this anger with three people who knew her boss's work style. She complained strongly about the decision and the inappropriate way the whole thing had been handled. In fact, she mentioned the issue at least twice to each of these colleagues. She imagines that they called it griping.

Marianne's typical way of dealing with her own anger in the workplace is to decide whether or not she wishes to share it. If she chooses to do so, she always gets "steamed" in front of colleagues, not in the presence of the offender. She believes that the major advantage of this approach is that she does not endanger her job or an important working relationship because she does not strain it by sending the anger "where it belongs." However, she reported that letting a few trusted colleagues know how angry she is helps a lot. She releases her feelings this way and sometimes receives support as well.

Marianne does not find this strategy particularly effective in helping the offensive situation to change. She understands that since the transgressor does not know of her anger, the chances of offensive behavior being changed are far less than if information concerning her thoughts and feelings had been given to the person involved. However, she does not expect that such information would change the person's behavior anyway. She explained that she tends to get angry with those who are irrational, or insensitive, or incompetent—not with the people she likes a lot. Therefore, she considers her offenders "beyond help" anyway.

Marianne's strategy is used by both men and women in the workplace. However, more women than men are likely to adopt this kind of style. Again, it seems to provide assurance for some that they can express powerful feelings of anger and still maintain the importance in their work lives of "decorum in public," as Marianne puts it.

### Martin, Richard, and Diana: Always Keeping the Lid On

Although they may feel angry at work from time to time, there are many who never—or very rarely—let anyone at work know that. If asked, they usually deny that they are angry, preferring to keep that information to themselves. We think of these people as *keepers*.

Martin, a federal court bailiff, is the kind of keeper who uses support people in his personal life to help him deal with his work-related anger. He has been known to keep his wife awake for a couple of hours while he "rants and raves" over something that someone at work has "done to him." She provides support and importantly, he said, a sense of perspective on the issue. Martin also made it clear that he does not trust people at work with his feelings. For Martin, emotions are personal things that he needs to keep to himself until he is in the presence of someone who is part of his intimate, personal life. Martin also turns to a brother and a good friend on some occasions when he needs to ventilate his anger. Despite the fact that he does share anger, we consider him a keeper because he does not display this feeling to anyone in the workplace, neither the one he blames nor any colleague.

As a campaign manager for a congressional candidate Richard, another keeper, had occasion to feel furious as a result of some mishandled publicity gimmicks that somebody had inappropriately authorized during a recent campaign. But he did not "blow off steam" over this in either his professional or personal life. He describes himself as a person who "absorbs" his own anger. By that he means that he occasionally gets an upset stomach or suffers from insomnia and that usually he can associate these physical discomforts with some anger that he is hanging on to pretty tightly.

Richard does not think that a person in his position can afford to "alienate" people. After all, he reasons, his job is largely a public relations position. Any angry outbursts that he delivers could be negatively associated with his candidate, and he can't risk that. After a good many years in politics he has begun to wonder if the price he pays in occasional physical ailments is worth the advantages of his job. Richard, like some others who deal with their anger in this way, usually decides that it is. Richard is committed to his work, and absorbing anger often seems like a rather small price to pay if he can be influential "where it counts."

Not everyone who absorbs anger in this way does so out of dedication to the work. Some just cannot reason their way through to a conclusion that anger at work is ever justifiable. We have discovered that both men and women, in approximately equal numbers, adopt the style that Richard's story illustrates. We estimate that a large number of people use this coping style with their own anger at work. A lot more people than we might have anticipated speak relatively easily of the physical discomforts they often—or at least sometimes—believe they experience as a direct result of keeping their anger to themselves. The experience is definitely not an uncommon one.

The third type of keeper receives a great deal of attention farther on in this book. There are many people who provide excellent examples of this kind of style. Diana, however, exemplifies several important variations within this style (many of which we discuss in detail in Chapter Five).

Diana, a restaurant owner/manager, told us about biting her lip in order not to cry when a meat supplier failed to come through with an order that he had firmly promised to her, even though she told him that failure to deliver on time would cost a substantial amount of her week's receipts. The restaurant expected to handle the biggest three-day lunch crowd it had ever accommodated because of a convention at a nearby hotel. Enthusiasm about this had been great.

Diana ended up going for a drive around the block so that she could release the tears. Later she realized that she was furious. Rather than deliver her anger, however, Diana had cried. In fact, Diana told us that she didn't even know she was angry at the time. We have come to discover that there are many women (and a few men) like her, who cry at work rather than get angry. Chapters Four through Six are devoted to a discussion of various aspects of this previously unacknowledged but important approach to anger or frustration in the work setting. As you will discover in those chapters, there are a variety of different ways in which many people experience the relationship between anger and tears.

### Ken: "I Don't Get Mad. I Just Get Even"

There are some people who express their angry feelings through a type of indirect action that provides them with satisfaction through vindication. In fact, this style is characterized by vindictiveness. In this culture we even have a label, of sorts, for it. This is, the *I don't get mad, I just get even* approach to angry feelings.

Ken manages a large frozen-foods operation in California. Years ago, as he was first entering the work force, he adopted the get-even method of dealing with his anger at work. After a particularly painful offense dealt him by his first boss during his very first week at work, he took steps to convince himself that feeling substantial anger and hurt at work was a silly and self-defeating thing to do. Rather than let someone else "get to him," he resolved that he would learn to control his angry and hurt feelings; he promised himself that he would "get back at" his offenders rather than suffer because of them.

Ken doesn't create the opportunity for revenge; he just waits for such an opportunity to come along. As someone else who shares his style put it, "You don't go out and bomb their cars or anything like that. You just wait. Sooner or later you'll find yourself in a position to get even." Most people who adopt this style are like that. They don't go out of their way to get revenge. As Ken said, a person who uses this method of coping "simply files the offensive event away in the mind somewhere" and, when the chance comes along, withdraws support from the offender at a crucial moment, tells an influential person about the offender's "true" character or abilities, fails to include the person's name on an important list of some sort, or follows some such other vindictive strategy.

Almost all the people we talked with who share this style believe that the *offender* is responsible for the retaliatory attack. "That's the beauty of this way of dealing with anger," Ken told us. "*You're* not doing the guy any harm; he's done it to himself." As an example, Ken told us about the time that a company vice-president, working out of the corporate office, visited his plant for a week, became impressed with the efficiency of some of Ken's production improvements, and raised his plant's quotas rather than offer praise or reward. Ken was seething but said nothing and did nothing, vowing "to get even at some point down the line." He observed: "What goes around comes around."

The knowledge that he would very likely be able to get even some-day helped him eliminate quickly his feelings of anger and frustration. He said that his "chest loosened" almost as soon as the thought he was not destined to be this man's victim forever came to him. About a year later, when this particular vice-president needed Ken's plant to put in some overtime in order to deliver a special shipment of frozen fruits that the vice-president had given his word he could deliver in half the usual time, Ken took advantage of the opportunity. There was a twinkle in his eye as he ticked off for us the reasons why that particular shipment was delivered to the customer much later, rather than much earlier. Among other unavoidable problems it seems that a couple of crucial processing machines had broken down that weekend and that some of his key employees had been unable to put in the extra hours.

Had Ken sabotoged the process? We couldn't be sure. Whether or not he had directly contributed to the emergence of the problems, it was clear that he had *not* intervened in order to get things back on track. To paraphrase Abbie Hoffman, he may not have been part of the problem, but he surely wasn't part of the solution. He hadn't gotten angry; he just got even. The vice-president was left holding the bag, and Ken is sure that "the people over at corporate never suspected this was revenge at its best!"

Some people who use this strategy for dealing with their anger do not feel its full satisfaction unless the target person has somehow real-ized who was responsible for the uncomfortable, hassling, painful, or embarrassing event that has occurred. Others seem to relish a private sense of satisfaction. In fact, like Ken, they prefer anonymity in these matters.

Unlike people who adopt most of the other ways we have described in this chapter of dealing with personal anger, those who adopt the method described here often seem to *enjoy* their style. They believe that revenge is sweet indeed.

How often do people who don't get mad really get even? We esti-mate that people who tend to use this strategy experience the vindication they desire on fewer than half the occasions when they have put this strategy into effect as a way of dealing with their anger. Time seems to be the important factor. Over time the offended person may begin to see other sides of the issue or more positive sides of the character of the offender. Or attention and emotional responses are diverted to other matters, and the desire for revenge begins to seem a little petty. In other words, over time people often come to forgive. "To err is human, to forgive divine" is a maxim that many people begin to endorse as they move farther in time from the offending event.

Another factor that interrupts the revenge process is that most people are unwilling to plan events that will provide for it. Most of us don't want to think of ourselves as someone who will orchestrate another's downfall—no matter how much that person is disliked. So the vast majority of people who use this style tend to wait for opportunity to present itself. And the opportunity doesn't always come. The offensive person may change jobs or locations, as might the person who is lying in wait to see justice come to fruition. Sometimes it's just that no good opportunity for vindication ever emerges.

Even though many often do not taste the sweetness of the revenge they expect, they report that they are happy with this style because it helps them manage their angry feelings. Almost as soon as they decide that getting even is a possible response, they start to feel better. Apparently they stop feeling like victims at that point. The people who tend to adopt this style are unable to use more direct ways of dealing with their angry feelings. In addition, they report that most of the indirect methods we've described don't provide enough satisfaction for them.

Most people believe that this style is adopted by more men than women. We agree but believe the difference is probably not large. Many more women use it than most people suspect. In many ways it is an aggressive strategy. Therefore, men are more likely to feel OK about adopting it. Nonetheless, we have discovered that almost as many women as men tend to adopt this strategy for dealing with their workplace anger. The major difference between the sexes seems to be that men will somewhat more easily admit that they adopt this strategy. Women are not quick to reveal that this style is one they use. In part this is because they are largely unaware of the preference. Given that such behavior is not considered "ladylike," women are more likely to develop other strategies in addition to this one and are less likely to pay attention to this revengeful aspect of their style. Many men who adopt this style tend to be proud of it.

Many men are comfortable with the idea of being used as an instrument for justice, an instrument for the redress of grievance. Most women are not comfortable with the idea of placing themselves in the position to be such an instrument at work.

### Carla: Getting Out, But Is the Getting Out Good?

Carla's style is the one most commonly found in work settings. While it is an approach that has been adopted by both sexes in large numbers, we estimate that more women than men tend to rely on it when confronted with their own angry feelings. We are also sure that almost everyone has used this strategy on at least a few occasions during the course of his or her work history.

Carla withdraws. When she feels anger, she physically removes herself from the precipitating situation. Most often she withdraws without comment, but on some occasions she has been known to huff off, letting her offender know her feelings through a cryptic remark or through nonverbal body language. As a typical example of how she deals with her own anger, she told us about a memorable day last winter when she "really lost it," as she put it.

Carla creates software packages for a middle-size firm on the West Coast. Both she and her boss have been with the company since its incorporation some fifteen years ago. They are very accustomed to each other's work styles. On the day in question Carla's boss, Bea, called her into the office to discuss a prospectus for a new statistics package that Carla had turned in several weeks before. Knowing Bea's style, Carla had assumed that when she hadn't heard anything about her outline after three weeks, the likelihood of Bea's being thrilled about the idea was slim indeed. As time had gone on and Bea had said nothing, Carla had grumbled to herself that her boss's approach to feedback was abominable. She resented not hearing one way or the other on Bea's evaluation of the quality of the work. Carla remarked to herself in the shower one morning that if Bea had waited all these weeks just to let her know that she considered the whole plan ridiculous, Bea was likely to "get a piece" of her mind. She fantasized telling Bea that all in all she was a terrific person to work for, but she needed to do some "work on herself" if she really ever expected to be a top-notch executive—one who knew how to instill enthusiasm and commitment in the people who worked for her.

As she headed for Bea's office that morning, Carla knew that she had been called to discuss the prospectus. The closer she came to Bea's door, the more anxious she became. The proposal was one she had worked on for about eight months. She thought it represented some of the very best work she was capable of doing.

Carla had settled in a chair and was participating in some rather stilted small talk when Bea abruptly changed the subject by saying, "This ASIC proposal isn't going to work, Carla. It's got some moments of brilliance, but overall it's just not the kind of thing we had in mind when we asked you to start thinking about this actuarial thing."

Carla was furious. Instantly furious. She sat impassively through a few more of her boss's remarks, then said, "I've got to get back to my office, Bea. If you don't have anything more to say on this subject, let's just cut this short." And without waiting for a reply, she got up and walked quickly out of the office. She recalled that she wanted badly to slam the door behind her but was aware of the need to control herself. While the door had been closed a little more forcefully than usual, she doubted that anyone could claim she "had actually slammed the thing shut."

On other occasions when she feels angry, Carla withdraws less dramatically. Sometimes her offenders do not know she is angry because she moves so quickly and quietly "within herself" when she feels this emotion. When Carla gets angry, she feels it pretty intensely, and she reasons that if she were to express it, she would do some things she would probably regret—and she would lose some things as well, like control, respect, and dignity. Or her job, perhaps, if she were to "make a habit of it." She shared her belief that if she expressed her anger every time she felt it, her work relationships could not tolerate the strain. She realized that she probably became angry about once every month or so over something around the office. But she was incapable of picturing herself *acting* angrily. The best she could do was summon up an image of huffing off, maybe slamming a door or two, or hurling a biting comment back over her shoulder.

Carla says that withdrawal—physical or emotional—provides her with at least *some* control over the situation. Usually her anger results from a sense that she cannot influence the proceedings, coupled with her knowledge of how important the particular issue is to her. Withdrawing at least makes a small point, she said. "When you just leave, you're saying that you have control over *something*. You're not just a victim."

Carla, like many others who adopt this style, has trouble reconnecting with the person she has abruptly left. She feels awkward for a few hours or days after the event has occurred. She reasons that since she has been mistreated, the other person should approach her. Yet she realizes that withdrawing as she does constitutes in itself an affront for some people and that perhaps she is then the one "at fault" and thus the one who ought to seek to repair the damages.

Few people we talked with who identified with this style were comfortable with it. Most reported that it feels very good for a short while—probably because at least *some* action has been taken. The feeling has been "registered" with the observer in some way. Problems seem to result later, however, with the realization that not much is known about the other person's position. These people were particularly aware that they don't know their offenders' reactions to *their* reactions, and no real progress on the issues has been made. Time after time, as we talked to people who tend to rely on this way of dealing with their own anger, we heard them remark that the biggest problem with it is the reconnecting. For some there is a sense of wanting their anger to be pursued by the other person. For others there is simply an awkwardness about returning to the conversation at a later time when no indication of the need for that had been expressed by either party because of the abruptness of the dialogue's end.

Carla talked about reconnection being easier when she has withdrawn quietly—or in a huff—from a group rather than an individual. She found it more possible to initiate the reconnection because she found it easier to approach a single person who had been a member of the group but seemed more in tune with her position.

It is worth mentioning again that no one we have talked with about anger at work failed to mention at least one instance of having "simply walked out" when they felt themselves becoming angry. Of course, there was wide variation in what people were accustomed to doing once that emotional abrupt break in the conversation had been made, especially within the groups of people who do not rely on withdrawal as a major technique for dealing with anger at work.

# 3

# Anger
## Being on the Receiving End

I know of no more disagreeable situation than to be left
feeling generally angry without anybody in particular to be
angry at.

—FRANK MOORE COLBY

J
UST AS there are recognizable ways of feeling and expressing
anger, so there are distinguishable styles of responding to it. We
are interested here in the responses of persons who are the targets
of somebody's anger in a work setting—not those who are merely
bystanders.

All of us who spend our days or nights somewhere out there in the
world of work have been in the position of discovering—either directly
or indirectly—that someone is mad at us for something or other. Being
on the receiving end of angry expressions is no less difficult, it seems,
than being in the position of sending them. Some, in fact, find it more
difficult.

Recall the last time you discovered that a colleague, employee, or
boss was steamed, and you were the reason. Many readers will remember angry outbursts aimed in their direction, while others received more
indirect messages that were conveyed through stony silence or work
slowdowns. We talked with quite a few people who reported that a
specific person in their work situation seemed mad *all* the time and
everyone had just become accustomed to the consequences. In most
job-related settings, however, anger is something that comes and goes,
cyclically in some cases such as those that are time-pressured, and
circumstantially in others where personalities and special tasks are
responsible for the variations.

People have characteristic ways of responding to angry messages.
Most of us have two distinct styles. We have a general way of respond-

ing if the message is indirect and circuitous, and we have a second way of reacting if it is clearly direct and confrontive. As you read through the following characterizations, you will probably find that you share some aspects of style with more than one person who is described in each of the two categories.

## Anger That Is Aimed at You Indirectly

When people let us know that they think we are at fault and they are angry with us but give that message in a circuitous way, we tend to have a different response from the one we have if the message has been clearly and unambiguously sent. We tend to respond in kind—i.e., we tend to respond indirectly. This is part of the reason many people choose more indirect routes of expression from time to time. Indirect messages do not require confrontation on anyone's part.

Indirect messages often provide the sender with an advantage that he or she values: They permit the sender to influence—in an important and practical way—the other person's response. Most people most of the time will not respond with anger to an indirect message of anger at work, at least not for a while. Indirect messages require more time for the receiving as well as for the sending.

An indirect message is an unclear message. In order for the receiver to appreciate it fully, some time and some thought need to be given to it. *Was that remark meant for me? Is she trying to tell me something with her silence this morning or is she simply preoccupied? Did I perhaps go too far in my criticism; am I not hearing from him because he's mad? Did he leave the meeting early because he was ticked off or because of another responsibility elsewhere?*

When ambiguous messages are involved, both the sender and receiver have some room to maneuver. The angry party need not take full responsibility for that anger, and the offending party is not forced to declare quickly what he or she thinks and feels. Consideration of the styles of Jed, Paul, and Leslie when faced with ambiguous anger provides opportunity for evaluation of the merits and disadvantages, in general, of indirect anger expressions among colleagues at work. In many ways, when people engage in indirect expressions of any important emotion and people respond in kind, an interesting set of dynamics begins to develop. Sometimes the very best analogy is to dancing. Often people seem to be "dancing around" an issue. The issue is definitely being dealt with, but not in a direct way.

### Paul: Preferring the Indirect and Acting on It

When circuitous ways of getting the message across are used, the person at whom anger is directed is much freer to choose whether or not to acknowledge the angry person's discomfort. He or she can also choose whether or not to participate in other indirect discussions that could result. Paul is the kind of person who is more than just willing to participate in an indirect dance of anger at work. He *prefers* this approach, and he *acts* on these messages. Confrontation is very difficult for him outside his personal relationships. So direct exchanges during the workday make him very uncomfortable.

Paul is just starting his own small plumbing repair company in a large southeastern city. He "will walk a country mile" to avoid an argument, and therefore, he truly appreciates it when employees or customers let him know in an indirect way that he has let them down somehow. In fact, this style of expressing negative information is so preferable to him that he makes it a point to be alert constantly for sidewise messages so that he can anticipate "trouble" before it develops into something that might require some direct confrontation. He rewards efforts at indirect communication by acting on them.

Paul told a story that illustrates the issues here perfectly. A few months earlier Selma, his receptionist-dispatcher-bookkeeper, had repeatedly routed phone messages to him much more slowly than she normally did. Apparently this had been going on for about three days before Paul "put two and two together" and realized she was angry about something. He told us that he spent considerable time trying to figure out what it was and eventually decided that Selma was taking action to let him know just how much she disliked the new plumber's assistant whom he had recently hired. He guessed that she was expressing her dislike by altering her speed of responding to requests. The new man had been asking her to do things for him more quickly than she felt she should have to do them. She had mentioned this fact to Paul, but he had not responded. He surmised that she was now slowing down in an attempt to let him know that her anger with the assistant was turning in her boss's own direction. As he usually does, Paul took steps to rectify the situation. He made a few suggestions to the assistant. Selma began getting his messages to him more quickly. No direct discussion of the issue ever took place.

Paul knows how to use indirect cues. And he prefers to operate indirectly himself. Thus, Paul's responses are usually the "right" responses as far as his accusers are concerned. In many ways he is the answer to the indirect message sender's prayers. He attends closely to the behavior of others, scans that behavior for indirect messages, and is motivated to change the things that he can change in order to alleviate the other person's anger. And all this "without a shot fired," as Paul says.

### Jed: Missing Cues and Ignoring Them

Jed ignores the messages. Often he doesn't even notice them. When he first started out as an automobile salesman several years ago, he often chastised himself for "missing" these social cues. Now he doesn't even bother to try to comprehend indirect messages, even though his current position as manager of five large auto dealership locations provides him with plenty of opportunity to pick up on people's backhanded angry comments and actions.

He told us of the time ten or twelve years ago when his boss had been so angry at him for botching a sales deal that he had taken Jed's company car home, forcing him to hitch a ride with someone else. This rather hostile act was followed the next day by the boss's orders that Jed deliver cars for the rest of the week rather than sell them. This was obviously a financially disastrous request, but not one that prompted Jed to put two and two together as Paul would have done. Jed remembers simply wondering if the boss was having a bad week and how much longer the mood could be expected to last. When he finally did figure out what the boss's motivations were, Jed was more embarrassed for having missed the social cues than he was for having dropped the ball with the auto deal that started the problems in the first place.

Jed told us that shortly after that incident he decided to stop trying to pick up on indirect cues since it never seemed to work for him anyway. He decided he was a failure when it came to that kind of social dynamic. He announced to the people he worked with that he was "lousy at reading personal messages" and asked them in a friendly and sincere way to let him know directly if they had a "beef" with him. As he has moved up in the organization, he has stuck with this approach. He says it works for him.

Jed thinks that he has become better at picking up on circuitous messages. However, despite increased ability, he noted that he has not increased his tolerance for this kind of approach. He told us that in his opinion, being indirect wastes time at best and is totally ineffective and annoying at its worst. "Give it to me straight, or don't give it to me at all," he says with an open grin.

Jed's style is a common one within the indirect category. It illustrates for us the difficulty that so many people have with indirect communication. They don't get it. While many people miss the message because they choose to ignore information that is communicated in this way, some just aren't skilled at picking up on verbal or nonverbal cues. Many people sense that *something* is going on, and wonder about it, but then forget it rather than work to figure out the meaning.

### Leslie: Meeting the Indirect with the Direct

Leslie's style is less common in work settings than are the styles adopted by Paul and Jed. She reports that she is pretty good at reading the cues that people send but that she has no patience with an indirect approach. Leslie refuses to dance. She knows that when someone gets angry with her, she is being blamed for something. Leslie firmly declared to us that people who blame her for an incident enough to get angry at her should do her "the courtesy" to let her know clearly what's going on.

Leslie confronts the person who appears to be sending indirect messages. For example, an accountant who shares an office with her recently reduced the amount of chitchat that was typical for them during a given day. The man "just stopped talking," she said. After experiencing this for only half a day, Leslie told him that she had noted the behavior, suspected that it had to do with some work she had done on a set of debit sheets given to her by a client they both worked for, figured that he was miffed about it, and said that she would appreciate it if he would directly let her know what was going on. She said that she let him know that she was "more than willing" to try to work things out, but she was unwilling to participate in any *nonverbal* conversation about how she might have messed up.

Leslie doesn't like sidewise messages because she believes people intend to "punish" others when they use that method of communication. She resents that intention. Leslie also believes that the indirectly angry person wants to send a message but is unwilling to hear a response or engage in "meaningful dialogue" about the problem.

Paul and Leslie respond to indirect expressions of anger in opposite ways. Paul resents confrontation, and Leslie resents indirect messages. And in further contrast with both of them, Jed originally just didn't pick up on indirect cues. Even now that he is more proficient at reading them, he simply finds the indirect dance too time-consuming and generally ineffective. While both men and women use all these styles, Paul's style is relied upon more often by women, and Jed's is used more often by men. Leslie's approach seems to be adopted by both sexes in equal numbers.

It is possible that from time to time all three of these strategies might seem useful to you. For example, perhaps you adopt Paul's style when you are dealing with indirect messages from your boss, while Leslie's approach may be more to your liking overall, and thus, you might use it within most of your work-related relationships. Whatever your approach, if you have trouble with the style you currently use for responding to indirect anger messages at work, you will find some suggestions for change in Chapter Ten.

## Anger That Comes Directly at You

Direct expressions of anger are confrontational. Even when the verbalizations are low-key and the message relatively nonthreatening, direct anger is basically confrontationsl because it almost *requires* that attention be focused on the issues of importance for the one who is angry. Little room for maneuvering is available. If someone comes right up to you and says he's angry at you, it is unlikely that you will ask after his mother, inquire about his health, comment on the weather, or turn attention toward the work issue of your own choice. You will likely respond somehow to the anger.

Those who prefer to deal with their own anger in a direct way tend to claim that they hang on to anger for a shorter time than they do when they adopt more circuitous or indirect methods. We are not sure that such a positive result can be solely attributed to the choice of direct strategy. Rather, we believe that the response style of the person who receives the anger has a lot to do with whether the angry person feels enough satisfaction and release to get over the whole thing fairly quickly. The other person involved in the anger transaction—the receiver—is important in determining how things turn out. The wide variety of responses people have to straightforward expressions of anger is well represented by Nancy, David, Ella, and Clark.

### Nancy: A Tinderbox Response

Nancy gets angry right back. She finds direct angry confrontations at work to be very disruptive and offensive, and she feels justified in "giving it back to them," immediately. In fact, she said she gets so mad sometimes that she is likely to be really unable to hear what a person has to say at all.

Nancy is the head nurse on a pediatrics ward, and a doctor, nurse, or parent is likely to confront her angrily two or three times a year. The last time it happened, a parent began yelling at her in the hall after he had found out that she was the one who had asked the physician to limit his visits to his terminally ill child, who took a turn for the worse each time this father appeared. Apparently the parents were in the midst of a difficult divorce at the time, and the father often came to the hospital hoping to convince his son that living with him after the divorce would be better than living with the mother. Immediately after each of these visits the boy experienced a severe setback. There were physicians and other nurses well within earshot as this man "unloaded" on Nancy, calling her names and using four-letter words. Nancy was angry in response to his anger. And she certainly didn't think his anger was justified since in her view, he had been further compromising his child's already precarious hold on life. Nancy told him that the kind of temper he was displaying might well be the cause for "many a problem" that not only this child but the rest of his children might face, that he was way out of line yelling in the hall like that, and if he didn't quiet down, she would ask him to leave the floor.

It was clear in our conversation with Nancy that she equates anger with aggression. She assumes that someone expressing anger toward her is intending to hurt her, and she responds in kind. As we talked, she began to reveal many other occasions when people in her setting had directly indicated to her that they were angry at her. But because they did not do so in an aggressive or hostile way, she did not immediately think of these occasions in response to our initial question. When she realized that we were asking for her characteristic responses to expressions of anger of all types, she thoughtfully replied that her style was probably basically the same no matter how people expressed anger to her—whether with hostility or in a more "reasonable" way. Nancy has a tendency to be aggressive—and thus to appear angry—when people confront her, even in calm and articulate ways, with their disappointment and anger over something she has done. She gets her back up. When someone actually yells at her, she is likely to raise her voice in return, while she is likely to match a more quiet style if the other person's display does not contain yelling. Nancy clearly does not like receiving any kind of direct anger at work. Anger makes *her* angry, and she responds in kind. While Nancy typifies this response style well, it's generally more characteristic of males than females in our culture.

### David: Listening and Responding

David's patterns are very different from Nancy's. He "toughs" through the situation toward the clearly defined goal of improving communication. David is a drummer in a well-known rock band. People lose their tempers with him fairly frequently—sometimes as often as once a week. He thinks the creative aspects of his business depend on access to emotions and thus does not think it unusual that so much direct anger is aimed in his direction during the course of a typical month. "It comes with the territory around here," he said.

David always feels uncomfortable when the anger flares. However, getting along with people, learning to understand them, and giving them a chance to express negative as well as positive emotions all are important goals for him. Therefore, when somebody starts telling him what he's done wrong—no matter what style he or she chooses for the telling—he makes it a point to do his best to *listen*. He asks his accuser for more information. He indicates that he understands that the other person must be pretty upset. He offers a point or two of clarification of his own position if that seems helpful. No matter what he's experiencing himself—sadness, confusion, anger—he tends to share those things only if he thinks the sharing might assist the goal of improving communication—that is, "finding out just exactly what this is all about."

David recalled a time when the lead guitar player in the band had abusively accused him of cutting one too many practices in order to meet with his accountant. The guy was furious that David would value the money more than the music. David began his end of the conversation by asking sincerely, "What do you mean?" several times. He then spent ten minutes or so listening while his accuser drifted off into comments on other aspects of the band's overall performance lately. Toward the end of the conversation David told the guitar player that he would probably feel the same way if he were in his shoes. He then mentioned that he had actually been "goofing off" in order to "be with a new lady" and had deviously said his accountant was involved so as not to have to take the inevitable "ribbing" that would occur if his partners were to know the truth. The conversation apparently ended with a discussion of how they could schedule practices at more convenient times and why there was such a general lack of creative fervor within the band these days.

"Getting angry is just part of living," David says. "I don't get angry a lot myself. But if I did, I'd sure want the other guy to listen and care about what I was feeling. I just try to give what I would want to get."

David's approach to an angry confronter is shared fairly equally by both men and women. While it is not as common as some of the other approaches we describe in this section, it is an approach that quite a few people we talked with wished they could learn to use. Someone else's anger doesn't usually hurt David. He uses it to help the work and the relationship prosper.

### Ella: Becoming Immobile

Ella freezes. We've seen her do it. The day we arrived at the department store where she is head buyer in Better Dresses and Sportswear, we walked into the manager's offices just in time to catch part of an exchange between Ella and her boss. It wasn't actually an exchange, however. To us, it appeared that Ella's boss was being quite tense and possibly accusatory for some reason, while Ella had become withdrawn—perhaps disdainfully—and was impassively looking down on her confronter.

Later Ella said that she had certainly not been disdainful or "above it all." Rather, she was immobile. Ella related that she has always responded that way to a direct expression of someone's anger. She cannot talk. Often she cannot even move. She simply feels trapped. Several people have told her that she appears to be cold and unapproachable during these moments. She is baffled by that information since her own experience of her response is so very different from the observer's. "The truth is," she said, "I get so taken aback and just plain scared, I guess, that I can't even move."

After one of these episodes Ella usually avoids her confronter until she is absolutely sure that the "trouble is over." Often she is unable to recall exactly what her accuser's point had been since she was mainly responding to her own perception of the person's angry emotion rather than the words. She guesses that this is true even if a person delivers an angry message in a straightforward and reasonably calm way. "I'm just not any good at handling other people's anger," she said.

Many people in the workday world, men and women alike, react as Ella does when faced with anger. Often they are not so easy to recognize because their appearance during the angry episodes may strongly belie how they actually feel. But they are so uncomfortable that they cannot do much at all—about the interaction or the precipitating events.

### Clark: Leaving the Scene

In contrast, Clark just leaves. He doesn't like to be approached with emotion at work. He doesn't "know what to do." So he just walks out if someone gets angry.

Sometimes Clark feels anger in return when he's confronted with someone's disappointment and fury. Sometimes he doesn't. In either case he refuses to respond to the person. Each time we pressed Clark, he could only offer that he leaves because he doesn't "know anything else to do." Clark's statement pretty much says it all for him. He, and others with his response style, react with confusion. They choose not to be in the situation. They leave.

Clark feels that the biggest difficulty with his approach is that his accuser is denied access to him. Often the person who is angry with him becomes further alienated as a result of seeing Clark just walk out. Usually the person has assumed, he is told, that Clark was angry in return. Clark has been accused of leaving in a huff when he really wasn't huffing. He was just leaving.

There is an adaptation of this style that can legitimately be referred to as huffing off. The accused gets angry in return and, when exiting the situation, often leaves a sharp retort or a slammed door behind. This approach is a variation on the one illustrated by Clark's remarks, but it is more rare. Clark's style is fairly common in work settings, and both men and women tend to use it in equal numbers. The huffing-off variation is more often associated with men in our culture.

In addition to great variation in the things people *do* when faced with direct and indirect anger messages at work, we have discovered that there is variation in the degree to which they are able to *comprehend* what their accusers are trying to say. The single most important factor seems to be the extent to which the receiving person is captured by the emotion rather than the substance in the interchange. Some people can only respond to the anger. Of all the variables in the situation, that is the one that most compels their attention. They concentrate so much on the feeling that is being directed toward them that they lose adequate access to the substance of the message. Others are able to concentrate more closely on the issues while controlling the impact of the emotions.

Another thing we have discovered is that almost universally people do not have goals or agendas for their own behavior in situations where they are confronted with anger and accusation. Very few people we talked with expected to be part of angry episodes at work, even though

almost everyone could claim a history of having been on the receiving
end of anger on at least a few occasions. Hardly anyone gave this kind
of work-related transaction the kind of attention that so many other
aspects of work life receive. Most people assumed that they have little
knowledge of their own anger response styles *simply because they have
not given the issue any thought.* We agree.

# 4

# Tears and Weeping
## Why Do We Cry?

It is such a secret place, the land of tears.
—ANTOINE DE SAINT-EXUPÉRY

ILEEN MORGAN is a veritable fixture in one of the Midwest's largest investment firms, where she is an administrative associate. She's watched the company grow from a promising local enterprise with three small offices dotted around Chicago to a company employing thousands in over 130 branch offices throughout the Midwest. At fifty-seven she's been with the firm for thirty years.

Eileen Morgan is a no-nonsense person at work. She's pleasant and extremely efficient. She knows the company inside and out.

In 1951, as a young bride just married to her high school sweetheart, Eileen had absolutely no aspirations to positions of power. Like most other young women of that time, she envisioned her future as full of her home and her family. But four years and two children later Eileen's world was transformed overnight when her husband was killed in a collision as he drove home from work. At twenty-five Eileen was suddenly a widow, the single parent of two preschool children, with no income and few job skills. She took a job with a fledgling investments firm as a receptionist/secretary. Over the succeeding years the partners agreed that it was one of the best hiring decisions they had ever made.

One of the cornerstones of Eileen's success in her own eyes was the fact that she was "in control" of herself and everything that went on around her. It was a quiet control, not aggressive or self-congratulatory but firm and deep. One of the things that Eileen never did, everyone agreed, was lose control. In fact, she could hardly understand how someone in the habit of yelling could command enough respect to get any work done. And she never cried at work. She had certainly shed tears at home, but it was a point of pride with her that those tears never saw the light of her office.

There were occasions when she had felt negative emotions rise; she was too involved and invested in her work to avoid that. But she had them under control. Well, there *had* been one exception, but she had pretty well put it away into the farthest corners of her memory.

She was then executive secretary to the vice-president for public relations, an area where one is frequently dealing with the public, with deadlines, and with some pretty eccentric and unusual people. During the time in question she had been working on a major report that was to combine information about many of the company's operations with new information on some of the joint ventures it was beginning to undertake with other firms. She had worked very hard on the report, which was to represent the "cutting edge" of the company's directions. Work on it had taken a major part of her time for several months, as she gathered materials, interviewed countless executives in and out of the company, brought the text gradually to a fully approved state, and made final photo selections.

The report had been sent out for preliminary printing, had come back for final proofing, and had been sent out again for final production. It was due in finished form in three weeks. At eight-fifteen one morning a harried and blustering man appeared at her desk, telling her loudly that he had to see the VP for PR now, *now!* Somewhat taken aback, she told the man politely but firmly that Mr. Johansen was not in at the moment and that he had a full schedule for the rest of the day. Perhaps there would be an opening tomorrow. "Tomorrow!" shouted the visitor. "Tomorrow! I need to see him *now!*"

Eileen grew uncomfortable but became firmer and more determined under the barrage of yelling. She repeated herself firmly and asked if there was something she could help with.

"I doubt it, honey!" snapped the visitor. "As I understand it, *you're* the problem!" Things went downhill from there. He stopped momentarily to confirm that she was Eileen Morgan, as her desk plate claimed. And then he roared: *Who* had given her approval to write what had been written about his firm in this fancy report? Where in the world had she gotten the information? Hadn't anybody ever taught her how to check her facts? Or was that little detail something she and this firm simply didn't care about? Had it ever occurred to her that she might have interviewed the wrong person about the information? A person who had been fired two weeks after the interview? Had it ever entered her mind to check back with them about the final draft of the report instead of assuming that if she didn't hear from them, it was OK? What in the world was she thinking of? And when in the world was her boss going to see him?

Eileen was amazed, furious, and scared. She knew she had done a good job with the report. But she also knew that somewhere along the line she might have made a mistake. In fact, a quiet but frantic run through her memory revealed that there *were* two companies with which she hadn't made a final check in person. Very uneasy now, she made one more effort to handle the problem herself and asked what the specific points at issue were. But the visitor's anger was hot, and he declined to deal with her any further.

Thirty minutes later Sam Johansen was accosted by the angry visitor as he returned to his office. Waving the draft of the report, the man yelled, "She never checked it out with me, she got bad information, she went to press with the stupid thing without double-checking anything!"

Eileen interjected firmly: "Mr. Johansen, could we discuss this in your office?" She knew that her careful control was now running on low.

Sam Johansen decided rapidly to bring both of them into his office. As he shut the door, Eileen was keenly aware that she detested this man and his incredible rudeness and was about to say so. She was also keenly aware of the gnawing anxiety in a pit at the bottom of her stomach—anxiety born of an awareness that she might have made a serious mistake that was going to cost the company a substantial sum. She felt shame and embarrassment rising as she sat down tensely. When Sam asked Ed Thomas to tell him more specifically what the problem was, Ed began less loudly but was still clearly agitated. Eileen looked on, angry, controlled, and increasingly uncomfortable.

Sam Johansen turned to her after Ed Thomas had finished and said, rather formally, "Well, Eileen, what's happened here?"

She opened her mouth to speak, but her anger at Ed Thomas's behavior, which had toned down considerably since her boss returned, got caught somewhere in her throat by an urge to clear her own good name and justify her behavior. She paused, swallowed hard, trying to get the lump down. Ed Thomas glared at her. Sam Johansen looked supportive but very businesslike and eager to hear her explanation. Her swallow only intensified the sense that she couldn't speak, and she felt tears—tears!—coming to her eyes. She looked up at the ceiling, acutely uncomfortable, stalling for time.

"Mrs. Morgan?" inquired Mr. Johansen.

And then the tears spilled. "I'm sorry," she managed to say to the two now-confused and awkward-looking faces before her. Rising, she murmured, "I think I'll excuse myself." She tried not to rush to the door. Once out of the office, however, she did rush to the women's room, locked herself in a stall, and cried and cried—silently, so that no one would know, she hoped. And she held cold water to her eyes before she left the bathroom sometime later, trying hard to erase the giveaway signs of her extraordinary break in control.

By the time she returned, Ed Thomas had gone. And through conversation that was at first very awkward, she and Sam Johansen worked out the problem. He was almost as concerned about her tears as he was about the project and asked if anything else was wrong. Mr. Thomas's rudeness had "just thrown" her, she explained. She was fine. It wouldn't happen again, she stated firmly.

Like thousands of other people, Eileen believes that she doesn't cry at work. However, for some people, like Eileen, there actually have been one or two memorable instances. But as a pattern of behavior? Never. Crying, she and many, many others would agree, is simply a behavior that's inconsistent with workplace expectations. In keeping with this belief, some people have never cried at work. But there are others, equally competent, who have cried a fair amount, covertly or openly.

Why do tears intrude? And where do they come from?

## Personal Tears; Cultural Tears

Tears are a mystery. They spring, in virtually identical form, from joy as well as pain. They may come from intense needs to communicate, but their very flowing may render a crier unable to speak. They are uniquely human, yet most of us ignore or suppress them for most of our lives. We accept them in the very young and—reluctantly—in the very old. But we do not have much patience with them (or even want to acknowledge that they're there) in the decades of life between child-hood and old age.

We begin life with a cry. And after that first lusty signal of success-ful entry into the world, we continue crying. We cry to let the adults in our world know when we need something, but scarcely does real language begin before the world starts teaching that tears are not an acceptable expression of needs or feelings. Having relied on cries for attention of all kinds, young children are told—albeit gradually—to bring their tears under control. The measure of adult maturity, in fact, is sometimes taken to be the ability to control tears, to "stand like a man" and take it, to be "adult" about events that are distressing.

Despite the common derogation of crying in our culture, almost everyone knows someone who sheds clandestine tears in public places or cries in the privacy of home at times. But as we learned some years ago when we first began delving into this topic, developmental psychologists don't know much or don't divulge much about tears in adulthood. In fact, one might conclude in concurrence with prevailing cultural attitudes toward crying that mature adults simply don't shed tears. Yet the world of literature is certainly replete with adult human tears. From mythology to contemporary biography and fiction, from John Steinbeck to Eldridge Cleaver, from grocery store romances to serious novels, the worlds created by writers are inhabited by characters who sometimes cry. And most of those who cry are normal adults. At major moments in their lives, and a few minor ones, in the midst of the intense times and occasionally during normal times, they cry.

In fact, our practices for accepting or rejecting tears in adults are not really as ironclad as the unwritten social rules might imply. Most of us don't like them and don't like to acknowledge them in adults, but we make exceptions. For example, we find (and perhaps sometimes eagerly seek) tears of joy streaming down the faces of strong and accomplished athletes; a burly hero who's achieved the pinnacle of NFL success hoists the trophy aloft to the shouts of his teammates as champagne and tears mingle down his face. Tears flow with joy. And we accept them. They also flow with desolation, as we know when we cry with the pain of losing someone we love, to death, to divorce, or even to "good" separations—a son's marriage, a daughter's move to college. We accept tears in ourselves and others in those instances as well.

More consistently we make some exceptions based on gender. In many circumstances, our culture believes, a woman's tears are more acceptable than a man's. For example, when fear or stress is involved, women often have more cultural permission to cry, and there is sometimes a fairly strong cultural expectation that they *will* do so. The husband who arrives home after a Saturday away and finds one child swinging from the chandelier, two others arguing to the brink of slugging it out, and the baby sloshing in the midst of an overturned bowl of spaghetti might not be surprised if his wife burst into sobs at the chaos all around before asking for help. If *she* were the one away, however, returning to her husband in the midst of the same Saturday family circus, she and he might be most startled if he began sobbing as she came through the door. Women's tears are often seen as normal in the confines of their private lives. Their tears may serve many social functions at home and in other areas of personal life. For example, their tears suggest vulnerability and closeness, characteristics that often promote interpersonal relationships and friendship. They suggest a need to be cared for, a need to be protected, and a need to be helped. And the role of men caring for, protecting, and helping women is often viewed as a good and natural component of normal male-female relationships.

But the differential expectations for women's and men's crying behavior often stop at the household door. For at work women and men are expected to behave in very similar fashion. And the similar fashion prescribed is not based on the model of acceptable and traditionally desirable female behavior at home. It is based, rather, on the model of traditionally acceptable male behavior: strong; resourceful; unemotional; determined in the face of adversity; independent; able to take care of oneself and others, if need be. At work we usually expect both men and women to behave like men. Men at work do not cry. And women who work out of the home, in what used to be the "man's world" of work, should not cry.

And yet many women at work *do* cry. Not every day, not every month, or even every year. But many cry occasionally at work. They cry because they've spent a lifetime being socialized into the expectation that it is all right to weep at some points in life. They cry because most of them continue to live full personal lives within which it's still OK to cry in some circumstances. It's hard to cut off the messages of a lifetime, even with iron-willed intent to do just that. It's often hard, too, to turn off the personal world and its styles in favor of the work world and its preferred styles, as if both were connected to some smoothly functioning internal tap that could be accessed at will. And sometimes, perhaps increasingly in these days, some women cry because—like some men—they have a growing commitment to work and to using their own styles there.

As we discovered, many men sometimes cry at work, too.

### Crying Comes in Many Sizes, Shapes, and Forms

One of the things we began to learn in our research on adult crying at work is that crying takes many forms. Most men and women think of crying as the shedding of tears, sometimes involving whole body movement—as, for example, when we sob and our shoulders and our whole bodies may shake. Or our crying may be quiet; it may simply involve the flowing of tears down the face—one tear or many tears.

When we ask women if they've cried at work, most of them say yes, they have. If we ask men the same question, most say no, they haven't. But if we change the phrasing of the question somewhat, if we begin to include some of the physical symptoms that often precede the active flow of tears, many of the men who initially said no change their response. If we ask, for example, "Have you ever choked up at work— i.e., felt a lump in your throat, felt an urge to suppress something that might turn into tears?"—many men say yes, they have. Like their female counterparts who experience crying, they are usually very quick to point out that this happens seldom; for example, they can think of only two, maybe three events at work where they choked up. They assure us that they definitely don't run around choking up all the time. If the question is framed still another way—"Have you ever felt tears come to your eyes?"—we're also likely to get more yeses from men. These affirmative responses are often followed quickly by a statement that they didn't "let the tears get loose," however. They stayed in control, wrestled the tears back in somehow. And as is true of many women who tear up, they'll often add quickly that they *didn't* cry.

However, there are several varieties of crying, only one of which is the classic tears-running-down-the-face version. The feeling of choking up is a form of crying. This may begin with a lump in the throat, an almost physical press to keep down and out of sight tears or the emotions that threaten to produce them. Choking up often comes with the sense that speech is not possible for the moment. It may be followed by clearing the throat, averting the face, taking a brief and almost unnoticeable time out to collect one's thoughts back into a rational and controllable place.

Tears in the eyes are another, quiet manifestation of crying. Eyes glisten and are noticeably moist. Tears begin to well up in the eyes, slowly or suddenly. People experiencing the forming of tears may struggle hard to keep them from flowing over. They may look up at the ceiling. They may suddenly "discover" a contact lens slipping or a speck of dust in the eye. They may simply avert the eyes and keep very still, hoping for the best, until the welling tears have subsided.

Crying may also take its more classic form, the quiet version, with tears spilling from the eyes. It may continue for a brief or for a long period of time. The person who experiences this kind of crying usually knows all too well that others around him or her are aware of the tears. If these tears come in a work setting, they're almost always accompanied by efforts, calm or frantic, to find a tissue or handkerchief to stem the flow and get them out of sight. The person may leave the scene (as Eileen did), may continue talking if conversation was in progress when the tears began, or may simply shut off the ongoing activity and let the tears come.

Another and more obvious classic form of crying combines the flowing of tears and body movement. The crier's tears overflow. He or she may cough to clear the throat, and the shoulders and the whole body may shake. The crier may feel "blinded by tears" and feel helpless to stop them. If the crier is at work, the feeling of being controlled by the crying may be accompanied by acute distress at being out of control, at looking ridiculous in front of others. Sobbing is the name often given to this kind of crying.

Finally, there seems to be a form of crying that has at times been called blubbering, and at others hysterical crying. This kind of crying occurs rarely in work settings. It involves the flowing of tears and whole body movement, described above, but at a much more intense level. It is so absorbing for the person that the crier may lose all sense of caring what others around may think of it.

Mostly the kinds of crying we experience in work settings, include the first three varieties: choking up; tears in the eyes; quietly flowing tears.

All the crying we've described above generally fits into a category that has been labeled "emotional crying." As William Frey, a biochemist who has studied tears, points out (and as most of us who've ever peeled an onion or felt a gnat fly smack into our eye can attest), emotional tears certainly aren't the only kinds of tears we shed. Frey suggests that humans experience two kinds of tears: irritant tears, tears that come to our eyes when noxious fumes or "foreign bodies" irritate them; and emotional tears, which seem to come as biological response to emotional stress. Irritant tears serve the function of excreting potentially harmful substances from the eyes ("washing" them). Emotional tears have functions that science is as yet unclear about. Frey suggests that emotional tears, which account for far more of the total tears shed in a lifetime than do irritant tears, may also serve an excreting function. They may wash away harmful substances that build in the body in response to stress. On the basis of his own research and other findings, Frey notes that emotional tears contain higher concentrations of some biochemical substances than do irritant tears. This evidence, he suggests, supports his thesis that emotional tears serve an excretory function, releasing substances triggered by emotional responses.

Biochemical analyses tell us important things about tears themselves, but they do not result in an understanding of the emotions and situations that precipitate tears and crying. For that we must turn to the experiences of people—in literature, in life, in work.

We cry for as many reasons as there are emotions. Any intense emotion appears to have the capacity to generate tears in human beings. Far from being a sign of weakness, as much of the common cultural myth would suggest, crying seems more accurately to be a way of giving overt or behavioral expression to deep feelings, feelings that are "beyond words." For the most part the tears we speak of have their genesis in feelings. There is, though, an exception: crying that is stimulated by physical pain.

In children physical pain in itself may produce tears. In adults bodily pain is often accompanied by emotional pain as well—pain at being insufficiently strong to suppress the tears; pain at defeat by an opponent or disease; pain at the knowledge of physical frailty that bodily injury or illness brings. But tears of physical pain may be among those that are most acceptable to others, because cultural messages about them aren't quite so mixed. Even a strong person, many agree, has a "right" to tears in the wake of intensely painful physical events. For men especially, tears from intense bodily pain may be among the few varieties that fail to mount a serious challenge to stereotypic views of strong manhood.

Other human experiences that bring forth tears are centered on loss and empathy for others who have experienced loss. As we grieve over the death of another, feel sadness at loss or disappointment, feel regret at paths not taken or words left unspoken, we often experience emotions so deep that they—and we—are beyond words. In these times tears may come, perhaps bringing release from the hold of overwhelming emotion.

In the grief born of emotional pain that comes when someone you love dies, there is sorrow for that which is passing and that which has passed, even when the loss is accepted as inevitable. The grieving and the emotional pain are often both for the passing of the person and for the aloneness of oneself in the face of loss.

In New Testament history Jesus received urgent word from close friends Mary and Martha that their brother Lazarus was gravely ill. Before Jesus arrived, Lazarus died. Two days later, as Jesus neared their village, Mary left her home of mourning and went out to meet Him. "When Jesus saw her weeping, and the Jews who had come along with her also weeping, he was deeply moved in spirit and troubled. 'Where have you laid him?' he asked. 'Come and see, Lord,' they replied. Jesus wept."[6] Jesus wept. He wept for the sorrow of his friends, for their emotional pain in loss; He was "deeply moved in spirit and troubled" by their tears and sorrow. And He wept for his own loss of a friend. Almost every adult experiences pain such as this in the death of loved ones. Life goes on, as everyone knows, but the pain and the tears may continue.

The mere anticipation of parting and death may bring tears to the eyes of adults. Fedor Dostoyevsky, in *The Brothers Karamazov,* records a conversation between an "elder" and his student. The elder concludes:

> "This is my last message to you: In sorrow seek happiness. Work, work unceasingly. Remember my words from now on, for though I shall talk to you again, not only my days, but my hours are numbered."
>
> Alyosha's face again showed great emotion. The corners of his lips trembled.
>
> "Why are you crying again?" the elder said, with a gentle smile. "Let laymen bid farewell to their dying with tears. Here we rejoice over the father who is departing."[7]

In the anticipation of parting from one who is loved, tears may come, even to one who is told that the passage through death should be cause for happiness, not sorrow.

Tears of grieving and loss may emerge for the passing of stages of life, too, even when they are replaced by something "better," something everyone wanted. Parents often shed tears, openly or secretly, as they send their children off to school for the first time. And sometimes mothers and fathers cry at their children's weddings even when they think the new sons- or daughters-in-law are truly wonderful. The tears are shed not because parents want the event canceled—rarely do we *really* want development stopped—but because a stage of life that has been enjoyed and loved is passing. That knowledge itself may bring its own tears and sadness, calling attention as it does to the realities of aging.

There may be sadness and grieving, too, at the passing of a project or a way of doing things. As change comes to institutions, new policy makers often mandate new ways of getting things done, and sorrow may follow for those who "remember when. . . ." When an industrial plant or a school, long outmoded, actually closes its doors, tears of sorrow and loss may be shed by those who once worked there, once went to school there, once lived a part of life there. In his classic series (ostensibly for children but loved by many adults as well) *The Chronicles of Narnia,* C. S. Lewis describes the end of a fantasy world. As those who've lived in Narnia watch its extinction from their vantage point in another world, Peter stoically says:

> "So . . . night falls on Narnia. What, Lucy! You're not *crying?*" . . .
>
> "Don't try to stop me, Peter," said Lucy. . . . I am sure it is not wrong to mourn for Narnia. Think of all that lies dead and frozen behind that door." . . .

> "Sirs," said Tirian. "The ladies do well to weep. See I do so myself. I have seen my mother's death. What world but Narnia have I ever known? It were no virtue, but great discourtesy, if we did not mourn."[8]

Events do not have to be personally experienced to produce tears of grief and sadness. Difficult experiences in others' lives may generate sadness and a vicarious sense of loss. A moviemaker who sets out to produce a "tearjerker" knows this, as does a novelist who wants readers to be "moved to tears" over the power of the prose. Many tears were shed over Brian Piccolo's death, powerfully recounted in the film *Brian's Song.* Many of those who cried had scarcely heard of Brian Piccolo or Gale Sayers. And yet the story—the way it was told, its basic appeal to human love and caring—generated intense sadness and tears in many people. Probably as many people shed tears again as the lovable character of another film, *E.T.,* lay dying, surrounded by modern medical technology. There were perhaps as many who choked up with joy as E.T. finally recovered and returned home.

Tears may come, too, as we think about events long passed, lives long over. Eldridge Cleaver, political activist and social commentator, described a prison teacher, whom he called The Christ, in *Soul on Ice*:

> He was drawn to those students who seemed most impossible to teach—old men who had been illiterate all their lives and set in their ways. Lovdjieff didn't believe that anyone or anything in the universe was "set in its ways." Those students who were intelligent and quickest to learn he seemed reluctant to bother with, almost as if to say, pointing at the illiterates and speaking to the bright ones: "Go away. Leave me. You don't need me. These others do."
>
> Jesus wept. Lovdjieff would weep over a tragic event that had taken place ten thousand years ago in some forgotten byway in the Fertile Crescent. Once he was lecturing on the ancient Hebrews. . . . "What is it that keeps pulling them back to this spot!" he exclaimed. He lost his breath. His face crumbled, and he broke down and wept. "Why do they insist on living in the middle of that—that" (for once, I thought meanly, The Christ couldn't find a word) "that—that—Freeway!" . . . He pointed to the trade routes on the map behind his desk, then he sat down and cried uncontrollably for several minutes.
>
> Another time, he brought tape-recorded selections from Thomas Wolfe's *Look Homeward Angel.* The Christ wept all through the tape.
>
> The Christ could weep over a line of poetry, over a single image in a poem, over the beauty of a poem's music. . . ."[9]

The tears of a victorious athlete and the tears of proud parents are tears that spring at least in part from another emotion, joy. We are often warmed to see evidence of special bonds of affection: the bear hugs of reuniting families at airport gates and bus stations; the sight of soldiers reunited with families. And many of us who witness or partake find lumps coming to our throats or tears coming to our eyes.

Even in early biblical history people shed tears of joy and emotional awareness, as Genesis recounts of Joseph. Joseph, eleventh child of Jacob by his wife Rachel, was much loved by Jacob. And being so specially loved, Joseph was also the target of jealousy among his brothers. Acting out of anger and jealousy, they sold Joseph into slavery and lied to their father about Joseph's ostensible death. Joseph made his way as a slave to Egypt and eventually into the confidence of the pharaoh, who placed Joseph in a government position second in power only to his own. From this powerful position Joseph oversaw the rationing and distribution of food to the entire population of Egypt and many who came to Egypt from adjoining countries during a great famine. As things developed, among those who came seeking food from Joseph were his brothers, who did not recognize him, although he knew who they were as soon as they appeared before him. He gave the brothers grain but, after they left, sent soldiers after them and had them brought back on trumped-up charges of theft by the youngest brother, Benjamin. Joseph's intention throughout was apparently to ascertain the current condition of his brothers' characters—and the presence (or absence) of remorse for their act of selling him many years earlier. One of his brothers pleaded with Joseph to let Benjamin return to their father and offered himself as a prisoner in Benjamin's place. Soon ". . . Joseph could no longer control himself before all his attendants, and he cried out, 'Have everyone leave my presence!' So there was no one with Joseph when he made himself known to his brothers. And he wept so loudly that the Egyptians heard him, and Pharaoh's household heard about it."

Joseph revealed his identity and explained all that had happened since they had sold him so many years earlier. The brothers, the writer notes, were "terrified," but they listened and gradually came to believe and trust Joseph's expressed intention to bring them all and their families and their father, Jacob, to live with him in Egypt. As this meeting came to an end, Joseph "threw his arms around his brother Benjamin and wept, and Benjamin embraced him, weeping. And he kissed all his brothers and wept over them. Afterward his brothers talked with him." The brothers returned to their own land to retrieve their families and Jacob, and in due course they returned to Joseph in Egypt. As Joseph heard of their approach, he "had his chariot made ready and went to Goshen to meet his father Israel [Jacob]. As soon as Joseph appeared before him, he threw his arms around his father and wept for a long time."[10]

Joseph clearly was a crier. And, one might add, he was no slouch. Rising from slave quarters in the pharaoh's household to a position of significant responsibility, rising again from palace imprisonment on false charges to a position whose authority was second only to the pharaoh's, Joseph was a foreigner in a new land who had a lot of strength, power, and faith. And with all that, he—as is true for so many of us—was moved to tears and sobbing by emotionally powerful events. It's interesting, too, that even then crying in adults was notable, as during the first reunion, when Joseph ordered his attendants out and the doors closed before he revealed himself to his brothers. Even through the closed doors his crying was heard. And all the pharaoh's household talked about it the next day. Not too unlike some few offices we've heard about from very contemporary adults who've cried or seen someone crying at work!

Tears come, too, from happiness over positive human relationships and perhaps a bit from the sadness we often experience at knowing the temporal limitations on friendships. Norman Cousins tells a story in *Anatomy of an Illness* of a visit with Pablo Casals when Don Pablo was in his late eighties. Casals tells Cousins about a valuable Brahms manuscript given to him years earlier by an old, old friend and then describes the last time he saw his friend: "The war came. He was in his eighties. He had no intention of spending the rest of his old age under Nazism. He moved to Switzerland. He was then more than ninety. I was eager to pay my respects. Just seeing him again, this wonderful old friend who had done so much for music, was to me a very moving experience. I think we both wept on each other's shoulder."[11]

In *The Best of Everything* Richard Yates writes about Ralph, someone any of us might know, someone you might pass every day. He tells of Ralph's wedding day, close at hand, and of Ralph's feeling a little (or more than a little) blue that the guys at work have made no big deal about it: "When Ralph left the office he felt vaguely let down. Somehow, he'd expected more of the Friday before his wedding. The bonus check had been all right (although secretly he'd been counting on twice that amount), and the boys had bought him a drink at lunch and kidded around in the appropriate way ('Ah, don't feel too bad, Ralph—worse things could happen'), but still, there ought to have been a real party." Ralph meets his friend Eddie for a drink, their ritual on Friday nights. Eddie, unbeknownst to Ralph, has planned a large surprise party.

Ralph doesn't have a clue, and Eddie plays up the fact as they walk along.

> Ralph stopped on the sidewalk, suddenly enraged, his damp coat wadded in his fist. "Look, you bastid. Nobody's gonna make ya come, you know—you or Marty or George or any of the rest of 'em. Get that straight. You're not doin' *me* no favors, unnastand?"
> "Whatsa matta?" Eddie inquired. "Whatsa matta? Can'tcha take a joke?"
> "Joke," Ralph said. "You're fulla jokes." And plodding sullenly in Eddie's wake, he felt close to tears.

Ralph and Eddie continue on to Eddie's house, under the ruse of getting Eddie's suitcase, which Ralph plans to borrow for the honeymoon. As they walk in the door to Eddie's place, Ralph is overwhelmed to see the room "packed deep with grinning, red-faced men—Marty, George, the boys from the block, the boys from the office—everybody, all his friends, all on their feet and poised motionless in a solid mass." The men strike up a chorus of "For he's a jolly good fellow" and shout out, "Speech, speech!" Ralph watches Eddie, now wading toward him through the crowd, holding high a new suitcase—a present from all of the guys. "Ralph couldn't speak and couldn't smile. He could hardly even see."

Later, after the party, the emotions continue as Ralph tells Gracie, his fiancée, about the party. " 'They was all there, Gracie,' " he said, " 'All the fellas.' " He tells her then about Eddie's presentation of the suitcase: " 'Here, Ralph," he siz. "Just to let ya know you're the greatest guy in the world." ' His fingers tightened again, trembling. 'I cried, Gracie,' he whispered. 'I couldn't help it. I don't think the fellas saw it or anything, but I was cryin.' He turned his face away and worked his lips in a tremendous effort to hold back the tears."[12] Ralph, like thousands of other ordinary people in life, men and women, knew tears that welled from feelings of being loved and being cared about.

As we saw in Chapter One, most of us think of anger as an emotion that leads to yelling, shouting, carrying on, and sometimes physical fights and attacks. But many adults, especially women, do not express anger in shouting, assertion, or aggressive behavior but rather in tears. Tears that spring from anger appear to emerge from frustration that what one is saying isn't being heard by another. Such tears may also embody grieving that one's ideas are rejected by another out of hand, before they've been given a fair hearing (literally). They may incorporate fear and anger that the other person does not really *want* to hear what you're saying.

Tears of anger and frustration at not being heard have been shed for centuries. Irving Stone, in *The Agony and the Ecstasy,* gives us his understanding of time early in Michelangelo's life when he had become aware of his passion for sculpture and might have thrown his energy into convincing his skeptical friends that sculpting is an exciting, vital art. Stone writes that one of Michelangelo's friends, Jacopo, "hooted" as Michelangelo spoke of his love for sculpting. As Stone continues to envision the scene. . . .

> "Jacopo jumped down from his perch. Sculpture is a bore. What can they make? A man, a woman, a lion, a horse. Then all over again. Monotonous. But the painter can portray the whole universe: the sky, the sun, the moon and the stars, clouds and rain, mountains, trees, rivers and seas. The sculptors have all perished of boredom."

Tears of frustration welled in Michelangelo's eyes.
Another friend picks up the attack:

> ". . . has it ever occurred to you that the reason there are no sculptors left is because of the cost of material? . . . Who would provide you with stone, who would support you while you practiced on it?" . . .
> Michelangelo turned away. If only he knew more. Then he could convince them of the magnificence of fashioning figures in space. . . . Without another word, he walked down the cool marble steps, away from the Duomo, over the cobbled streets to home.[13]

Within this story Michelangelo perceives clearly that he is not going to be heard. Tears come to his eyes. Then, in a behavioral response all too familiar to many of us who try to be heard but feel stymied in the effort, Stone has Michelangelo make one last effort to explain himself. Then Michelangelo leaves, perhaps unable to speak because of tears or perhaps having decided that the argument cannot be pursued or won at that point.

Tears may also come in blinding anger, anger that is a cumulative response to a sequence of events—extended over time or compacted into the space of a few minutes. That anger may flare at another who has so ignored or misconstrued what we are saying, or have been trying to say, that there seems no recourse but to let the fury fly.

### Tears at Work

Former talk show host Mariette Hartley introduced a nationally televised discussion of tears in the workplace with this question: "Tears on a love note, tears on your pillow. They're understandable, even poetic. But tears in the executive suite?"

Most people grant that adults cry, perhaps more often and for more complicated reasons than we usually admit. But do tears really belong at work?

The answer may reside not so much in a consideration of whether tears ought to be in the workplace as in the reality that they *are* there. *Tears are at work because adults experience emotions in all aspects, times, and places of their lives.*

As we know, where there are emotions there is also the possibility— and often the reality—of tears. Not always and certainly not in all situations. But in offices and work settings across the country many highly capable professional women and men find their emotions occasionally leading them to tears. Like Eileen Morgan, they may cry very, very seldom. But from time to time their tears fall. When they fall, those who see them may feel a need to respond. But many of us, criers and observers alike, often find ourselves woefully inadequate to the task of responding because *we don't understand where the tears come from or why they came. And without knowing that, we can't figure out what to do about them.*

On her own "day of infamy," as she once ruefully referred to it, Eileen Morgan's tears came from anger at the behavior of her adversary, Ed Thomas. She felt frustration from the fact that he wouldn't listen to her and deal with her about the issue at hand, and she felt fear that she might, after all, have made a serious and costly mistake.

Eileen Morgan certainly didn't begin her day or even the interaction with the angry Ed Thomas with any intention of crying. In fact, she struggled intently to keep the tears down once she realized they were on the way. She hated that they came. She was profoundly embarrassed for herself, for her job performance, for her boss.

Perhaps worst of all, although she didn't think of it as the worst thing at the time, *her tears brought the entire interaction to a halt.* They stopped it cold. She, for one, dropped all her intentions to defend her actions, explain her position, work her way through to a solution, and secure an apology from Ed Thomas for his inappropriate behavior and language. When she felt the lump in her throat, when she couldn't get it down, and when the tears came to her eyes, she left the substance of the conversation emotionally and mentally. All her energy moved frantically to keeping the tears from falling down her face. When she failed to hold them back, she thought only of how to get out of there, how to remove herself from the scene, in order to spare herself and these two men further embarrassment. Indeed, what she saw of the two men through the blur of her tears only reinforced her need to leave. They both had stopped what they were doing, too. Gone was Mr. Johansen's businesslike, supportive expression. Gone was Mr. Thomas's blustering, angry glare. Instead, there were looks of amazement, confusion, and awkwardness.

Seldom do any of us choose to cry at work, and most of us suffer considerable embarrassment when we fail to control our tears. The major questions are: What can we do about all this? How can we get rid of tears if we don't like them? More important, how can we deal with tearful feelings productively in ourselves and others when they do come?

*Tears in themselves are not nearly as damaging as their all too frequent consequence: the stopping of the business at hand, the dissolution of focus on the work task at issue, and the stalemating of productive action.* Tears often stop action that could resolve the problem, address the counterproductive feelings involved, and enable the continuation of effective and efficient work activity.

Unlike anger, *tears are not an emotion. They're a behavioral response to or a manifestation of emotions that are actively moving within a person.* Tears may mean any one of a number of things to someone who is crying, just as they may signal any number of things to a person who observes the crying. As we've already seen, tears may spring from extremely diverse emotions, from profound grief to joy, and they may come from the full range of emotions in between these most negative and positive of human feelings. But why do people experience tears at work? What are the emotional roots of *workplace* tears?

The experiences of employees in a large, diversified organization provide some partial answers. At the time of the study the organization was free of major crises that might have precipitated more emotions than usual. The two hundred people involved included professionals, managers, secretaries, and technicians.[14] Occupational status, however, seemed to have little bearing on reports of tearful behavior or on their responses to the tears of others. Nor did age make a difference. Gender, as we'll see shortly, did play a role in some interesting and potentially important ways.

Seventy percent of the sample said that they had cried at work at some point or several times during their working lives. Considering that crying is an emotionally loaded issue for so many people, this percentage in itself suggests that workplace tears are at least on occasion an important issue for many, many people.

The most frequent reason for workplace tears was grief (56 percent of those who had ever cried at work). This includes sadness, feelings of loss, grief about a person who has gone, an opportunity missed, or a sense of loneliness for a person or a way of doing things. In our interviews and in recent stories throughout the media recounting tales of workplace tears, grief also emerged as the most reasonable and respectable excuse for office crying. Grief-born tears seem to have a degree of acceptability, a space and place in the panoply of personal behaviors that we accept, if reluctantly, and tolerate for a time, even at work. As a culture we seem to understand that grief arising from serious cause is a part of human life that may transcend place, at least for a while.

Often the source of grief implicated in workplace crying is outside the workplace itself. Many of us could tell personal stories of times when we found our own grief to be no respecter of place. "For no reason at all," said one project manager, "I'd suddenly remember that Dad was dead, and I'd feel overwhelmed, and the tears would come. In the middle of my office, in the rest room, looking at my secretary's pictures of her parents' fortieth wedding anniversary, even once at a meeting that had nothing to do with anything Dad had ever done. I just thought of him, and the tears came. I really thought I'd be through with the emotional stuff sometime after the funeral, you know, after a few weeks. In fact, I cried very little at the funeral. I don't know why. But there I was, even months later, suddenly remembering Dad at work, realizing with an awful start that he's gone, and there would come the tears again." For the most part this person experienced acceptance of tears when they came in public (actually an infrequent occurrence). This manager thought other people either ignored these "sad times" or understood the loss. Workplace tears of grief may also come, however, from more private and work-based sources, for example, from feelings of disappointment or sadness triggered by a sense of having failed at work, having fallen short of a goal. Such tears are often less easily accepted.

Frustration and not being heard were also important sources of workplace tears for over 40 percent of our sample. One hospital admin- istrator found himself in tears of frustration—quiet, private and very brief, but "definitely there," he said. Prolonged contract negotiations were "eating away" at the capacity of his hospital to provide the quality service on which its reputation rested. "We'd been negotiating for weeks, and we were close. And then there was a new demand out of the blue, something no one had ever even *mentioned* before. It all broke

loose. Weeks of work disappeared. And nothing I said made a difference. *No* one was listening. I felt sick that everything we'd done for
days, weeks, months in preparation was down the tubes, right there in
front of our eyes. I argued till I was hoarse. Nothing I did made any
difference. I walked back to my office, shut the door, locked it, and
cried." Five minutes later he went back out and reentered the fray.
Negotiations came to a "reasonably successful" conclusion two weeks
later. He never told anyone about the tears; to the best of his knowledge
no one knew. He laughed in retrospect and said that he probably could
have screamed, pitched a fit, and sobbed out loud on that particular day
and still not received any attention.

Another important cause of workplace tears was anger (40 percent
of our respondents). Tears of anger at work seem to involve anger
turned inward in part, blocked by an individual's view of acceptable
emotions and emotional expression, as, for example, when an employee
believes that you simply shouldn't get angry at other people, especially
at work, or when an employee fears the consequences of becoming
angry with a superior. Tears of anger may be brought on, too, by a
person's inability to recognize angry feelings as such. In these circumstances, we suspect, tears come because the person can't or won't let
the more "accurate" emotion through. Tears come from anger then
because *something* has got to give.

The personnel director of a city government recounted a time when
what she only later identified as anger temporarily destroyed her normally cool professional demeanor. But her anger didn't come in the
raised voices she was accustomed to hearing in the political debates that
often swirled around her. It came in a sudden sensation of choking up
as she began to summarize her position on a very controversial issue
before a large public meeting. As if her sudden descent into inarticulate-
ness weren't bad enough, her effort to deal with choking up quickly
produced tears, which welled in her eyes. But tears and "softness" were
the very *last* things she wanted to convey at that moment. "I wanted
to sway opinion, turn the tide in my direction. I knew it was going to
be a rough meeting. I knew that I'd have to be convincing. But I'm
*used* to carrying the day, you know. You don't get as far as I've gotten
in this business without winning most of your battles."

She was used to carrying the day by the force of cool logic: "I can
outfact and outfigure almost everyone else around here, and they know
it." But on this day, for many reasons—among them her intense interest
in the issue, the heat of the debate going on around her, and the failure
of almost everyone to pay much attention to her "fact and figuring"—

she found herself launching into an impassioned speech. Before she'd gotten halfway into the first sentence, she "choked" on it and couldn't continue. When the tears filled her eyes, she wiped them away, drew in a deep breath, and continued. She "got it under control" and made her points. She *did* carry the day. She concluded later that what caused those most unwelcome tears was her fury at the posturing going on by most of the people at the meeting, their failure to pay attention to the serious issues involved, and their apparent uninterest in data related to the issue. "They were playing the part of fools," she said, "and it made me angry." But her anger, as is true for many who've felt tears come at uncomfortable moments without understandable cause, was not immediately identified or directly expressed. Tears, rather than directly angry behavior, flowed from the feelings.

Other causes of workplace tears include feeling emotionally hurt, feeling that personal standards—related to the way things ought to be or the way one ought to be treated—have been violated. Tears of hurt may come in part from frustration, but they seem to come, too, from a sense of sadness for a vision of the way things might have been, the way things once were in an earlier time. Lee Iaccoca describes workplace tears caused by hurt and offense in his autobiography. Recounting the events surrounding his involuntary departure from the Ford Motor Company, he tells of going to the office designated for his use after his official "retirement": "My new office was little more than a cubicle with a small desk and a telephone. My secretary . . . was already there, with tears in her eyes. Without saying a word, she pointed to the cracked linoleum floor and the two plastic coffee cups on the desk."[15] While some might feel that Iacocca's situation didn't warrant empathy and tears, the point of importance here is that his secretary *did* experience sadness and tears. The distance between what he deserved and what he was given, in her eyes and in his, was immense. And the immensity of the gap was almost too large for anger; its magnitude rendered an aggressively angry response inadequate to the grievance. Tears of hurt and dismay came for her from the realization that things as they had been and things as they *should* have been had been so repudiated.

Being emotionally moved in a *positive* way by events at work is also a source of workplace tears for some people. These kinds of tears, very infrequently shed, are acceptable (or at least not cause for professional embarrassment) in many offices. They can come from the happiness and sadness found in farewells to a good friend who's moving on to a another job. They may come from simple pleasure at a co-worker's delight, as when a lawyer told us of tears she shed while her law partner, with whom she'd worked for several years, described (with tears in his own eyes) his joy at his first child's birth the previous night. She was simply very happy for him, and she cried. Tears of positive emotion may come, too, from personal honors and recognition. Several people identified such situations as their only tearful times at work. Tears came when they tried to say thank you for an honor, an appreciation banquet, an award, a surprise birthday celebration.

Many people, especially in two-earner and single-parent families, often identify exhaustion as a precipitator of tears. Expressions of "doing too much," "trying to do it all (and wondering if I really *can*)" wove their way through many tales of workplace tears. At issue here is not the ability or professional capacity of the person; many of these employees were extremely well regarded and notably successful in their work. Nor was it an issue of style; these were rarely people who claimed to be "all-the-time criers" in the workplace. What *was* at issue was a periodic confrontation with the very fullness and intensity of the demands in their lives. "Every now and again," one architect and mother of two said, "it seems like everything that *could* go wrong in one day *does* go wrong. When it feels that overwhelming, I can tear up on the slightest provocation. Something that I'd handle easily on a normal day can precipitate tears almost immediately." These tears come more from tiredness than the independent working of any specific emotion.

## Are Tears a "Women's Issue"?

Questions about tears and women may seem strangely rhetorical at this point. The capacity for crying, after all, is a *human* capacity. Men *and* women experience tears. And crying in the workplace transcends sex and gender. Even the toughest business settings know tears—the crying of both men and women. Terrence E. Deal and Allan A. Kennedy, coauthors of *Corporate Cultures,* describe four generic cultures they believe characterize many contemporary companies. One of these is the "Tough-Guy, Macho Culture," which incorporates, in addition to toughness, a focus on competition, risk, winners and losers, war games, aggressiveness, outrageous behavior, and other king-of-the-mountain attributes. Here is one of the personal behaviors often central to success in a tough guy-macho culture that Deal and Kennedy describe.

> A newcomer in one macho business asked what sorts of things needed to be learned in order to succeed. The senior staffer replied, "Learn never to cry in public. No matter how bad it hurts, go back to your office and cry in private."

The junior staffer seemed mystified by this: "But why do you have to cry?"

"Ah, because the bastards will get you when you're down."

"Who are the bastards?"

"They're all over the place," said the senior staffer. "They're your colleagues, your customers. They'll get you down, especially when you're depressed. But don't cry. Cry and they'll just tear you apart."

"Well, what else is there?" the junior staffer felt brave enough—or perhaps just scared enough—to ask.

"It's o.k. to shout, scream, and curse. It gets frustrating, and while you're not allowed to cry in public, it's all right to express emotion that can forcefully affect the situation. So, if you really get upset, say some outrageous curse word and storm out of the person's office, rush back to your own office, and then cry. Just remember, don't do the crying first."[16]

Of greatest interest here is the acknowledgment that even in the toughest of the tough-guy work settings, presumably populated by men *and* women, the *urge* to cry is a sufficiently frequent occurrence as to warrant so much advice. In short, the potential for crying at work does not seem to be gender-specific.

And yet something about crying just *seems* more like women than men. As a culture we certainly believe an assertion that women cry more readily than we do a companion claim that men cry. We "know" that women cry, but we have to prove it if we want someone to believe that men cry. A magazine editor suggested not long ago in a television interview that tears are the "vocabulary of women." A former mayor of Phoenix, Arizona, recently described the history of women chief executives in major cities and observed, "We have prospered and we have gained humility. [And] we have altered the 11th Commandment so that it now says, 'Thou shalt not cry until thou hangs up the phone.' "[17] This is not a commandment one would likely attribute to a man reviewing men's experience in chief executive roles!

If tears in the workplace are experienced by both men and women, why, then, do so many think of them as a women's issue? The answer to the question lies in some of the differences between men's and women's experiences of workplace crying, for men and women *do* demonstrate differences—of degree, not kind—in access to tears, reasons for tears, and experience with tears.

Eighty percent of the women and 50 percent of the men in our study reported having cried at least once on the job sometime during their working lives. Those women and men who have cried at work have cried most often in response to feelings of grief and sadness. But many women and men have also cried on the job out of frustration and the feeling that their ideas are not being heard.

Most striking among the differences between males' and females' reasons for crying is the feeling of anger. Women appear to cry out of anger much more frequently than men. The reasons women more frequently resort to tears as a means of expressing anger stem from many sources. Among the most important are the messages our culture gives most women throughout their lives about the need to suppress overt, direct expressions of anger.

Men and women also differ in the extent to which they are likely to find tears emerging as an expression of positive feelings. Men are much more likely than women to report tears when they feel "emotionally moved" at work. Reasons for this difference may lie in the possibility that many women, who are usually raised to be freer and more at ease with emotional expressiveness than men, have access to (and use) a wider and more varied range of responses to emotionally moving events. They hug, laugh, talk, listen, "shout for joy," and so on. The same reasoning probably applies to men's more frequent report of "joy at achievements" as a cause of tears.

As women have entered the out-of-home workplace over the last decades in increasing numbers, many of them have brought their collective emotional socialization histories with them. That history includes permission to cry. And the workplace is now meeting that history.

In the end tears in the workplace are neither a male nor a female issue, but a human issue. Most of us now spend a good portion of our adult lives "at work." And most of us experience emotions throughout our lives at home (as we have known for ages) and at work. If we are to experience dignity, vitality, and effective productivity in the workplace, our emotions—and the tears they sometimes produce—will be part of the mix.

# 5

# Tears on the Job
## Styles and Patterns

To every thing there is a season, and a time to every
purpose under heaven;
  A time to be born, and a time to die; a time to plant, and
a time to pluck up that which is planted;
  A time to kill, and a time to heal; a time to break down,
and a time to build up;
  A time to weep, and a time to laugh; a time to mourn
and a time to dance. . . .

—ECCLESIASTES 3:1–4

TOM JEFFREYS had been awake the better part of the night, and
he resented that. Things were tight enough around the office
without the added burden of a groggy headache, scratchy eyes,
and a brain that felt as if it had been left on low. He shaved
and dressed absentmindedly as thoughts of the day ahead turned over
in his mind. His nine-year-old daughter, Jenni, bounced into the bedroom, saying something excitedly as he straightened his tie. Without
looking at her, he grunted some response. Most of his energy at that
point was focused on the tie.

Soon he flung his jacket over his shoulder and headed downstairs.
His preoccupation slowly gave way to an awareness that someone was
crying in the kitchen. He realized with mild surprise that it wasn't their
two-year-old. He stepped into the kitchen and was met by Jenni's hurt
and accusing eyes, brimming over with tears. *Now here's a problem,* he
thought, then: *Brilliant!* He congratulated himself silently and sarcasti-
cally. It emerged quickly that *he* was the problem, alone to blame for
the miserable state of Jenni's entire world at that moment. How could
he have forgotten their long-planned father-daughter Girl Scout cookout this afternoon? she asked accusingly. Tom quickly realized that
must have been what she was talking about in the bedroom. He remembered it now; indeed, it had been on his calendar for over a month. He
was irritated with himself and chagrined. He bent down and apologized

to Jenni, promising her he'd make it. She rewarded him with a weak and tearstained smile of thanks. He told her to hurry with her breakfast, then gave Sarah, his wife, a quick hug and tousled their little boy's hair. Sarah reminded him she had to go in early this morning. Ten minutes later she and their son were in her car, headed for the care giver's and then on to her real estate office. Tom and Jenni left a few minutes later. He dropped her off at school with a promise to be there at three forty-five to pick her up for the cookout.

He eased on out into the major traffic artery that would take him to the corporate headquarters of the health care services firm he'd been with for twelve years. Seven years ago the firm began serious expansion and then mushroomed at an astonishing rate as the market for private provision suddenly expanded. But the boom didn't last. A combination of intense competition from outfits that hadn't even existed when his firm began expanding and several ill-advised purchases of major hospital plants a year earlier had put the firm in a rather precarious position.

Tom had taken over the hospital division six months ago, but his best efforts there to turn things around led him to the difficult decision that they simply had to cut back. His conclusion was duplicated in several other divisions of the company as well. "Pruning" lists were developed and finalized. The reality that Tom and several of this colleagues were about to fire (or "retire") many good employees began to sink in. The knowledge didn't make any easier the day-to-day interactions with colleagues and subordinates who knew that their jobs might be the next to go.

He pulled into his parking place and rode the elevator up to his floor. He greeted the floor receptionist with his usual polite "Good morning!" It was an extra effort today, but he had long thought that habits like this were important to general staff morale. She nodded back, silently, with a tense smile and returned her attention quickly to her work. Tom thought absently that things were getting tighter and tighter around the place.

He walked down the hall to his office and greeted his own secretary, Katie. She spoke with him—a little nervously, he thought—as she handed him several letters and a draft report he'd given her late the day before. Katie swallowed hard as their conversation lulled, then asked hesitantly if a particular hospital was scheduled for a decision at the ten o'clock meeting this morning. Tom suddenly understood that she *was* nervous. The hospital was indeed one of those up for decision today; it was Tom's own opinion that it should never have been acquired in the first place. He wouldn't have shared that opinion freely outside the inner circle and certainly not with Katie, who'd told him proudly when he first came up to this office that she wasn't the only one in her family who worked for the firm. Her mother, her husband's mother, and her brother-in-law all were employed at their hometown hospital, the only one for miles around in that rural area. But today there were no proud smiles as she asked hesitantly about its fate. She knew, as did Tom, that if the firm decided to sell it, it would probably close down for good. The likelihood of finding a buyer interested in that remote area of the state was very low. Tom told her it would be on the morning agenda. He noticed a brightness in her eyes as she bit her lower lip.

Tom was torn between a sudden wish to give her a hug and tell her it was going to be OK and a wish just to get the whole thing over with. But he simply continued on into his office.

He groaned inwardly as he looked at the stack of proposed "retirement" offers he still had to work on before the afternoon's meeting. Then he noticed a form in the sheaf with "Leonard T. Jenkins" typed into the top corner. He'd overlooked this one yesterday. Len! About to be eased out? Len, who had shown Tom the ropes during his early days in the firm; Len, who'd enthusiastically touted Tom's skills and advancement potential in those early years. When Tom was promoted over his level, the older man had taken it with grace and good humor. They still ate lunch together every now and again, and Tom continued to appreciate Len's quiet, competent, and supportive way. Tom knew that Len's wife had recently battled with cancer and that Len was planning on taking retirement at age sixty. He had even toyed with the idea of retirement at fifty-five but had decided against it. It made no financial sense, he said. They'd have time but not enough money for all the traveling they hoped to do. Len was now fifty-four; he had six years to go.

And here was a termination paper, signifying that in all probability Len would be taking retirement earlier than he'd ever anticipated. He grew sad and angry that it had to be this way. He decided to plead Len's case at the meeting this afternoon; maybe he could buy some time and things might even out before the next round of cuts affecting Len's shop.

He began making quick notations on several of the papers in front of him. When he left for the ten A.M. meeting, Katie nodded at him. He wanted to tell her it would be OK, but he knew it *wasn't* going to be OK. He simply said, "See you around noon."

He returned a little after one o'clock. The meeting had been even more difficult than he had anticipated. His own tiredness hadn't made

him any more lucid when he was called on to justify his recommendations on specific hospitals, and there had been some heated debate about
which units to let go. In the end his recommendations had been among
those adopted. He had delayed coming back to the office; he didn't want
to tell Katie. But when he returned, he walked to her desk directly and
told her gently, "It's going up for sale next week."

Katie looked down at her desk, then up at the ceiling, biting her lip.
This time tears came. "I guess it's for the best," she whispered quietly
through the tears. "But it's going to be so hard for Mom. And Bill's
brother . . ." The tears continued, quietly, as Katie sat in her chair.

Tom almost wished she'd get up and come around to the front, so
he could give her a hug and tell her he was sorry. But he didn't want
to hug her either. He stood by for a few moments, feeling helpless, then
went into his office.

He sank tiredly into his chair. He glanced at his watch. *Great
. . . thirty minutes till the next party!* he thought. He remembered then
with a start that he'd have to leave the two o'clock meeting by three-
thirty to get Jenni. He knew that he *shouldn't* leave at three-thirty, not
this meeting. But that was that. He turned his attention again to the
sheaf of retirement offers and tried to concentrate on them.

Fortified by a stale sandwich, he entered the conference room a little
before two. He stopped briefly by Sam's chair to tell him he'd be leaving
at three-thirty for a prior, long-standing appointment.

Sam looked at him somewhat incredulously. "Can't you cancel or
reschedule?" he queried quietly with raised eyebrows. "We've got new
stuff on the agenda; we'll be lucky to get out of here by six."

Tom groaned inwardly but said, "No, I can't." And then, firmly:
"We'll just have to get through my things first. I'll look over the rest
of it and leave you some notes before I go."

"OK," said Sam, in a tone clearly conveying that it wasn't.

The meeting began. Patricia was on the warpath, sharply demanding justification for several recommendations. Things droned on, uncomfortably and querulously. Patricia noted more than once that the
issue here was making cutbacks that were going to save the most
money; pet projects and personal preferences had no place in the process at this point.

At two-fifty Sam asked Tom to present his recommendations, on a
case-by-case basis, for the early-retirement proposals he'd been working
on. Tom had decided to go with most of them but held three out for
reconsideration. These he saved till last. The first group went unevent-
fully, but now, as he raised the few problematic ones—at three-fif-

teen—several questions came up. With one eye on his watch Tom responded to the concerns. They accepted his recommendation to withdraw the proposal on Dora Hughes for the time being. They overruled his recommendation on Bill Cunningham, returning him to the group to be offered early retirement.

And then Tom raised Len Jenkins's case. Patricia immediately jumped in. "Of any we've been considering in this group, Tom, I'd think Jenkins is a cut-and-dried case for early retirement. We'd have been better off if we'd let him go years ago."

"What!" exclaimed Tom. "What do you mean by that?"

"He's been in a backwater for years, Tom," Patricia replied coolly. "Or is there some sterling part of his performance I've been unaware of?"

Tom looked quickly at his watch. Three-thirty. He inhaled deeply. "Patricia, I've got to leave. Your crack is unfair and uncalled for. Len Jenkins is one of the most . . ." and to Tom's utter astonishment and dismay, a lump formed in his throat, and his words stopped, blocked. He swallowed hard, suddenly aware of several eyes on him where he stood, having risen to leave. He looked down at his papers, putting them into his briefcase, trying desperately through the shuffling of papers to clear his throat and continue. "I think . . ." and the choking sensation came again. "I think," he said, forcing himself to continue in as regular a voice as possible, "that we need to consider his overall value to the firm from the beginning." He snapped his briefcase shut and nodded to Sam. "I'm leaving. I want to save this one again until the next meeting." "I don't think we have that luxury, Tom," Patricia said coolly.

Tom glanced again at his watch. Three-thirty-six. Jenni was going to be waiting on the school street corner by herself. "Well, take the luxury then, Patricia!" he snapped. "I want this one on the next agenda. Have I made myself clear enough?" He lowered his voice, which had risen to a shout, and turned to Sam. "I'm leaving. Do whatever you need to do." He pushed back his chair and walked out.

He stepped off the elevator on the ground floor and hurried to the stairs that would take him to the next parking level. As he flung open the door, he suddenly stood face-to-face with Len Jenkins, preparing to come through. "Tom!" Len said with a startle. Tom shut his eyes momentarily and groaned silently for what seemed the hundredth time today. "Tom," Len repeated haltingly, his eyes averted. "They're going to let me go."

Tom stared at him. How had he heard that? Were there tears in

Len's eyes? Tom put his hand on Len's shoulder. "I don't know, Len," he lied. "I don't think so. How could they?" A quick glance at his watch. Three forty-two. "Len, I've got to go. I'm late to pick up Jenni. I'll come down and see you tomorrow."

"Fine, Tom," said the older man absently, turning away. "Tomorrow."

Tom ran on down the stairs and to his car. He started it, pulled out of the garage in a fury, and gunned his car into the traffic.

At the first red light he felt tears sting his eyes. He saw the light change through the blur, and he gunned his engine again. A few tears fell and then subsided after several more lights. Tom felt his anger, frustration, exhaustion—and, finally, some release. Ten minutes later he arrived at the school corner where Jenni was waiting, forlornly. "I'm sorry I'm late, sweetheart," he said, reaching over to open the door for her.

"It's OK, Dad," she said quietly. They drove on to the cookout.

Tom knew many tears that day: Jenni's, Katie's, perhaps Len's, and his own. And he experienced many styles of workplace crying: Katie's hard-fought tears, finally brimming over and spilling; Len's stunned and halting speech, tearful eyes averted; his own choking up, his barely controlled anger and frustration welling up in tears that flowed when he was safely away from the office.

It was obviously a rough day. It was an unusual day. But were the circumstances all *that* unusual? Most of us don't have days like Tom's very often. Companies aren't cutting back, tempers aren't flaring, working lives aren't being cut short, and children aren't being offended every day of the week. But most working adults do have days when some of these things, all of them, or other kinds of things, very similar in nature, *do* happen. When we experience events like these—events that threaten our sense of self, our ability to do things well, our ability to live life the way we want to—we're at high risk for uncertainty and change in our "normal" behaviors.

In the normal course of things, times and places for weeping do not include the workplace. We usually no more think of (or plan for) crying at work than we think of crying on the golf course, in the grocery store, in the subway, at a PTA meeting, at the gas station. We just don't think of tears coming to us in public settings.

But when events seem overwhelming or "larger than life" and threaten the control most of us struggle to build in our adult lives, emotions, both positive and negative, well up. And emotions can produce tears.

### Variations on a Theme: Elements and Patterns
### of Workplace Crying

As we explored the emotional roots of tears in Chapter Four, we saw many variations in people's styles of crying.

• Some experience crying as choking up; others as tears welling in the eyes; others as quietly flowing tears; others as sobs.

• Some let their tears come wherever they may be; others struggle, often successfully, to put the tears off until private spaces are available.

• Some cry for a few moments; others feel their tears going on and on . . . and on.

• Some, once they are aware that crying is a possibility, announce that fact to anyone present, almost as a warning ("I'm going to cry!"); others give little attention to anyone else around them as they turn inward to deal with the incipient tears.

• Some people apologize for their tearful behavior; others simply let the tears happen without voluntary explanation or excuse.

• Some continue speaking through their tears once any blocking lumps in the throat have dissipated; others find themselves speechless (or assume that they are) until the crying is over.

• Some follow up on their tearful episodes (for example, was the message behind the tears clear? What did other people think? Is there any further business to take care of?), while other criers put the tearful event as far behind them as quickly as they can, often vowing never to bring it up or let it happen again.

• Some assume that with the act of crying they have forfeited control and power in a situation; others make it a point *not* to give away situational control when and if tears come to the fore.

• Some react to their own tears with mortification, some with simple embarrassment, some with amazement, some with acceptance (even if reluctant!); and many experience shades of reaction in between.

Across these many elements of crying behavior people express their individual approaches to tears. Most of us tend to mix various choices as we grapple, rarely or frequently, with our own "urges to cry" in the workplace. Individual choices, if fairly consistent across tearful workplace times, come to constitute what can be thought of as a style for handling our own workplace tears.

The patterns or styles that we describe in the following pages are shaped primarily by two factors: personal attitudes toward one's own crying behavior and individual perceptions of the frequency of one's own tears at work.

We begin the discussion of styles with a person who represents a relatively small number of adults, men and women, in today's workplaces. Marlane has never cried on the job because she has never felt emotional responses at work strongly enough to lead to any form of crying.

### Marlane: The Well Never Fills

Marlane is a college dean on a bustling urban campus of twelve thousand students. Her responsibilities focus primarily on student life, and her office is among the busiest places on campus. She began academic life many years ago as a young Ph.D. assistant professor of English. She shifted to an administrative position four years later, when her skills with students and well-organized ways caught the attention of the college president. Overall Marlane likes her job, and she especially enjoys the student contact associated with her role.

She is described by most of her colleagues as a no-nonsense, pleasant, and efficient administrator. She is matter-of-fact about almost everything. Her approach, viewed by some as unemotional and sometimes cold, is one that she worked hard to cultivate in the early years. "I was the only woman around the place then who wasn't a student," she said. "I felt like I had to be very serious and 'masculine' in my approach to things." She is very glad there are finally more women in academia. In truth, however, she confessed that developing a no-nonsense style wasn't hard for her. "I've never been the kind to get emotional about much of anything," she said. "It's just the way I am."

Marlane reports that she has never cried at work. She's never felt tears well up in her eyes, she's never—to the best of her recollection—choked up or felt even the beginnings of a lump in the throat during any of the moving events that she's witnessed or participated in during her working life. She's certainly been involved in interactions with the potential for emotion, and she's been through many times at work when emotions were flying around her. For example, there are professors. "Most of them," she said with a smile, "prize rationality, but most of them can go into orbit over their own projects or pet ideas, especially if they're challenged. I've seen more than a few shouting matches. But they usually pass," she said, "and things go on pretty much as usual."

She has known myriad student crises over the years. She described many, with ease, as a "small sample" of the problems that pass through her door: health emergencies, fights with roommates, irate parents, suicide threats, tear-filled and earnest pleas for "just one more semester or probation; I'll die if I can't come back!" "They don't die," Marlane said with a slight smile, "although at nineteen, most of them have a

hard time believing that. We try to be as accommodating as we can, and
when we can't help out here, we try to help them—and their parents—
see the other choices they may have. We don't want them to hurt any
more than they already do."

Through all the events of her working life Marlane passes with
careful attention, considerate listening, and efficiency. Her efficiency is
usually pleasant, but she's been known, too, to knuckle down. "I guess
people think of me sometimes as more grim and heartless than pleasant," she said. "But that's part of the job. I couldn't be effective if I gave
in all the time. It's important for someone in this role to make the hard
decisions as well as the easy ones. Most of the kids we actually see in
this office," she observed, "present hard decisions. The ones who are
doing just fine don't come our way very often!"

What kinds of feelings does she experience on the job? "A sense of
satisfaction that I do it well. And enjoyment. Sometimes frustration,
but that usually passes. When I get frustrated, I try to remember not
to expect too much."

Has she ever felt close to tears at work? "No," she said, "I haven't.
I feel concern or sympathy when one of our students is upset and in
difficulty, but I don't feel like crying. I get irritated and frustrated with
them sometimes, but I don't get close to tears then either. I *do* have
feelings about it all. I just don't cry."

Marlane has never experienced tears on the job because she rarely
experiences strong emotions that might lead to tears. It's not that she
has tearful feelings and puts them down. She just doesn't experience the
events or the people in and around her job as leading to feelings that
might come out for her in tears.

Her style is found more often among men than women. But few
people in either gender group hold the characteristic central to her
style: a low level of emotional response to issues at or about work. More
often men and women in several of the style categories that follow *do*
experience strong feelings at work at times but choose to suppress them,
fight them, or ignore them in order to keep any threat of crying away.

### The Submergers: Dorothy and Jennings

There are many people who lay no claim to workplace tears who
have in fact experienced the urge to cry at work—usually on relatively
rare occasions—and who have successfully developed effective ways of
putting that urge down. Some have developed these control techniques
out of a strong belief that they simply should not ever cry at work.

Others have responded to their perception that the emergence of tears and any underlying emotions would seriously impair their ability to carry on with their responsibilities. They do not want to risk that. Everyone in this category, whatever the motivation, has the ability to suppress potential crying responses when and if he or she feels them emerging.

These noncrying styles are more characteristic of men than of women. Everyone in this category, however, has been successful in keeping tears from emerging in working life.

### DOROTHY: "I DON'T LET MYSELF CRY"

Dorothy is manager of a men's clothing store, one that specializes in classic and often expensive menswear. Her store handles some merchandise that is more trendy than classic, but the mainstay of the firm's business is a large and stable clientele that looks to her store for excellent clothing that is generally conservative. The firm has been in business for decades and is very well established. Among the regular customers are many of the city's "leading citizens."

Dorothy has been in her present position for eight years. Before she assumed that position, she had worked for a little more than ten years at various lower-level management duties in the store. She has enjoyed most of her time with the firm, finding it a pleasant and interesting place to work. She has consistently appreciated the level of quiet formality that pervades both the "floor" and the business offices at the store.

The topic of emotions at work brought a smile to Dorothy's face and an affirmative nod. "It's an interesting subject," she said. "I know some workplaces are very different from mine. I imagine that in the pressure cookers some of our customers work in, emotions *must* run strong. We get people in here, very respectable, well-known people, who fly off the handle at any little thing. We get others, of course, many others, who are as polite and pleasant as anyone could want. But the ones who are 'hot' give us more than a few challenges."

Dorothy believes that handling these challenges is a critical part of her job. She also believes that she has important reputations to uphold as she conducts business on a daily basis: her firm's reputation as an outstanding menswear store and her own reputation as an efficient, effective, successful businessperson. She gave several examples of times over the years when someone, usually a customer, moved into angry yelling and threats in response to a delay in the store's receiving of a promised order—for example, "What do you mean, they haven't come in yet? I need it now! You may think you're the best store in town, but

I can't imagine how you rest on those laurels when your service gets as sloppy as this!" Dorothy paused from relating the heated reaction and said, "They can say a lot of other things, too, and they can get pretty personal. It's not easy to take, but I simply *can't* respond in kind or with anything but understanding and letting the customer be right, always. It would never do. I dislike those responses intensely. Sometimes they make me *feel* like crying. But I put my mind into automatic when that happens and let it roll off my back. I simply *can't* let myself get riled up or tearful in return. It wouldn't do any good and would create many more problems than are already present when that happens." There has never been any doubt in her mind, from her first day on the job many years ago, that "emotional control," as she puts it, was going to be a primary requisite of success.

"I doubt that I've ever thought about my own emotional control very much," she said. "I just know that it's simply part of the way I have to be if I'm going to do my job well. I *can't* fall apart, ever, on this job. I *couldn't* cry." When asked why, Dorothy thought for a few moments, then shrugged her shoulders and said, "It just wouldn't do. Can you imagine anyone who works in a store like this—let alone the manager—getting seriously upset in any way that a customer could see or overhear? Or crying? It's one thing if a customer gets upset, although I can tell you I work very hard to insure that that happens rarely. But it would be unheard of for the manager to do so!"

Dorothy doesn't think very often about her emotions on the job, but she believes that her career and her firm's reputation depend in large part on her careful control of her feelings—especially any negative ones—and she controls them.

Unlike Marlane, who doesn't feel emotions in sufficient strength to prompt any urges toward tears, Dorothy *does* experience feelings that might lead to tears. But she's combined her ability to put the feelings down and her beliefs about appropriate on-the-job behavior to create her "never cry" style.

Her style is shared by somewhat more men than women, although people in both gender groups are clearly represented here. It's important to note that the category is probably relatively small; many people—male and female—who at first identify themselves with having Dorothy's style often find in reality that their style is more accurately reflected in those that we discuss in the next major categories.

Before going on to those groups, however, we consider the other *submerger* style, exemplified by Jennings. Unlike Dorothy, who hasn't thought a lot about her feelings at work, Jennings has given considerable thought to emotions on the job. Despite the differences in processes leading up to their decisions, however, Jennings, like Dorothy, never cries at work.

### JENNINGS: "I DON'T HAVE TIME FOR TEARS NOW OR LATER"

Jennings is a pediatrician, senior partner in a group that's been together for twenty-five years. In spite of the fact that his practice is located in a fast-growing suburban area, he embodies a good deal of the stereotypic old-time country doctor. He began his career with a general pediatric practice but gradually began referring many of his would-be new and "normal" patients to his partners. About half his own patient load now consists of children with problems, problems caused by genetic anomalies, environmental hazards, congenital disease, birth trauma. Because of this, Jennings has some pretty close relationships with many of his patients' parents, who look to him not only for medical advice but for ideas about the hundreds of large and small problems that daily confront the families of handicapped and chronically ill children. He believes that successful medical treatment and health care for children such as "his" must involve the whole family. He's not shy about saying so when he thinks that one or both parents of a patient are too reluctant to become full participants in the child's progress.

Jennings's style with "his" parents, his partners, and any other adults who come into his office arena is most charitably characterized as gruff, sometimes abrupt. He is not a man who exudes joy for all the world to see, or laughter, or even much of an overt sense of caring. He often appears preoccupied, and the nurses know to stay clear of him when the warning signs of an overloaded day go up. But with his patients themselves, Jennings is funny, caring, clowning, stern, and warm. Adults who've been around long enough to see him with the kids time and again usually identify him as a "teddy bear." In fact, his waiting area and examination rooms offer tribute to this opinion. For there resides a large collection of teddy bears—stuffed, in pictures, in clay, you name it—gifts from "his" kids and their parents.

"Emotions? At work?" he asked, his attention caught by an unlikely topic. "We're full of 'em around here. I don't imagine I've had a day *without* emotions. You want to *see* some emotions? Sit out there," he said, gesturing to the waiting room. "Or come sit in here," he said, looking around his own cramped office, "when I tell mother that her kid's got a real problem, not just slow development. Or when I tell a father that his boy's illness means he's probably not going to walk, let alone play baseball. Or tell a sister that she just has to toughen up and accept the fact that her little brother with cystic fibrosis needs more of Mom and Dad's time now." He paused reflectively. "No, I don't think you'd like it. I can't think of anyone who *does* like it. A lot of times it's rough."

Jennings does not cry at work. He never has. And he says he never will. "I don't think my patients or their parents would like that too much," he said. "More to the point, I don't think they could take it. It's not what they come to me for; they've got enough tears in their lives already, heaven knows." Furthermore, he quickly volunteered, he doesn't cry about anything or anyone related to his job when he goes home. And he certainly doesn't cry at the hospital.

"Do I ever *feel* like crying? Of *course* I do! But there's no time. If I let everything I feel get in my way, I'd never get anything done. I'd be no good for my patients if I cried. You *can't* cry in this business."

He was silent for a moment and then continued. "I know what tears are like. I see them more than most people would ever want to. But I can't afford to cry. Tears are a part of life. But I just can't cry. And I don't."

Jennings, like Marlane and Dorothy, does not shed tears. Like Dorothy, he has feelings that he simply won't let out in tears. Unlike Dorothy, however, he has thought a fair amount about emotions and tears. He's *had* to think about emotions and tears and what he should do about them.

Like many others who share his style, an approximately equal number of women and men, he works in a job setting where human dramas of life and death and personal well-being are played out daily. His decision, as is true of many people in occupations where one confronts often life-threatening needs, has been to put his own tears down. But he has done so with considerable awareness that he has the potential for them.

### The Deniers: Kyle, Maria, and Susan

Many people experience crying at work—in some form—very, very seldom. But the urge to cry does come, and they struggle with it. For people in this style category—the people we think of as *deniers*—the struggle ends, at least sometimes, not in the suppression of those unwanted tears but in serious denial that the tears ever happened. As a group deniers intensely dislike their tears and their potential for tears. Most of them believe that crying at work reflects very badly on an individual's competence. And these people as a group do not intend to have their professional competence impugned by such unwelcome intruders as tears in any form.

KYLE: "I DON'T BELIEVE IN CRYING!"

Kyle is head of a large and expanding firm, a man who impresses almost everyone he meets as powerful and tough. He prides himself on this reputation and uses it to excellent advantage in running the business. He started many years ago and steered his fledgling company through some initially rocky times to its current extremely successful state.

Kyle has changed his work habits over the years, from his early days, when he routinely spent six or seven days a week in the office, to his present "relaxed" schedule of five days a week, most of them with late nights. He disclaims the label of "workaholic," but his wife and several close associates disagree. In many ways his business is his life, and he loves it. He's an avid hunter in season, but other than that his outside interests are limited. Everything he is is bound up in the business. He likes it that way and says frequently that he wouldn't have it any other.

Like many other people, especially men, Kyle was at first incredulous about the topic of emotions in the workplace. He made it abundantly clear that he viewed the issue as at best amusing. When asked specifically about *his* experiences with crying in the workplace, he raised his eyebrows with a look of disgust and said emphatically that he could do without hysterical secretaries. "If they cry, they haven't got what it takes. I don't like it. If it happens more than once, I'd just as soon get rid of 'em."

Asked if *he* had ever cried at work, Kyle gave a loud laugh and a derisive "NOOO!" He listened attentively as we told him about our observation, garnered in previous interviews, that sometimes men who report never crying do sometimes experience choking up, a very real or even dim realization that they *might* cry if they don't control their emotions very tightly right at that point (control which most of them report quickly and emphatically they *do* keep in the situation).

Had he ever choked up at work? "No," he responded, but more thoughtfully this time. After a few moments of silence he added quietly, "There was one time." His silence continued. He finally said, looking out the window, "It was about my son."

"His name's Gavin. He doesn't want much to do with me. He's twenty-eight and mad as hell at me. He told his mother three years ago that I'd been at work all his life, and he had no feelings for me now. He doesn't know who I am, he said. And he's not interested in finding out anymore. 'It's too late,' he says. He hasn't been home in years. That picture," he said, pointing to one of three photographs on the bookshelf behind his desk, "was a Christmas present to his mother last year. That's his wife with him. They got married overseas; I've never met her. If he knew his mother brought the picture in here for me, I suppose he'd stop speaking to her, too.

"We had this planning meeting in January, right after Mary brought that picture in. I told her I didn't want it, but you know how women are. And mothers. So I said OK. The next day I came into this meeting in the conference room and several of the guys were laughing around with Ed; you know, big-time congratulations and all that stuff. His boy's wife had a baby, first grandchild, and old Ed was proud as a peacock. And I don't why—I looked at him and how proud and happy he was, talking about the baby, holding him, all that stuff, and I suddenly thought of Gavin and how bad things are between us and I just—" He swallowed hard and continued. "I just couldn't say anything for a few minutes. I stood there, pretending to get my papers in order." He paused for several moments. "I don't know if I had tears in my eyes. I might have." He paused again, for a long time. "I didn't cry. I guess," he said, his voice now back in firm control, "I guess I was envious because I don't think I'll ever have that. And I guess I felt sad, wished things could be different. But it's too late. I can't make him spend time with me. Or like me. I'm used to it now. I wish I'd done some things differently when he was little. But I don't think about it now."

Kyle continued looking out the window. After a few minutes, spent in silence, he turned to us with his characteristic booming voice and asked, with half a smile, "Well? Anything else I can do for you?"

Kyle's style, adopted much more frequently by men than women, is based on his belief that he doesn't cry at work. He doesn't believe that tears or any of "those feelings" have any place at work. He asserts firmly that any businessman worth his salt has to be tough. He reacts with aggressively expressed anger when either of these standards are violated. "If a guy doesn't want to be tough," he opined derisively at one point, "let him do social work or play with little kids!" These are *not* opinions calculated to endear Kyle to a good many working people. But in Kyle's view there's simply no room for tears at work.

Far beneath all his experience, his beliefs, and his ideology, however, Kyle has the capacity for feeling deeply about some things. But he does not believe in tears. And if anyone had the temerity to ask him again about tears at work, he'd more than likely snort, "Me? I *never* cry at work!" He believes that only the weak cry. And he, above all, is not weak.

MARIA: WHEN PERSONAL TEARS AND PERSONAL<br>TOUGHNESS COLLIDE

Maria is a woman with a prodigious record of achievement. At twenty-nine she was brought into her firm, a private contract research corporation, to "fix it up," to bring some of the magic to bear that she and her reputation of extraordinary competence had worked in the two firms she was with previously. Maria is verbal and assertive; she can also be very aggressive when the situation demands. Highly committed to doing the job she's been brought in to do, she has no doubts that she *can* do it. It's just a matter of how long it's going to take—the one year she had originally hoped for or the two years that several people in the firm told her during her interviews (and have continued to tell her) that she'll need to accomplish the job.

She had been on the job for just a few months when several negative factors about her reputation began to develop. She was still well respected for her abilities but had become a fairly controversial person in that short time. Some of her co-workers were increasingly open in their comments about aspects of her style, which they found abrasive. Although she was aware of the controversy swirling around her, to all appearances she had disregarded it completely. This, too, provoked controversy. Some people believed Maria genuinely didn't care about others' upset feelings, whereas others thought she relished them. For her part Maria continued to insist on the validity of her own position and of her own approach to doing things.

Maria's boss, Whitney, "let this go on" for some time, feeling that the organization needed the kinds of questions and "shake-up" that Maria was precipitating. Furthermore, she thought that Maria was "right on target" with the substance of most of her concerns, recommendations, and decisions, even though she agreed that a little *less* intensity and self-righteousness on Maria's part at times would make things a lot easier for many people, herself included. Her few talks with Maria about modifying her approach "haven't gotten very far." But as far as Whitney is concerned, Maria's successes continue to outweigh her liabilities.

Maria spoke with great enthusiasm about her job in the firm. But she shifted quickly into her own frustration with the "reception I've gotten. I don't understand it," she said intently. "They said—they *all* said—they wanted me to come in and clean house . . . do this, do that. They were ecstatic that I took the job. But in some ways the only thing I've gotten since I've been here is grief. I talked with Whitney about it a few weeks ago. That's when I cried. If you'd asked me about this emotion stuff up till then, I would've told you I *never* cry. In fact, I think most people who cry at work are simply too weak to be interesting or worth the time. I still think so," she said ruefully. "Not that I cried for very long! Whitney is the only one at work who knows about it, and I certainly don't want it to happen again, I can tell you that!"

Maria felt hurt over the difference between the way she thought things should be—the way she expected them to be—and the way things were. She was angry about the discrepancy, and she cried. And she was angry about her tears. She was angry and hurt about the way things were going at work, and she was deeply embarrassed that her emotions were expressed in tears.

Like the others who share her style—some women, fewer men— Maria had never seen herself as having tears or needing them. They don't match her idea of the way she or anyone else who is competent should be at work. But she knows she has the potential for them, and she doesn't quite know what to make of that. Unlike Kyle, she can't fully ignore her tears. She's uncomfortably aware of the discrepancy between her beliefs and her behavior. She sees a need for redoubled toughness—or reassessment—down the line. She's not very pleased with either possibility.

### SUSAN: THOSE HATED TEARS

Susan is president of a well-respected public relations firm. PR work has been her chosen field since she graduated from college two decades ago, and she's made an excellent career for herself. She began life in the PR world with a "girl Friday" position in a small firm in her college town. She slogged through months and months of filing, typing, making coffee, running errands, taking notes at meetings, cleaning desks, you name it. All the time she was picking up a great amount of knowledge about the substance of the work. When she was given a small opportunity to try her hand at something beyond gofer work, her "feel" for the job was evident. The head of the firm noticed, and she was soon given a more substantive slot.

Susan had some trepidation about taking that job, but she decided that her fears were "silly." They were related to the fact that she was the only "girl" in the office, and she wondered about "proper" behavior

anyone . . . !' 'Understood, boss!' she said, and was gone. But the tear
weren't. I just kept thinking about all that time, for nothing. And I kept
crying. A vacation down the tubes, for nothing. And a backlog, right
up into the holidays, for nothing. Yes," she said with a trace of bitter-
ness, "I cried. But I don't believe in crying. And it won't happen again,
for a long, long time. You can't *let* things get to you that way."

How do you keep from crying if and when the feeling comes? She
laughed. "I could've written the book on biting your tongue, digging
your shoe into your foot, taking a deep breath to the count of ten. You
name it, I've done it. Those techniques may sound corny, but they
work, let me tell you! I wish I could teach them to some of these young
kids, especially the girls, coming out of college these days, assuming
that they don't have to toughen up for the real world of business. I had
an intern in here last semester. She was good, did things efficiently,
caught on pretty quickly. But she missed the boat on an assignment just
a week or two before the end. I told her so. I was real irritated about
it, because I'd heard that the interns sometimes leave before they're
really finished. Graduation and all that, I guess. But she broke down
in tears when I started with her about it.

"Tears!" she continued. "Good grief! What would've happened to
me if *I'd* cried the first time someone chewed me out? I'll tell you what
would've happened. I would have been out of there so fast it would've
made your head spin. And there she was, over some little thing, crying.
I couldn't tell her a thing! She looked at me as though *I* ought to feel
bad for making her cry! I told her she'd messed up, but it wasn't worth
tears. I was disgusted, though. One of the first things I learned in this
business is to keep the lid on your emotions. She's never going to make
it if she doesn't learn that, too."

Susan claims that she never cries. In reality she means that she
rarely cries. Tearful episodes are very powerful for her, and their occurrence, rare though the occasions may be, is usually followed by renewed
resolve to suppress them. And denial that they ever happened.

Susan's style is more common among women than men. For many
women it seems to come out of a sense of having struggled "to make
it in a man's world." Susan made it, she paid a price for doing so, and
others should be willing to do the same, she believes. Like the small
number of men in this category, she's willing to be quietly supportive
of the few others who struggle with the issue, too, but she doesn't
believe a different resolution of the issue is acceptable.

Although Susan gets angry with herself when she fails to keep her
feelings down, especially if they're likely to produce tears, she is in some

for someone in a "real" job at the firm. She didn't dare reveal h
ignorance and ask direct questions about it; instead, she began studyi
carefully the behavior of those around her. There was a lot of serio
ness, a lot of bantering, some jokes and backslapping, very little ov
uncertainty, and a decided lack of tears.

Susan did well, and before too many years had passed, she was hi
away by another, larger firm. After eight years with that company
"took the big leap," left the firm, and started out on her own. Her sk
contacts, and innate good sense were responsible for the early
continuing success of her business. Susan is well known in her cit
both her business skills and her community involvement. "I ha
good life, all in all," she said, "and my work is definitely a big pa
it."

Do any tears ever fall on that good working life? Susan's resp
was an immediate and vehement "No! They don't. Not mine, any
Tears are inappropriate." When people cry at work, she believes
lose their credibility, their right to be taken seriously, and their p
tial for promotion. "You just don't cry, at least in my field, ai
ahead." Had Susan ever *felt* like crying at work? "Sure! Plenty of
Well, actually not *that* many, but enough to know how uncomfc
it is. I'm not a person without feelings. Things get to me sometim
like they do to anybody."

Susan paused briefly, took a deep breath, and said, "Let me
my answer. I *have* cried at work, I'm sorry to say. But rarely. 1
time was two and a half years ago in November, right after Tha
ing.

"I'd been working hard on a proposal for a major accoun
an excellent chance to take it away from one of my biggest com
because the client wanted something completely new, a differen
and he didn't know if the old firm was up to it. I worked my
I canceled my Thanksgiving plans to stay home and be sure ev
was done right. I got it to them exactly when I said I would. T
me they'd let me know in a week. I knew I'd get it; the con
great, I took a day off just to relax, even though the other v
really piled up while we got that package ready. He called me
later. I thought at first, *Oh, help! I left something out!* Ar
thought, *I know I didn't leave anything out—they've bough*
paused. "Ha! Poor, unsuspecting Susan. They called to tell me
no. I couldn't believe it, but there it was. Even after all the ex
and excuses—no. I hung up the phone and cried. Geri walke
I was blubbering away. I took one look at her and said, 'If yc

ways ambivalent about those feelings. Unlike Kyle, she hasn't put her feelings quite so far away that they never emerge. Like Maria, she is aware of her potential for tears, and she is afraid of that and what it represents. Her irritation at the intern who cried when reprimanded and at the other "kids who think they can cry at work and it'll be just fine" reflects both her anger and her ambivalence about it all. She believes she spent a lot of energy learning how to do the "right things" with her emotions and her emotional behavior at work. It simply seems unfair to her that newcomers could change the rules "just like that" in order to avoid the hard work of entering life in the business fast lane.

### Strangers in a Strange Land: Bob and Larry

A third group of crying styles is characterized not so much by overt and angry denial that tears have ever emerged in the working lives of competent people as by surprise about tears. Most people who evidence these styles, more men than women, simply have never noticed tears at work—their own or those of others. They have usually ignored the tears that might have fallen around them. And their own urges toward tears, which most people in this category experience infrequently, are also usually ignored and often forgotten.

#### BOB: "I'VE NEVER REALLY THOUGHT ABOUT CRYING"

Bob is in his early thirties. He grew up in the era of "emotional expression"; letting it all hang out was a big deal when he was in high school. He's now head of accounting for a major convention and entertainment center. "I like the job," he said, but added quickly, "I don't think I'll be in it forever. It's good training, a good stepping-stone for the next one."

Most of the people with whom Bob works think he's capable, fair, and easygoing; a little quiet, but a good guy. Bob acknowledged that he likes to cultivate that reputation: "It makes things a lot easier when everyone gets along well—assuming they know their stuff!" Bob is frequently called on to make presentations to his own superiors and to development groups proposing similar centers in mid-size cities across the country. He likes that part of the job. The traveling gives it some variety.

Bob looked momentarily shocked when asked if he had ever cried at work. He shook his head and laughed. "No!" He grinned quizzically and added, "I've never even *thought* about it!" He pondered the issue for a few minutes and then asked earnestly, "Do you *really* think people cry at work? *Really?* That's hard to believe." We asked Bob if he'd ever *seen* someone cry at work. "No. Maybe accountants never cry." He went on to say that his office, indeed his whole firm, was pretty formal and "polite." "I double that anybody here has ever *thought* about crying. I guess I could be wrong, but I don't think I've ever heard anybody even talk about it." Maybe, he suggested, "that's just the way the office is."

Have you ever *felt* like crying at work? Or have you ever choked up about something? "You mean, like the first time I went out to do a seminar and there were ninety people there instead of the twenty-five I'd been told to expect?" he asked, laughing. "Yeah, that was a choking time. I came close to gagging, as I recall. It wasn't," he said, rolling his eyes slightly, "my most brilliant performance." He smiled, shook his head; "I really don't think there has been a time, though," he said slowly and reflectively.

Suddenly he said, "There *was* one time I *did* choke up. I just couldn't say what I had to say. Is that what you mean? I had to fire someone who wasn't working out. She was young, really didn't have the skills needed for the job. I shouldn't have hired her in the first place, but she was so eager. And she was the only applicant," he added. "I knew when I decided to let her go, she'd be upset. She'd been trying so hard. I started to call her in, but I had to put the phone down; I realized I couldn't say anything. I had this little speech all ready for her, and it just kind of got caught in my chest. You know? I knew I wasn't going to be able to tell her, not then. I waited till the afternoon, now that I think about it, hoping that it would be easier then. I finally told her after lunch. It wasn't easy. I didn't like doing it. But I got through it. She *did* get teary, I remember now. But she just sat there and listened, didn't really cry or anything."

After thinking more about the topic, Bob initiated two more conversations. It had become apparent to him that he had at least a few experiences with choking up at work. He had also seen tears, in others, in his work setting. When asked why had he been unable to remember any of those incidents at first, he offered the observation that perhaps he had just not been aware of the "signs." He doesn't like things to get unpleasant at the office, and the "signs of tears" often mean something unpleasant.

Bob's style is more common among men than women. Like many men, Bob tends to see himself as one who never cries at work. But he feels emotions with the potential for tears sometimes, and he has experienced some of the subtle forms of crying, especially choking up.

He has an ability and a preference to let his "close to tears" emotions and times fade out, both as they're happening and after they've passed. He does the same with tearfulness that he sees in others. He's not angry about tears; he simply doesn't *think* about them at work. He tries to ignore them. And they fade quickly from his attention and memory.

LARRY: "TEARS? THE SURPRISE OF MY LIFE!"

Larry is in his mid-fifties, genial and usually at ease in public settings. He works for a large department store chain with outlets throughout a major region of the country. You can tell on meeting him that he's accustomed to being with the public. He has a firm handshake and an easy smile, and he obviously enjoys conversation.

He's been with his present firm for about fifteen years. He "jumped ship" from a competitor when he was in his late thirties, seeing the move as the best way to "get ahead in the game." But Larry's star didn't rise quite as fast as he wanted it to in this new firm. For a while he was alternately angry and depressed about it, particularly when he came to conclude that at his age—and with his family situation—he'd better stick with what he had rather than try again for greener pastures. So he stayed with the firm. He's been relatively satisfied with it overall.

Recently a much younger man was "imported" into an upper-level management position, one to which Larry himself had aspired. In fact, it was a job for which Larry, according to all reports, had been a serious contender. After the decision was in, and the new man on board, Larry tried hard to give him a wide berth. He also tried to be generally supportive, although it wasn't easy. The hiring of this young outsider over his head signaled to Larry with sterling clarity that the highest levels of management had decided he had gone as far as he was going to go. That knowledge wasn't easy to take, but Larry has adapted over the months. He currently believes he's in this job "for the long haul."

At a recent meeting, however, the "new kid" was openly arrogant toward Larry. According to two other sources who were also there, the man was clearly derogatory about Larry's work and abilities. Larry was stunned. He hadn't counted on the "kid turning obnoxious." The attack, Larry said, was just that: an attack. Unprovoked, calculating, unnecessary.

After that meeting Larry returned to his office, fuming about the incident. He felt mostly the immense unfairness of it all. He'd worked many good years with this company. He'd done a good job, and he was still doing one. Good enough to have been considered a candidate for the position the new man was given. And then, without an apparent justifiable reason, "this guy attacked me!"

Larry was angry. But he was also hurt because the situation seemed unfair, and he felt there was no way to win the fight the new man seemed to be picking with him. Larry felt he shouldn't "have to mess with that stuff at this stage of the game." As all this went through his mind in the privacy of his office, he was amazed to find tears coming to his eyes. "I was crying!" he said, still with some amazement. The tears passed after a few minutes. Had he been in public, Larry is sure he would have fought the tears back. But in the privacy of his own office he allowed himself to cry.

Larry had never cried before at work and doubts that he will again. Although it was all right with him that he cried then, he was emphatic in asserting that he would not have done it in public and certainly not in presence of "that kid." He added that he'd noticed a few women crying at work over the years, and he thought maybe he understood a little more of what they were going through: "I guess tears come when things get rough. Pow!" he exclaimed suddenly. "It was like getting hit in the gut!"

Larry believes that the tears were justified right then. And it's important to him that he *can* justify them. He certainly doesn't want to think that he cried because he was "falling apart." And as is true of many people who cry rarely at work, the flowing of tears brought a fleeting vision of total personal disintegration. But Larry's not an alarmist, and his assessment of the situation quickly led him to conclude that almost any private expression of emotion under the circumstances at that point would have been understandable.

Men and women share Larry's style in about equal numbers. Like most of those in his style category, Larry is at heart pretty matter-of-fact about his emotions and his experience of crying at work. Unlike the deniers, Larry does not become angry about tears in himself or others. His own experience of tears, despite the fact that it was immensely surprising to him, has simply led to somewhat more awareness and understanding of crying on the job.

### Holders and Keepers Until . . . : Vernon and Sandy

There are many people who know and acknowledge, usually privately, their own capacity for crying at work. Their tears do not bother them personally. But for a variety of reasons they hold or keep their tears "until later." For some, "later" means until they can get to a private spot at or near work; for others, "later" means waiting until they are well away from work—on the way home, at a friend's, etc.

This category of *holders and keepers* is also well represented among workplace criers. There are more women in this category, but there are a surprising number of men as well. The men, however, usually have a much stronger tendency than the women to treat the tears as purely private, secret matters. That's why the presence of men in this category is surprising to many people—even to many of the men who share this style since each assumes he's the "only one." As a business consultant observed, "There aren't many men out there willing to admit to tears at all, let alone occasional ones. You have to be pretty careful how you handle it if you're a man."

People in this category tend *not* to view their workplace tears as a challenge to their competence, although they may have worked hard to achieve that attitude. The change in attitude usually has to do with coming to accept their tears and treating them as a part of who they are. As an award-winning commercial artist explained, "For years, I was embarrassed by my tears, even though they were *very* infrequent. I think I assumed they must say something extremely damaging about my abilities or my character. I remember thinking, *Who else do you know who cries at work? No one, dummy! Get it under control!* When I finally began to discover that other people—competent, well-respected, successful women—cry at work and live to tell the tale, I began to think, *Well, if* other *competent women do it, it must be OK!* I only wish I'd come to that realization years earlier."

Like the two people whose stories are below, people who hold and keep wish to keep their tears secret. They usually do not want anyone else to know about them, even though they personally feel OK about them. They often expend considerable energy holding and keeping them for private out-of-the-office moments—the park during lunch, the car on the way home.

### VERNON: KEEPING THE TEARS FOR PRIVATE TIMES

When asked if he had ever cried at work, Vernon looked around to see if anyone else was nearby and then said slowly, "I never used to. But I have a few times. Let me tell you, though," he added emphatically, "I'd *never* let it happen where anyone else could see me! I wait till I'm good and alone."

Vernon has been with the U.S. Postal Service for sixteen years. He began with it right out of the army, as soon as he'd finished his overseas stint. He has some complaints about the bureaucracy, as do many of his colleagues, but he likes his duties as a supervisor. He doesn't talk much about his job, and he rarely discusses personal things at work. His co-workers know he's married, has three kids and a boat that he loves to take out on the lake on weekends. But other than that Vernon is a private man. He's well liked around the office largely because he's seen as fair and hardworking, ready to back up his people. He gets a little uptight now and again, especially during the heavy-duty times that are the bane of postal workers' jobs, but he's usually reasonable and patient even then. He's not what anyone would describe as very emotional, but he's not "cold" either, just pretty even-keeled.

Vernon is well aware of emotions in the workplace. He laughed, saying one should visit the lobby of the main post office two weeks before Christmas, or the airport (twenty-four-hour-a-day service) office two days before Christmas, or any post office station on April 15 if one wants to see emotions "on parade."

When emotions come around the office, Vernon tries to be very calm. If a customer is upset and he gets called in, he tries to be reassuring and take care of things. Sometimes all they want, he said, is to know that they've got the boss. "If I listen (and tell my people to be cool if they're there while I'm listening), a lot of times they'll calm right down. I usually tell them the same things they've been told before. And I try to help them understand the situation. But you know how people are. If they're really irate, I might spend a long time with them, but I get them out of the main area, where other people can get upset just watching it all. If it's a phone call, we just keep talking till they're cool about it."

Sometimes his employees "break down" in tears. When that happens, he usually gives them a break, tells them to get off by themselves for a while if they want to, and tries—then or later—to figure out what the problem is. Usually, he said, they're just tired. If it's more than that, he tries to get the problem worked out.

As for his own tears, he said adamantly that he'd never admit them to anyone else at work. In fact, he never let himself cry until a few years back. But things are changing, getting bigger, more pressured, more hassled. "Mind you," he said sternly, "this *doesn't* happen but once or twice in a year." And when "it happens," he knows what to do. He saves the urge toward tears until he can get into his office. Once there, he'll lock the door and let the tears come, very quietly, for a few minutes. After he's finished, he usually feels better, and he comes out, ready to go again. If he can't use his office for some reason—things are just too hectic—he'll hold them until his lunch break, go walk in the park, get to a deserted place, and let the tears come there. Again not very long and no noise. Then he's ready to go back. No one else knows about the tears, of that he's sure.

He told of a time—last April 15, in fact—when too many things had gone wrong. Two key people had gone home with the flu, and he had no one to replace them. A car hit one of the outside boxes, and the traffic lineup was terrible; angry people came in yelling, and one too many people told him that if *he* were competent, things wouldn't be in this ridiculous mess. "I'd *had* it," he said. "I told my assistant to hold things together for ten minutes. I got out of there, went down to an unused packing room, and let 'em come. I pounded on the wall, too. And then I went back. I felt better. We got through it all, and no one knew about those tears." Asked why he doesn't want anyone else to know, he said simply, "I just don't want them to. It doesn't look good. It doesn't sound good. 'Vernon cried?' Noooo . . . I don't think so."

So Vernon cries about work-related events from time to time, but he sheds tears only in private. Like the many women and some men who share his style, Vernon is able to "save" his tears, and he does so. He's had tears at work, but only in places and times of his own choosing.

Unlike Sandy, whose style is discussed next, Vernon has no ideological commitment to the value of emotions or tears at work. He simply knows that they come from time to time, and he knows that he's worked out a satisfactory way to deal with them when they do.

### SANDY: WHEN IDEOLOGY AND BEHAVIOR CLASH

Energetic and capable, Sandy currently is the youth minister in a large urban church. She's been in the position for almost two years. Before taking it, she served as the full-time "circuit" pastor for three small rural churches. Although she knew she wouldn't stay in that rural area forever, she had been eager to get into a more "home-based" position. But it was with a great deal of sadness that she left those little congregations.

The new position was good, but very different. She was now in a very junior position, part of a large staff (fifteen), in a congregation of thousands rather than dozens. Her work with the youth groups got off to a good start. She enjoyed the kids a lot, although she was known to admit from time to time that they could stretch her patience, as when she invited the senior highs to her home for the Super Bowl and was still finding popcorn all over the house two months later. The arrival of her first child eighteen months ago complicated her working schedule, as she knew it would, but things have worked out pretty well.

Sandy talks easily about her emotions on the job and off. They're a part of her life that she values. She has some sense that she's even doing a little trailblazing in this area on her job. "Ministers," she explained, "sometimes run with the occupational hazard of listening to everyone else's feelings, and problems, and joys. But many of them turn right around and assume *they* shouldn't have any of those feelings— especially the downers. I think part of it is just endemic to the helping professions. I'm working on educating my colleagues." She laughed, then added, "But some days it's slow going."

It would seem likely, in view of Sandy's awareness of and openness about emotions, that she would be relatively comfortable with tears, her own or others', at work. But her answer to the question about crying at work is "complicated," as Sandy put it. "I talk a lot about the need to be more emotionally open, especially among ourselves as a staff. I guess 'honest and caring' would be the most accurate way to put it. But I don't often let myself cry at work. Most of the other staff members don't either, I suspect. Does that contradiction totally discredit my position?" she asked with half a smile.

What does she do when she feels like crying? "I tell myself, 'Later, Sandy, later . . .' And then I wait till the drive home. *Then* I can cry you a river! There've been a few days when I didn't even get out of the parking lot before the tears were streaming down my face. They're always over the time I get home. They have to be. . . . I can hardly come moping through the door with a miserable-looking face to greet Jason. Life's rough enough at age one without having your mom in the middle of a downer when she gets home!"

Sandy recounted a recent experience in which she held back tears at work only to release them later. "It's actually one I'm a little embarrassed about. It wasn't a time of feeling sadness or grief for someone else; it wasn't a time of being righteously angry about a principle. This was good old crying because I was hurt. And I was surprised and offended—and scared, too, that I might lose my job. I knew I wouldn't, but I felt like it for a while.

"We've been having annual performance evaluations this month. The senior minister came to my office for my appointment. He started with the good stuff. There was lots of it, and although I was pleased, I was not terribly surprised. I've gotten a lot of positive feedback about a lot of things I've been doing, and it pleased me that these things were making it into the evaluation.

"But then he said, 'Now we come to a more difficult area,' and my heart just sank. I could feel it drop like lead into my stomach. I kept my cool, though, and nodded, trying to look like 'Well, of *course*, I knew we'd be discussing this problem. I'm *so* glad you raised it.' I doubt I really looked like that . . . but I tried. He said that several people were concerned that I wasn't doing enough liaison work with the other areas of church ministry—staff people and adult church members. At least I *think* that's what he said. Everything else he said that had been positive dropped through the bottom when he said, 'Here's the difficult area.' I kept thinking, *I've failed.* I know he wasn't saying that or meaning it, but that's what it sounded like right then. And I was angry. . . . I confess some pretty uncharitable thoughts went through my mind. Like *Well, if any of* them *ever took the time come to me . . .* and *I'm running on all four burners now just to do my job with the kids. And now I'm supposed to add two more burners just to tell everyone else what I do?* Not good thoughts, but I just felt overwhelmed. And I could feel the tears coming. I looked intently out the window, willing the tears to stay put. I bit my tongue. I did manage to say, 'Thank you,' when he finished. 'That's very helpful' or something like that. I kept the tears back. I don't think he noticed. He didn't say anything if he did. I didn't cry even after he left. I did piles of paper work . . . with speed and efficiency that shocked even me. But when I got in my car that afternoon, I had a doozy of a good cry. All the way home and then some."

Sandy has thought a lot about her emotions, her tears, and ways of integrating her personal and professional life. She's achieved a lot of success in that effort. She's also the first to admit that she's got a way to go. She accepts her emotions in almost all arenas of her life, but tears—especially at work—are a little bit different. Although she recognizes her emotions at work and is willing to claim most of them (at least in speaking about the topic), she pushes the off button when it comes to tears. What she believes should be OK doesn't square with what she's comfortable doing in part because she feels that she's already challenging the "way things are done" in other important areas of her work. She doesn't ignore the need to cry but saves tears until she's on safer, private ground, where she works to understand their meaning for herself and her next course of action.

Sandy's style is shared by many more women than men. Sandy and the others who have adopted her style are somewhat like Vernon in that they save their infrequent tears "for later," until they're alone and out of sight or hearing. In some other important ways, however, they differ. Vernon accepts his tears because they come and he believes they solve some useful tension-releasing purpose. Sandy, who believes she *should* accept her tears, has a hard time doing so, and the discrepancy concerns her. She wishes she could be more at ease with her tears when they do come, but she hasn't worked her way to a resolution yet.

### Accepters: Carol, Anne, and Deborah

Last among the crying styles, the *accepters* category is the smallest. It is also the one populated most heavily by women. Few men fit into this category, although some said they know what some of these specific styles are like because they see them pretty frequently!

Accepters have simply learned that they cannot, or choose not to, suppress, deny, or hold their tears back on some occasions. Some accepters, like Carol, hold jobs that are not constantly pressured. Others, like Anne, hold jobs in settings that are time-pressured and stress-producing, such as the media or the performing arts, or understaffed, where too few people continually have to get all the work out. Other job settings that tend to have accepters are pressured in a different way. The stakes are often high, and what one does matters in an important, often life-threatening way.

Accepters may differ in the extent to which they allow their usually frequent tears to "show" to those around them. As a group, however, they know and usually accept that their tears are a part of who they are. Not all of them started out that way; but their tears came often, and they believed strongly in their own abilities despite the crying. They concluded logically that they had better not spend much time stewing over the tears or berating themselves for shedding them. Part of that conclusion, for each of them, was a decision to develop a reasonable way of dealing with these frequent episodes of crying in the workplace.

#### CAROL: OCCASIONAL TEARS, LITTLE DISCOMFORT

Carol's a fashion buyer for a well-known firm, headquartered in the West. She's in her mid-thirties, mother of two elementary-school-aged children, usually crazy about her job, and pretty tolerant—as is her family—of the frequent trips she has to make. Her favorite destination is San Francisco largely because she grew up in the Bay Area, loves the city, and enjoys visiting her parents, who still live in her childhood home. In the last two years her mother's health has been failing, and Carol is candid about admitting that she tries more than ever before to find business excuses that enable her "to pop in on the folks." Recently her mother has weakened visibly, and Carol has experienced some times of profound sadness over the loss of this energetic, vigorous, and high-spirited woman she credits (among many other things) with developing her own interest in fashion and her "innate" sense of color, style, and design—essential tools of her trade.

Many of Carol's reflections about her mother have crept softly into her working days. Sometimes she thinks about the "things that have driven me nuts!" adding, "They're probably far fewer than the things I've done to drive *her* nuts. I think getting close to forty is giving me new perspective!" But overall the reflections are punctuated by sadness. When she came home from her last trip, she talked seriously with her husband about her mother's condition, and they talked with the children, so that the kids would be prepared for a quieter time during the next family trip down there. She went into her office the next morning, still preoccupied and tired. A longtime friend and colleague came in to check over the decisions from the trip with her. After they'd finished the business at hand, Peg asked Carol how her mother was doing. Carol told her briefly, appreciating Peg's interest, and added that she was ready for a break—from work, from home—and was really looking forward to their two-week vacation on the Coast this year. "Nothing to do but play and let someone else do the cooking and make the beds. We all need it," she said softly.

Suddenly she thought of her mother. She remembered the annual camping trips to the mountains, and she realized—strangely, as if for the first time—how much work "vacations" had been for her mother all those years: camping, with five children; three meals a day cooked on a Coleman stove; laundry (someone was in diapers for more than a few of those years); keeping constant watch over all of them in camp, at the lake, on hikes. Suddenly she felt tears. Her tears were brief and quiet. Peg saw them and sympathized quietly with her. The tears were spent before the two of them left the office for lunch.

Carol is a woman at ease with her own, infrequent workplace tears whether they come from personal issues or work problems. "Not that I always felt OK about them. I remember clearly the first time I cried at work. I'd come back from a trip; I was very new to this game then. I was excited about the things I'd seen, and I was feeling pretty good about some choices I'd made. I brought them into my boss for review, expecting a fine compliment for all of my efforts . . . and talent! He looked at them; he looked at me; he looked back at them; he looked at me again. And finally, he said, 'We'd better team you up with somebody more familiar with our market for a while.' No smile. Just a nod, which I figured out after endless seconds, meant 'You can go now.' I was crushed.

"I left his office without a word; I didn't know what to say. I ran with as much dignity as I could muster to my office, opened the door to fling myself into my chair and flop my head onto my desk. But there was my office mate, who looked at me in surprise. I turned around without a word and ran out, looking for any place to be alone. The tears were coming then. I felt frantic. I saw a small conference room, and opened the door. I looked around quickly, saw that it was empty. I went inside, locked the door, sat down on the floor, and sobbed. I sobbed into my skirt to muffle the sound. I cried and cried. I couldn't believe I'd blown it so badly. I was sure I was through forever. An entire college education down the tubes! I felt in my pocket for a Kleenex, anything to blow my nose on. Nothing. I couldn't stop crying and suddenly realized that if I ever came out of that room, I was going to look awful. I wound up using my slip to blow my nose and dry my eyes. Half an hour later, I snuck out of the room.

"I survived—obviously. And I thought a lot about those tears and what they meant. I came to conclude that I'm a fairly emotional person, even at work. And I decided, after I had talked with a good friend, that I didn't want to go through that kind of scene again. Slowly I experimented with relaxing more about my emotions. I still usually try to hold off till I get to my office, but it doesn't always work. So I'll cry every now and again right where I am—*if* I'm not in a big meeting. But that's about the only exception. I've even cried in front of my boss. I'm a quiet crier. I've learned to tell people why I'm crying, that the tears will be over in a few minutes. People are pretty accepting," she reflected. "It doesn't bother me too much anymore."

Although, like Vernon and Sandy, Carol pretty much accepts her tears as part of the way she is, in several ways her specific style with tears is different. For Carol, getting to a private place is a preference, not a necessity. Unlike Sandy, Carol hasn't thought much about her tears in any "ideological" sense. She might agree that some changes in typical workplace responses to emotions would be nice, but she doesn't think about furthering that effort as an explicit part of her own agenda.

Carol's crying doesn't happen often, and she believes that it's simply not that big a part of her working life—or "that big a deal."

ANNE: "CRYING IS JUST SOMETHING I DO"

Anne is an editor with a major newspaper. She's been in the print media all her professional life. She began with a regional magazine, rose to an editor's position there, then left after a few years to join the staff of a major evening newspaper in a large city. She's been with the paper for the last ten years. She loves her work, and she loves the pace of it.

She's a self-described high-energy person. "I can drive myself crazy in just one day of vacation if I don't have enough to do," she said earnestly. Her high energy and love for her work both are strongly implicated in her success.

The subject of emotions in the workplace is one to which Anne responded with enthusiasm. "I'd love to talk about that! We're crying *all* the time around here!" she exclaimed. Emotions run high in media environments, she explained. There are so many deadlines, so many time-pressured situations, so much running around, so much competition, so much raw energy, and so many demands to do it "faster, quicker, better than anyone else and maybe win the Pulitzer Prize while you're at it!" Somebody, she said, somewhere in her outfit is crying all the time.

"There are so many open spaces in a newspaper office," she continued. "*Any*thing that happens may turn out to be anybody's business. So if someone cries—or yells, anything else for that matter—dozens of people know about it. And wonder about it. 'What happened? What'd she do? What's going on? Did you see the look on his face? Where's she going? How does he get off acting like that?' and on and on and on. It's like being in a fishbowl. It's not just that the emotions are here. But whenever they are, everybody *knows* it. And then it just keeps on going."

Anne is very matter-of-fact about her tendency to cry often at work. "I didn't think of myself as crying easily," she explained. "But it's obvious—and has been since I got here—that I do. I think it's mostly the pressure. There's always a deadline just around the corner. Now don't get me wrong. I like the pace, and the deadlines are part of that. I think, in fact, that most of us here who are really good are as successful as we are because we *need* the pressure to produce. We do our best when things are really tight.

"It's not the pressure of deadlines itself that makes me cry; it's that I get so focused on meeting the deadline, doing what's necessary, getting it out, checking the last facts, making one more contact, deciding if we can afford to run it as it is . . . or if we can decide *not* to and get scooped for holding it. I get so focused that any little thing that comes up and throws the effort off or slows it down really gets to me. Sometimes I pound around, sometimes I yell, and sometimes I cry.

"I'd rather yell than cry, frankly," she continued, "but I don't always have the choice. Sometimes I just feel the tears coming in spite of my best efforts to hold them back, and I'm all of a sudden crying. I still don't like it very much. 'Weeping woman editor' is *not* the image

I have of myself! If I can't hold the tears—and I can sometimes—I'll leave the scene for a few minutes. Go to the women's room, take a quick walk around the block. But sometimes they just come, right in the middle of everything. I usually say, 'I'm sorry, give me a minute,' then turn my back until I've got myself composed again. I may explain what's going on, but I usually don't. If they last longer than a minute's worth of turning around, I'll just go right on ahead with the business, through the tears. I may say, 'Look, I'm crying because I'm frustrated with how late in the game this is all getting. The tears are no big deal.' And then we get on with it. I know people talk about it sometimes. I'm not real crazy about that. But it's the best I can do. I know I'm good at my job. And everyone else does, too." She smiled.

Anne's tears, like those of others in this style category, don't happen literally "all" the time. But most of our common expectations for workplace behavior are so far from including the idea of *any* tears, even every now and again, that people whose tears come fairly predictably are indeed prone to feel that "it's happening all the time!" Anne may cry two or three times a month—and that feels like all the time to her. Tears and other emotions are so much in evidence so much of the time in her work environment that by the time she and the others put it all together, many of them agree that the label is almost true.

Essentially Anne acknowledges her tears and then goes on about the business at hand. "If we're going to cry 'all the time' around here," she said with a laugh, "we sure can't stop for long while we're weeping!"

### DEBORAH: "LETTING THE TEARS COME OFTEN, AS I CHOOSE TO"

Deborah, at thirty-four, has been on the police force in her hometown for almost a decade. She fought her way to her present position, detective, through some tough times. She was one of two female recruits in her class. The training was hard, much harder than she expected and harder than anything she'd done before. She still has clear memories of struggling to pull herself up one wall during the last round of physical endurance testing after training and of thinking, *I can't do it anymore. This is crazy. It's not worth it! You were a fool to think you could do this!* But something got her through it. Something, she suspects, related to what she describes as the "gritty, rock-bottom stubbornness" that pulled her into the force in the first place, against all advice from her family. And something perhaps related to an earnest wish to prove a point to several cousins who bet her she'd never make it. She went over the wall, and she was in.

She's had second thoughts about her chosen profession a few times.

Like most people in police work, she has a hard time with some of the downsides of life that she confronts on a day-to-day basis. But so far she's decided that it's worth it. She sees herself in police work for a long time to come.

Deborah's response to the issue of emotions at work is immediate. "Is there anything *but* emotion around here some days?" she asked rhetorically, sweeping her hand through the air to encompass the whole place in one gesture. "But you know, it's funny. Feelings are here all the time, but most of us try hard to deny that they're anywhere around. Some of us, in fact, spend a lot of time trying to forget them completely. If you let your emotions get to you on this job, you're as good as dead, sometimes literally," she said soberly.

Do people around here ever cry? "Oh, yeah! Some days every other person who's brought in here is crying. The other half are screaming or so p.o.'d they're just glaring, fit to kill. Other days it's mostly calm, business as usual. But the officers? Nah, not many, not often. It's pretty much an aberration. When somebody cracks under too much strain or has been into something awful, you'll see it. But not often. We spend a lot of time joking around, clowning it up.

"I'm afraid I'm the exception around here." She smiled. "I'm the one detective who *does* cry. Almost anytime. You name the time, I've probably cried then. *Except* when I'm out there. I do *not* cry in front of anyone to whom I'm the detective. I'm in ironclad control out there. But in here? Ah, that's a horse of a different color. I *do* cry. Not lots, but often.

"Before I came on the force, I'd never seen myself as one to cry. I've always been the tomboy in the family, the tough one, the one who'd take on anybody who even looked to threaten one of my brothers or sisters or cousins. I'd stand up to the biggest bully in school and usually win. Not because I was bigger or stronger but because I had better bluffs. And I was faster." She laughed. "But I never dreamed when I came on the force that I'd cry. In fact, it was a point of pride with me in the early days that I was as strong and as tough, as able to take it as *any*one. But after a while some of the things on this job begin to get to you. You *have* to deal with them. You can get hard-bitten, or cynical, or obnoxious. You can really get into other things during your off time, like your family or backpacking or bowling, or drinking, or yelling at the cat. Anything to get your mind off some of the stuff that comes with this job. What did *I* find to do? In my own inimitable way I found crying!

"I cry when things get to me," she continued. "When it first happened, I was mortified. I thought, *Turn in your badge, Deborah, you're through!* But as it happened, the officer I was with when I cried just said, 'Yeah, things get to me, too, sometimes. Anything I can do for you?' I was so shocked I stopped crying. 'Are you *serious?*' I said. 'Sure am,' he said. I looked straight ahead and said, 'I guess all I needed was just to cry for a minute.' 'You gotta do something,' he said. And that was that.

"Really," she continued, "I don't want you to get the idea that I'm a basket case. For one thing I don't *really* cry all the time. And for another it's just gotten to be the way I deal with things sometimes. I feel better after a good cry. Even a little one. I save the big ones for more privacy than we usually have around here. People know I cry at times. That's the way life is. I don't think it gets in my way, though. I'd work on ways *not* to cry if I was afraid of that. But I think in all honesty it helps. After the tears are gone, I'm usually ready to go."

Deborah was straightforward and unapologetic about her workplace crying. "That's the way it is, and that's the way I am" is her approach. The others in the style category she represents usually presented their stories and opinions with more overt reflection. Many indicated it was a considerable struggle for them to get to the point of saying (and believing) that the style embodied in "It's who I am, and it's what I do sometimes" is all right. But most of them know and accept, as does Deborah, that tears can coexist with great professional success and competence.

Before we leave the accepters styles, there are three important issues that need consideration. None of them applies to the styles represented by Carol, Anne, or Deborah, but they may apply to you.

The first issue is related to the fact that some people find themselves responding to a serious but usually temporary personal crisis with many more tears than usual. (Remember that *crisis* is personally defined. What constitutes a crisis for one person may not seem like much of a big deal to another. The kinds of events referred to here are crises defined as such by the individuals experiencing them.) Many people have gone through personal crises at some points in their working lives that put them on the edge—or very squarely in the middle—of frequent workplace tears, even though this is not their normal style.

The second issue is related to the fact that people sometimes undergo work-based crises that provoke more tears than usual. Such events might include major company cutbacks; threatened across-the-board layoffs; heavy and serious infighting for a promotion; the "right" to stay in a current position; or an emerging lack of fit with the prevailing corporate culture.

In short, there are many temporary situations that may change the frequency of even an *accepter's* tears to an unacceptably high level. Suggestions in Chapter Ten may be helpful for people who find themselves temporarily in such a state.

A third important issue is related to people who wish they could accept very frequent tears but feel completely out of control over the emotions leading to the tears. Continual weeping at work—over time and with no apparent link to any personal or professional crisis—can be dysfunctional and debilitating. Accepters understand pretty clearly why they cry more than "every now and again" at work. They have developed ways of dealing with this propensity for tears, ways that enable them to function efficiently and productively on the job. It took Carol, Anne, Deborah, and many other people in this category quite some time to come to those effective ways of dealing with the tears, but they eventually did. People who cry *"all* the time" at work, who feel that they don't know why, or who are unable to develop ways of bringing some control to the situation may need to explore the issues with a professional who can assist in bringing the feelings and the behavior under more personal control.

## *Variations on a Theme*

Styles of workplace crying are made up of several different elements. Some of these elements have variations that fit specific styles pretty closely. Other elements, however, have very little connection with specific style. They transcend style.

*Form* of crying refers to the way we cry. It includes choking up, tears in the eyes, quietly flowing tears, sobs—and all points in between. Form is often connected with style. Deniers and strangers usually experience more subtle and less obvious forms of tears; they tend to choke up or get tears in the eyes. Holders and keepers and accepters may be anywhere on the form spectrum, but people in these categories often experience freely flowing tears at least occasionally.

Where a person cries—*place*—is pretty strongly associated with style. Deniers have a strong tendency to go somewhere else, out of public view, for their crying whatever its form. Most of them go to their own offices, rest rooms, or out of the office altogether before they cry. Strangers and holders and keepers may cry anywhere. Most are intensely private about their tears, are able to "save them for later," and do so. Accepters most often find their tears rushing forth in public, even if they try to hold them for later.

*Duration* of crying—how long a tearful episode lasts—is pretty independent of style. The one exception is some deniers, whose rare episodes, in whatever form, tend to be short. People in all other style categories may experience any duration of crying: momentary tears, tears that seem to go on and on, and any point in between.

*Acknowledgment* of crying—the extent to which a person announces tears, ignores them, or works hard to keep them secret—is associated with style to some extent. Deniers and holders usually keep their tears a secret. Strangers and accepters may be anywhere on the spectrum. They may announce tears ("Oh, no, I'm going to cry!"), try to ignore them, or try to escape a situation altogether before they have to acknowledge them. Accepters more often show the greatest tendency to acknowledge their own tears (e.g., "I think I'm going to cry, but let's get on with the business here").

*Apologies and explanations* for tears transcend style. People in any style category may feel that their tears are an unprofessional intrusion for which they should apologize or explain. Similarly, people in any style category may omit apologies and explanations altogether, assuming that the tears are something for which they don't have to seek sanction or forgiveness.

*Speech through tears*—the extent to which a person is able to continue talking through tears—also transcends style. Most people, in whatever style, believe that they cannot cry and talk at the same time. Despite beliefs to the contrary, people in any category can learn to talk through the tears (see Chapter Ten). Those who have learned this usually continue to talk with others *as they cry,* so that the interaction continues through to an acceptable conclusion.

Tendency to *follow up* on tearful behavior includes several different behaviors: checking to see what the reactions of observers were, talking with other people directly involved in a tearful episode to finish whatever business was interrupted by the tears, and so on. Many deniers have tearful events so seldom or experience them in such barely noticeable form that they do not follow up on them. Some of them, though, and people within the other style categories show variations within this dimension. Those who are embarrassed by their tears may do a lot of checking to ascertain reactions of others present (or to assess the damage they assume has been done). Others, who've given more thought to their potential for crying behavior, may develop the habit—whatever the frequency of their tearful episodes—of following up on them to be sure that the business at hand has been completed even if it was interrupted by the tears.

Assumptions about *control* in tear-producing situations also transcend style categories. Some people in each category are defined in part
by their control over tearful feelings; even when they feel potentially
tear-producing emotions, they assume that they're still in charge of
themselves, the situation, and the outcomes. Other people, across style
categories, however, assume that their tears mean they've lost control
of the situation. In other words, *they assume that if they cry, the crying
in itself gives away control of the situation to anyone else who is present.*
People in each category who have learned that crying does *not* automatically mean loss of control and power in a situation usually retain
or regain control before much of the crying episode has passed. Those
who haven't learned this, regardless of style category, usually assume
that their tears have washed away any control they may have possessed
in the situation. The latter assumption isn't necessarily accurate, and
in Chapter Ten we'll talk more about techniques for maintaining control of a situation even when tears come.

*Embarrassment* over tears also varies across style categories. People
in any category may feel embarrassed about tears or may also simply
accept the tears. We found that most people have a natural tendency
to feel embarrassed by tears. But many have *learned not* to be embarrassed about them. Techniques for lowering embarrassment about tears
and increasing acceptance of them are discussed in Chapter Ten.

Finally, as evident in the stories described within each style, the
*causes of workplace* tears vary across styles. People in any style category
may cry for any reason. The emotional causes of tears are not connected
to style. Deniers are as likely as accepters to cry out of sadness, anger,
or frustration or any of the other emotional causes of tears.

### Individual Differences

As you think about your style of workplace tears and the questions
above, there are a few other important things to keep in mind.

Your own personality—who you are, how you behave, how you
react to things—is going to play some role in your crying style and in
the changes you'll find desirable or easy to make. For example, if you're
a pretty reserved and quiet person by nature, one who prefers formality
to informality, caution to abandon, it's not very likely that you'll be able
to transform yourself into an accepter like Deborah very easily even if
you want to. But there may be some things about Deborah's acceptance
of tears that you'd like to emulate for your own quiet, possibly very
infrequent tearful times. Similarly, if you're an outgoing, gregarious,

and emotional person, it's not likely that you'll easily make your way to becoming a "never cry" person of Marlane's "I just don't cry" persuasion. However, there may be some tips about reducing the urge to cry that you can gain from Marlane's matter-of-fact, quietly helpful approach to emotional crises around her.

In other words, if your crying style is going to be right for you and work for you, it's got to be pretty close to "who you are" and what your general personality is like. Within that ball park there are probably a lot of changes you can make to bring your handling of workplace tears more into line with the style you *want* to have.

### Work Culture

The nature of your workplace and the specific demands of your job influence your crying style to at least some extent. As we explore in more detail in Chapter Nine, work settings often have distinct cultures. They have "personalities." Work settings that are time-pressured, don't have enough resources, or consistently undervalue employees' work efforts are likely to produce more environmental press toward tears than do more evenly paced, adequately supplied, positively reinforcing work settings. You may feel that you'd like to change your crying style so that you experience workplace tears less often. If you're in a work culture with constant time pressure—where everything is due yesterday and always rushed—and a habit of devaluing employee work, it may be harder and take more effort to make changes than would be true if you were in a less pressured, more positive setting. Anyone, in any work setting, can certainly make adjustments in style by following the suggestions in Chapter Ten. But the nature of your workplace and the specific demands of your job will probably influence the amount of effort and energy you'll have to put into making changes, just as they influence some specific elements of your style in the first place. You may also find, if you're in a pretty negative work environment, that your efforts will need to focus to at least some extent on changing particularly difficult elements of the work setting. If you're in a very negative setting, it may be, too, that the changes you'd like to effect in your own style would be much more successfully undertaken in a different job or in a different work setting.

As our review of crying styles illustrates, tears on the job are not a problem in and of themselves. *The problems come when those who shed tears and those who see them stop the action, leave the task at hand, and shift the focus away from productive, effective work.*

So the problems with workplace crying come from two sources: the crier and the observer(s). The crier's best path to integrating tears and productive work lies in the development of a crying style that's personally "right"—one that fits both personality and job.

But the crier is just one of the people implicated in the relationship between tears and workplace productivity. In many circumstances there is an observer of the tears, a real observer (i.e., he or she sees the crying) or one whose presence is merely a possibility (e.g., your boss, who might walk in when your tears are falling, your colleagues who might notice the telltale signs of a tearful episode). As there are different styles of workplace crying, so are there also different styles of responding to workplace tears.

# 6

# Why Are They Crying?

## The View from the World of the Observer

Only your own hand can wipe your tears away.

—EGYPTIAN PROVERB

RUTH PULLED INTO THE LOT, parked her car, and began walking toward the building. She waved absentmindedly to a reporter and camera crew loading equipment into a station van. She walked up the steps to the station entrance and pulled the heavy glass doors open. Immediately she had the feeling it was going to be one of those days.

She turned to look back at the reporter and camera crew, now pulling out of the lot. What were Calvin and Lori doing in there? They had been assigned to her for the nine-thirty taping. Why were they going out with Vicki? If she could get to Jack quickly enough, he could call them back for her and send another crew out with Vicki. She stepped briskly into the lobby and began hurrying past the glass trophy cases. Many of the awards and honors bore her name. Some were accolades for her work as host of a weekly program of political commentary and analysis; many of the others were in recognition of her work on several topical specials.

She really needed Calvin and Lori for this nine-thirty assignment; she couldn't imagine why Jack would make a change. She had made a point of the fact that she wanted the two of them. She couldn't have any screwups with this taping, which was going to take place in the cramped and noisy offices of the director of emergency services at General Hospital. The director had put Ruth off for days. He was busy, he didn't want the attention, and he was nervous about her investigation. When he finally agreed, very reluctantly, Ruth had promised that it would take no more than thirty minutes. She had no doubt that any problem at all—being late, taking too much time to set up—would be excuse enough for him to pull out, even at the last minute. She couldn't afford to lose him. Her upcoming special on allegations of mismanagement in the city's funding and operation of emergency services needed direct comments from him.

Her schedule this morning was particularly tight. In addition to the nine-thirty taping, she had agreed weeks ago to fill in for the host of the station's noontime live talk show, beginning at eleven-thirty. As she hurried through the lobby, a voice suddenly startled her out of her preoccupation. "Ma'am? Ma'am?" someone was demanding. Ruth turned and realized that the woman behind the receptionist's desk was calling her. She realized, too, that it wasn't the regular receptionist, Ellen. "Ma'am," the woman was calling to her, "you can't just walk in. Who's expecting you? Come over here! It's station policy, ma'am. All guests have to sign in and wait for an escort."

Ruth was too startled to respond for a moment. Then she recovered and explained, "I'm not a guest. I'm Ruth Carden." She fully expected that to take care of the matter and turned to continue on her way.

"*Ma'am!*" demanded the woman again, now walking toward her. "You *can't* go back there!"

"I *work* here," Ruth repeated, with exasperation.

"I'm sure you do, ma'am," responded the woman, her voice now deliberate with an effort to be patient. "May I see your ID?"

Ruth decided to fish for her ID and protest later, but on second thought she counterdemanded, "Who are *you?* Where's Ellen?"

"I'm here from temporary, ma'am. I've been told that no one goes in without an ID."

Ruth pulled out her ID victoriously, held it up, then turned on her heels to head for the offices.

She arrived in her office and put in a quick call to Jack, which produced the information that he'd left minutes ago for a dentist's appointment. "Oh, great!" she shouted into the phone with exasperation. Then she asked Jack's secretary about Calvin and Lori. She learned that they were en route to the state capitol, fifty minutes away, scheduled to be there for the full morning. Pete and Richard had been assigned to her for the nine-thirty taping. *Wonderful!* she thought. *The two new kids! Jack, how could you do this to me?* "OK," she said to the secretary, "but tell Jack I want to see him when he gets in."

Promptly at nine Pete and Richard arrived in her office, gear in tow. They left for the hospital, Pete and Richard following Ruth, who had decided to drive her own car. At nine-twenty Pete and Richard got lost, having forgotten Ruth's directions for getting through the construction around the hospital. At nine twenty-five Ruth pulled into the hospital parking lot. At nine-forty Pete and Richard arrived, full of apologies. She rushed them through the noisy hallway filled with patients and staff. They all arrived, breathless, at the director's office. He was obviously nervous, so much so that Ruth began to wonder if he'd be able to talk. "You know I have to leave at ten," he reminded her.

"We'll be finished in no time," she reassured him, turning to look meaningfully at Pete and Richard.

The two of them hustled, setting up lights, reflectors, readying the camera. Ruth thought the director was going to bolt as he watched. But then they hooked up the microphones, and Pete said, "We're ready." The doctor swallowed hard.

Ruth was one sentence in to her lead-in when Pete interrupted, "Hold on a minute!" Ruth stopped in amazement. The doctor looked sick. "Richard," Pete said, "you have a new tape in there? Something's wrong with this one."

Ruth rolled her eyes. The doctor looked at his watch and exclaimed, "We're running out of time." Ruth looked at him grimly and glared at Pete.

"I can't find one," came Richard's plaintive voice. Pete left the camera to search through the bag himself. Ruth shook her head.

"I've got to go in five minutes," said the doctor.

Pete looked up. "Ruth, we'll have to go to the van for another one."

Ruth restrained her urge to tear off the microphone and fling it in the direction of her crew. She managed a professional smile and asked the doctor if he possibly had any time, *any* time, this afternoon. He was sure he didn't. His secretary came to the door to remind him of his next meeting. The doctor asked her rhetorically, "I'm all booked up this afternoon, right?"

She looked seriously at him and said she believed he'd had a cancellation at two.

"Put me down," said Ruth as the doctor looked on in disbelief. "We'll have everything under control when we return, sir. It'll take less than fifteen minutes. Thank you so much!"

The doctor scowled as he stalked out. "Well, see that you remember to bring some film next time!"

Ruth snapped at Pete and Richard, "Good advice!" and she walked out.

When she arrived back at the station, the noon show producer told her that there had been a last-minute change in the guest lineup. "No sweat, I can talk with anybody," she said with a rueful laugh. She began reviewing the program notes on her way back to her office. She looked in on Jack's office as she passed by; he still wasn't back.

At eleven-fifteen, she headed down the hall to the noon show studio. En route she told Jack's secretary, in "don't mess with me" tones, that she really did want to see Jack as soon as he got in. She went on into the studio and stood in the wings, letting the familiar bustle of pre-airtime work go on around her. She wished that she'd not agreed to do this. It was a lineup of dull guests, and her mind was still on the morning's fiasco. She turned to her guest list again, trying to get the order of the whole program set in her head.

Don, who produced Ruth's weekly political show, suddenly burst in to the studio. "Ruth! I've been looking for you!" he called. "I need to go over some things with you about Saturday's show. I thought we could do it over lunch. But clearly"—he paused, his voice heavy with disappointment—"you can't." He shook his head. "Things are getting really tight. How about two?"

"Can't." said Ruth. "I've got to go back out to do the hospital interview again."

Don shouted at her, "I can't do the show without you, Ruth! Something in this schedule of yours has got to give!"

He stomped out of the room. Ruth looked after him, amazed and then angry.

"What's *with* him?" she asked angrily of another producer nearby, stifling an urge to run after Don.

"He's had a rough morning," she answered.

"Well, welcome to the crowd!" Ruth muttered. She looked at her watch. Six minutes before airtime. She'd chase Don down later. She walked to the set and sat down to get the mikes set and checked.

Suddenly she heard Jack's voice at the door, demanding, "Where's Ruth?" He spotted her and came rapidly toward the set. "If you think I'm going to hold down the best crew I've got for some favorite assignment of yours, just because it's you, you'd better reassess the situation!" he shouted.

"I *asked* you for them!" she yelled back, pinned now into her chair by the mike cord. "And you *said* I could have them! Why didn't you tell me you'd taken them off? At least I could have rescheduled before I went out there with your two rookies and made a fool of myself!"

The first guest, being ushered on to the set at that moment, looked amazed and overwhelmed. Ruth saw him out of the corner of her eye and wanted to reassure him, but she hadn't finished saying her piece to Jack. As she turned her attention back to Jack, she suddenly felt a lump forming in her throat. *Oh, no!* she thought desperately. *Not now!* But it was too late. Tears came to her eyes even as she warned herself. They fell, and she called out to Jack, "Who *are* you to come in here yelling at me anyway?" She put her head in her hands, then looked up again, searching for the studio clock as tears rolled down her face. "I don't believe this," she muttered through the tears.

"Bring me a tissue," she ordered a technician standing nearby. He jumped and came back with one in a moment. Ruth wiped her eyes. The makeup woman, who'd been standing at the studio door when the shouting began, ran in with a damp cloth and new makeup. The first guest, now being seated opposite Ruth, was simply staring at her. Ruth looked at her watch again and wiped her eyes for the last time, taking care not to rub the last of the fresh makeup being applied at that moment. She smiled weakly at the guest. "Don't worry, we always do this right before a show." He laughed weakly in return and looked confused. She yelled after Jack, "I'll deal with you later!"

The makeup woman finished, with one eye on the clock, and whispered to Ruth, "It's going to be OK, honey." Twenty seconds.

Ruth looked toward the cameras. "Where are we starting?"

"Camera two," came the reply. Ten seconds. *I'll kill Jack,* she thought, smiling into the camera. She winked at the guest. "It'll be fine," she mouthed to him with a smile, pleading silently, *Don't freeze up on me!* Suddenly, she thought frantically, *What is his name?* She glanced down to look at her notes again.

The producer groaned, "Great!"

But on the split second Ruth was smiling into camera two, bright, poised and friendly. Perfect for the noontime show. "Good morning! Ruth Carden here, sitting in for my friend David Barrett. . . ."

The show went on.

And so did her colleagues' reactions to Ruth's tears. For better or worse, Ruth didn't get to sample those reactions right then. But the reactions were there.

Sophie, the makeup woman, who happened by the studio door at the beginning of Jack's diatribe, felt genuine sympathy for Ruth when she saw her cry. *Poor thing!* she exclaimed to herself. *What has that man done to upset her like that?* She immediately wanted to help. She ran for makeup, hurried back with it, and cared for Ruth in a way that was genuinely helpful at that moment.

Ron, the technician standing near Ruth when the tears started, reacted with amazement and stood transfixed. He thought—to the extent that he *could* think—*What is she doing?* And then, with much greater intensity; *What am* I *supposed to do about it?* He felt a lot of pressure to do something. But he had absolutely no idea what. Ruth was a famous person, and here she was in tears. He felt pulled in two totally opposite directions. He wanted to get out of there, and he wanted to help. But he didn't have the foggiest notion how to help. When Ruth told him to get a tissue, he was immensely relieved. At least he had *something* to do.

The producer of the noon show, Ed, watched from the studio floor as the scene unfolded. His eyes widened in amazement and then panic. "Why *me?*" he implored under his breath, rolling his eyes heavenward. Ed felt intensely persecuted at that moment. First, he was dealing with substitute hosts three out of five days this week, three different hosts at that. He was always nervous about substitutes. The regular host was so good that Ed could just relax, knowing that everything would go according to plan. Ed had felt fine about Ruth's hosting today, but he knew there might be little hitches just because it wasn't her usual thing. And then he'd had last-minute changes in the guest lineup. He didn't like that at all. And now Ruth was in tears! Had any producer anywhere ever opened a live show with a weeping hostess? He was in a panic, but like Ron, he felt completely immobilized. He didn't know what to do. To begin with, he didn't like emotions—*any* emotions—at work. He'd had no better reaction to Don's and Jack's yelling than he did to Ruth's tears. He just stood there, watching to see what she'd do next. He wished he could tell her to take a break and get out of there until she was finished sobbing. He felt immense relief when he finally saw her smile at camera two and knew the episode was over.

Mary, a station executive, was in one of the control rooms, scanning several of the screens, when the cameras began transmitting the image of tears falling down Ruth's face. "I don't believe it!" she muttered. "Ruth Carden!" She was instantly disbelieving. She looked more closely and asked incredulously, "Ruth Carden in tears?" She knew Ruth well, and she liked her. Ruth was the kind of woman that you could feel very good about in this business. But Ruth in tears? Mary shook her head, silently willing Ruth to get it under control. "We lose two steps for every one we've gained with something like this!" she muttered to no one in particular. She shook her head and shot an exasperated, disbelieving look at a colleague who came walking in. She didn't want him to think that she condoned this sort of behavior. What could Ruth be thinking?

Samuel, the evening news anchor, was in an adjoining area of the studio, checking out a new set for the news program, when he heard the commotion. He went over to have a look. He was a little taken aback by Jack's yelling. He was even more surprised when Ruth yelled back. But he was astounded when she began to cry. He said nothing but looked on in amazement for a few moments. Like Mary, he hardly believed it. He'd thought that Ruth was above that sort of thing. *She must think she's got to pull out all the stops to get what she wants from old Jack,* he mused to himself. *I guess I shouldn't be surprised; she's a woman. But I thought Ruth would be above the old turn-on-the-tears trick.*

Jack probably would've turned down Samuel's sympathy if he'd known about it. Jack was surprised at Ruth's tears, too. But he was well aware of his own anger, and he figured Ruth was angry, too. He shook his head as he walked back to his office. *Brilliant, Jack . . . you come back to three messages that she wants to see you, she yells at you, she cries at you, and you figure out she's angry? Way to go!* He regretted having yelled at Ruth, but *he* really was angry about the attitude he assumed was behind all her messages. And his whole face ached. He hated dental work; he had hardly needed this work headache waiting for him when he got back to the office. He figured that he and Ruth would work it out. It didn't occur to him that she might cry again later when they talked about it, but if she did, he would continue to work it out, feeling convinced (as he did) that they both needed to get the issue of her crew assignments straightened out once and for all.

Bill Cosby's book *Fatherhood* recounts an episode in which his daughter is crying:

> There is . . . one sound from my own children that I cannot bear: the sound of one of them crying. And the most piteous crying comes not from an injury to your daughter's body but to her feelings. It starts low and then heart breakingly builds, with fluid flowing from a variety of outlets: her eyes, her mouth, and her nose. Desperately you try to calm her while wiping her face and seeking the name of the person who reduced her to this state. But your plans to kill that person are changed when you learn that the person is another daughter of yours.[18]

Now a father-daughter family crying episode may seem an unusual point of departure for exploring responses to workplace crying, but its "personal" nature reflects a point of basic importance about reactions to workplace crying.

In our collective heart of hearts most of us in this culture believe that tears are really a private event, something that goes on between parent and child, between spouses, among siblings, maybe even between friends. But tears, we believe, are *not* something for all the world to see. So when we observe tears at work, we tend almost immediately to assume that a professional workplace relationship is being transformed—suddenly, ambiguously, perhaps against everyone's wishes—into a relationship that's potentially much more personal than anyone wants it to be.

The situation is often worsened by the fact that the only responses most of us have when someone else cries are those that we learned in personal (often parent-child) relationships—intimate gestures of hugging, patting, comforting, taking care of things for the crying person. None of these options feels very "right" to most of us in most work situations.

Cosby's episode depicts tears being shed by a female, who looks to a male for help, and this theme, too, strikes a strong cultural chord. Tears often evoke strong images of culturally appropriate male-female relationships. Women frequently grow up with the idea that it's all right to cry in some situations, especially if you're with someone "close." In fact, girls are often taught that occasional crying in such circumstances facilitates culturally valued male-female relationships. (That is, under the right circumstances, crying may be good for you!) For example, when a woman cries and leans on "her man" for comfort and help, strong emotional bonds may be forged and formed. If a man is moved to help "his woman" out of her sadness and tears, this, too, may forge strong emotional connections. For many people in our culture the image of women who cry when things are rough and of men who take care of them through it all is deeply ingrained in basic ideas about the "way things are." And despite the fact that many people, male and female, reject this idea to the extent that it connotes a one-way street rather than a mutually interdependent relationship, it's an image that's also strongly ingrained in many of our traditional cultural assumptions about the way things *ought* to be.

As a consequence, many men—and women—grow up with the assumption that if and when a woman cries, she should be helped, protected, and taken care of by a man. But while the assumption *may* work well in private life, its application at work can—and usually does—create considerable awkwardness, for both the crying person and the observer, especially if the crier is a woman and the observer is a man.

The crier may feel strain because personal nurturing from a work-place acquaintance (or boss, or subordinate, or colleague) may be the very *last* thing she or he wants at that moment. For example, who wants a parental pat on the back from the very person whose antics have "reduced" you to tears of anger? Who wants to be "taken care of, like a baby," when tears have already threatened to wash you right out of workplace power and authority?

The awkwardness born of traditional beliefs about male-female be-havior around crying may also be difficult for the observer of tears, especially if the observer feels a need to do something that is tradition-ally parental and comforting. For example, should you, as an observer, give a crying colleague a hug or a pat on the back? If so, why? Further, are you supposed to stop work and say comforting things to the very person you've just been reprimanding for poor performance? If so, what in the world should you say? Should you say, "It's all right," even when it's *not* all right?

Responses that we've learned for dealing with tears in personal relationships—parent-child or intimate male-female—usually fall far short of anything we consider comfortable or appropriate when we're confronted with the tears of a co-worker.

Not the least of the ironies here is that usually *neither the crying person nor the observer wants to get or give nurturing, intimate, comfort-ing responses at work. What both usually want is to get through the problem creating the tears and on with the business at hand.* But because the very sight of tears—or even the anticipation of tears—triggers so many man-takes-care-of-woman (or parent-takes-care-of-child) im-ages, it can be very hard for an observer to shake off an impulse to "take care of" the crier. That impulse in itself may be surprisingly uncomfort-able when it springs up at work. *(Why do I want to hug her? Why do I feel like putting my arms around him? Why do I want to tell him or her that it's going to be OK?)* The urge to help may lead to even more confusion and no small amount of irritation when the observer realizes that the urge is not producing bright or wonderful ideas for *how* to help.

As Bill Cosby describes, crying is also a mess. When tears come to us, most of us lose all ability even to imagine that we look professional or anything close to acceptable. Certainly in those moments we have nothing approaching the in-control look and feeling most of us aspire to at work. Many people who shed tears on the job often turn their attention almost automatically from the work at hand to how they must look. In this pull toward preoccupation with one's own appearance, matters like budgets, plans, projections, disputes—anything related to the business at hand—may seem suddenly quite irrelevant, clearly secondary in importance to appearing to be in control again.

Observers, too, are often thrown by the "mess" of tears. It can be shocking to observe someone who's normally calm, cool, collected—or even someone who's not quite so polished—making "piteous" sounds, having "fluid flowing from a variety of outlets." It can be hard enough to view someone you love (and have seen in all manner of moods) in such a state. But a colleague? An employee? Small wonder that observers of workplace tears often respond with a frantic press to get the crier to a private place out of the way. "Take a break, go calm down, dry your eyes." We feel the pull to do something even if we decide immediately or later that we chose the wrong thing to do. Even an observer who steels him- or herself *not* to respond may find it an extraordinary effort.

But when you combine an urge to do something with an inability to come up with something appropriate, you often have frustration, confusion, and awkwardness. Like Cosby, whose "urge to kill" over his daughter's tears wound up with an awkward target, the observer of workplace tears may feel that whatever he or she does is bound to be wrong. Should you pat her on the back and get slapped with an harassment lawsuit? Should you sympathize, send for a tissue, hand it over solicitously, and discover later he now thinks you're "interested" in him? Should you tell her to take a break and discover half an hour later that she thought you meant a break until she recovered while you really meant a break to blow her nose? Should you ignore tears and find yourself labeled cold and heartless? Episodes of workplace crying often are perfect setups for confusion and failure.

## How Do People Respond to Tears at Work?

When we surveyed people about their experiences with tears at work, we were, of course, also interested in their *responses* to the tears of their co-workers. As you may recall from Chapter Four the survey drew on the experiences of over two hundred employees, male and female, in a large, diversified workplace.

Just as our respondents' reports about their own tearful feelings produced a few surprises, so, too, did their revelations about their reactions to workplace crying.

By far the most commonly reported response to the sight of someone else crying at work was an impulse to comfort the crying person.

And the second most frequent response was feeling "emotionally moved or touched." More than 40 percent of our respondents reported this feeling. Tears in others, even at work, seem to "touch" many observers and often evoke a need to respond in a way that will provide comfort. Although many people reported feeling moved to respond to the tears of others, they do not always act on those feelings. Many hold back out of embarrassment, an inability to come up with the "right" action, or fear of doing something inappropriate.

Perhaps most intriguing and surprising in these findings, however, are the data on the two most negative responses to workplace crying. Very small proportions of the survey group claimed either feeling manipulated or being angry and disgusted when they see others cry at work.

Yet a great many people believe that crying is likely to evoke such reactions in others. After interviewing many people, we came to realize why such attitudes may be more apparent than real.

Assume that someone is talking with a colleague (or boss or employee—anyone at work) and begins to see the signs of tearing up. These signs, for the perceptive observer, may be subtle: a catch in the voice, a sudden pause, or a quaver. They may also be powerful and direct, as when what seemed to be a reasonable conversation dissolves suddenly in a wash of unexpected tears. When most of us see the signs of tears, we begin to feel a need to comfort the person. But almost simultaneously we run into the reality that we don't know what to do. If we have an inkling and try to act on it, many of us immediately begin wondering if it's "appropriate."

So most of us act hesitantly or not at all—doing nothing or taking a best-guess action—and these are two responses that can have their own negative consequences. Most of us are used to feeling that if there's a problem on our job, we know how to handle it. But here's a problem, and it's one we *don't* know how to handle.

Who among us likes to come face-to-face with our own incompetence? If we're so able, why can't we do something appropriate to take care of these tears? We move from feeling responsive to being irritated by the evidence of our own inability to help. From that point it's a very small step to feeling irritated with the person whose tears put us in this uncomfortable predicament in the first place. This irritation may come *after* the tearful episode, as the observer tries to figure out what happened. The frustration over inability to respond "successfully" may shift easily into blaming the one who cried: *Why did she do that to me? Why did he make me feel that way? Maybe because she or he wanted to get something? Well, that's pretty unfair and manipulative and irresponsible . . .* and so on and on.

The important point discovered in our survey, however, lies in the fact that a primary response of *most* people who see tears at work is an essentially positive impulse to help out. As we'll see in Chapter Ten, there are several ways in which the observer of workplace tears can take an urge to help and do something positive and productive with it.

## *Do Men and Women Have Different Reactions to Workplace Tears?*

While many people believe that males and females have different experiences with crying at work, fewer have definite opinions about possible male-female differences in responses to the tears of others on the job. The difference suggested most frequently by the many people with whom we spoke was that women might be more sympathetic toward workplace tears and men more often angered by tears. But the survey data indicate that there's more myth than truth even in that suggestion.

Most men and women (63 percent and 71 percent) report feeling a need to comfort a crying person when they see tears in the office. Women and men (41 percent and 42 percent) also report feeling emotionally moved or touched by the tears of others. Only a few men and women (4 percent and 3 percent) claim feeling anger or disgust upon seeing a co-worker's tears.

Men and women differ in some patterns of reaction, however. Men are more often left feeling awkward and confused by a tearful episode than are women (43 percent versus 28 percent), while women report more feelings of helplessness than men (36 percent versus 26 percent). Men confronted with a crying co-worker may well feel more acutely the confusion that often attends efforts to draw on personal experiences for responses to individual needs in the workplace; women may well be quicker to perceive that "someone else can't take care of it" when tears surface. A final difference emerged in reports of feeling manipulated. Among the few people who reported this response, there were more men (11 percent) than women (4 percent). Some of the difference may be related to the prevailing assumption that men are supposed to feel manipulated by tears. But we suspect it has more to do with the powerful combination of responses apparently experienced by many men: a sense of responsibility for helping, mixed with confusion about how to do so appropriately. Add to that mix the reality that many women cry from anger—which men typically express more directly in shouting and yelling—and it seems unfortunately logical that a man might well interpret a female colleague's tears as an attempt to get through indirect means what she can't or won't fight for directly.

Before turning to solutions for problems with workplace crying, however, we take a more detailed look at common patterns of response to tears at work.

## Styles of Responding to Tears at Work

The different responses to Ruth's tears at the beginning of this chapter were those characteristic of *most* people who experience someone else's crying at work. While personal style is important, so are circumstances. For example, you may have one kind of reaction if someone cries in your private office, but quite another if someone cries in a large meeting. You may feel most inclined to respond with one style if your crying co-worker is an employee and quite another if he or she is your boss. Similarly, you may experience differences in response tendency if the weeping co-worker is a friend, or merely an acquaintance, or a woman, or a man. It is probable, nonetheless, that you will find yourself moved to respond on *most* occasions in ways that are pretty close to one or two of the styles described here.

### Sophie: "Poor Thing, I Just Want to Help!"

Sophie, the makeup artist who saw Ruth crying, ran to get more supplies so she could repair the damage the tears had done to Ruth's camera-ready face. The fact that she could do something so concrete at that moment was serendipitous. If makeup had not been needed, Sophie would have found something else to do to express her take-care-of-it response style.

Sophie's way of reacting to workplace tears is the way most parents respond to the "genuine" tears of their children. The tears tug at your heart, and you act immediately to fix it, to make it better, take care of the problem somehow. Adding to her parental style are the facts that Sophie enjoys the parental role and doesn't mind at all, even at work, being viewed as a good, caring parental person. She considers herself highly competent in her work, an opinion her colleagues share. Caring and competence are at the core of her self-image, and she builds her job skills and her interpersonal relationships at work around that center.

She, and many others like her, do not spend a lot of time thinking about her role with others; she simply acts out of the way she is and the way she thinks a decent human being *ought* to act. She may experience a few tremors of doubt about running right in to take care of a co-worker's tears, but she doesn't doubt very often. And regardless of her co-worker's role—her boss, an employee, someone she knows well, or someone she's barely met—Sophie responds to tears in essentially the same way.

Sophie is most concerned about helping the tearful person feel better. If she suspects she was involved in causing the tears, she'll check that out and may try to fix the cause. But usually she assumes that tears reflect a temporary breakdown in the system, an insult, a grievance, a problem that will take care of itself over time (as is often true with children's tears). She's at ease offering pats on the back and even hugs. She listens sympathetically and usually agrees with whatever interpretation a crier puts on his or her tears. She's not being simple or simplistic, but she believes that tearful circumstances are unique; the crier alone knows what's wrong and eventually what to do about it. She believes that people who cry need comfort, a shoulder to lean on, an ear to listen, and she provides these aids with a very matter-of-fact sense of caring.

The one difficulty that she has with her style of response to workplace tears is that sometimes she can't "fix it." Sometimes a shoulder and sympathy aren't enough. She feels a little inadequate then, although she usually assumes that the person will be able to go on and "feel better" through some other means. Her difficulty springs from the same source that sometimes brings problems for the recipient of Sophie's sympathy. A tearful person may experience her response as being too focused on taking care of him or her, too "easy" in its quick slide over the real problems at the root of the tears. Every now and again a crier may feel a bit insulted at the implicit assumption that the problem underlying the tears isn't more serious than a hug and a tissue.

Sophie's style is somewhat more characteristic of women than of men in the workplace perhaps in part because its parental base fits the traditional mother-parent role more closely than it fits the traditional father-parent role. But men use this style, too, especially if they, like Sophie, are overtly caring or paternal people.

The dominant theme in this style, for both men and women, is moving in to help the crying person feel better. Usually people with this style assume that they know what will make the person feel better, and that usually involves giving comfort and reassurance that everything *will* feel better, will be OK. The comfort is usually offered and given without reference to the causes of the tears. Indeed, people with this response style often assume that tears simply come in the natural flow of life and will pass on in the natural course of things, especially if caring people are around to give (temporary) comfort.

### Ron: "Oh, Help! Now What'll I Do?"

Ron, who was standing near Ruth when her tears began to fall, was simply paralyzed by them. He soon concluded that he wasn't responsible for her crying, but for a panic-stricken moment he had wondered what he'd done to upset her so much. He was immensely relieved when a quick run-through of the possibilities ruled out any fault on his part. But he felt very strongly that he should *do* something about her tears. Here was a woman crying and here he was, a man. But he hadn't the vaguest idea what to do.

Ron, and people like him, aren't accustomed to seeing tears at work. Much more important, however, most haven't imagined that tears could (or should!) be at work. Many of them think of tears within personal relationships as problematic, raising issues and uncertainties that are often difficult to deal with. The idea that someone might cry at work just poses too many "strange bedfellows" for them, presenting—as they perceive it—a request for personal help in the context of a professional relationship.

When "Oh, help!" people see tears in the office, they usually assume that something awful and probably personal has gone wrong for the person who's crying. And strong though they may be in other situations, many find themselves very hesitant at the thought of helping a co-worker solve a major personal problem. They may know the usual responses for tears—tissues, hugs, offers to sit and talk about it, a retreat until it's over—but they tend to believe that these responses are inappropriate at work since they assume that tears almost always spring from intensely personal sources.

Ron was greatly relieved when Ruth told him to get her a tissue because he sincerely wanted to do *some*thing. Without her permission or instruction, though, he believed that any action on his part would probably be wrong and intrusive and quite likely would make the problem worse instead of better. One corporate auditor we interviewed who claimed to be an original "Oh, help!" reactor explained, "It's like this. I don't know anything about flying airplanes. If I was in a plane and the pilot had a heart attack and shouted, 'Take over!' before he passed out, I'd probably spend half the time descending to earth shaking him, trying to get him to wake up. Then I'd spend half of the remaining time trying to figure out what to do. At the last second I'd do something. But I doubt that I'd be able to describe it once it was all over. And you wouldn't catch me up in an airplane again!"

Like the auditor in the hypothetical plane, Ron would just as soon not be there when the pilot passes out or when the tears fall. He doesn't like to think he'd turn away from someone in need. But he doesn't know what to do. So he looks on, waiting for it all to be over.

If "Oh, help!" people are pressed, they tend to ask awkwardly if the crier *needs* something. Like a break. Or they may suggest nervously that the crier *do* something. Like take a break. Usually their response is motivated by a sincere belief that the crier is no more eager to have the offending tears seen than the observer is to watch them.

Ron's "Oh, help!" style is more typical of men than women. Although many women, too, feel this way about someone else's tears at work, most have had enough experience with others' tears during their own growing up that they know a few useful responses that they can pull out in the clutch. They're somewhat less likely than male counterparts to find themselves frozen with ignorance. As is true of "Oh, help!" men, however, women with this response style may find themselves very uncomfortable about their urge to do something when they doubt that anything they can come up with will be appropriate or helpful.

The idea of asking the crier what she or he would like them to do rarely occurs to "Oh, help!" responders. Their strong belief that *they* are responsible for helping somehow and their assumption that crying comes from personal issues that they shouldn't be aware of seem to preclude the possibility of so direct a question to the crier. The "Oh, help!" responder's obvious distress over the crying may in itself add to the problems experienced by the crier. Many criers have reported a need to get their tears—and the precipitating problem—submerged, at least temporarily, so they can concentrate on reassuring the hapless observer!

### Ed: "Why ME?"

"Why *me?*" responders, like Ed, the producer of the noon show, most often react to workplace tears with disbelief and sometimes more than a little sense of unjust persecution. Like most of his "Oh, help!" counterparts, Ed knows that tears fall occasionally even in the best workplaces. He's been around long enough to realize that tears are neither rare nor confined to personal and intimate relationships. In the course of life, he knows, there are times when things break down. "Things just happen," Ed said, "I know that. And I know that it happens at work, too. I just wish the breakdowns would happen somewhere else. I hate dealing with emotional outbursts!" he exclaimed.

Some "Why *me?*" people specifically dislike tears. As one oil company executive said firmly, "The normal emotions are fine; anybody can yell every now and again at work. It's just tears. It's impossible to deal with someone who's crying!" What he considered normal may vary across workplaces and workers. But some of his companions in the "Why *me?*" category dislike emotional outbursts of *any* kind. Some fear the lack of control, others get angry about it, and most feel strongly that emotional behavior does nothing but divert attention from the work at hand, very unnecessarily.

Many people with this response style can often think of something to do in response to tears, but they'd simply rather not have to deal with it at all. "Tears? While we're working on this project?" Ed was dismayed by Ruth's tears because he was in a time-pressed spot. The show had to go on, and he knew he couldn't begin if the guest host was sporting tears at the very moment of greeting the viewers. He felt helpless because of the time crunch. If Ruth had been in his private office after hours when tears struck, Ed would have pulled out one of his stock responses like "There, there, it will be OK." But he would have continued to feel the same way. "Why *me?*" Why now? Who needs this?" Ed *can* deal with tears at work, but he'd simply rather not at any time.

Many people, across many response styles, agree with "Why *me?*" people that there's never a good time for office tears. We don't after all, have institutionalized emotion breaks the way we have coffee breaks. But some "Why *me?*" people, in an interesting paradox, acknowledge that there *might* be times when tears at work are justified. But the time is almost never in front of *them,* in the midst of one of *their* projects. "It's not the right time if *I* have to deal with it!" Ed exploded in frustration. And then he added, "It's not logical, but it's what I think."

A few more men than women claim this style, but women are certainly present here. Regardless of sex, most "Why *me?*" people believe fundamentally that they don't have time to "waste" on workplace tears. Part of this reaction comes from the fact that some of them, like people who have the "Oh, help!" style, aren't really sure what to do about the tears. They believe that their responses will probably be wasted effort, especially if they wind up doing the "wrong thing." Much more strongly than "Oh, help!" responders, however, "Why *me?*" people focus on what they believe to be the wasted time and effort involved in any tearful episode. They believe pretty strongly that tears come from personal issues or internal states that only the crier can rectify. It seldom occurs to "Why *me?*" responders that the tears might emerge legitimately from a work-related problem that needs to be solved. Tears, in their view, rather than provide a perhaps crucial indicator of a significant problem at work, simply eat up time and energy that would much better be spent getting the job done.

### Mary: "I Can't BELIEVE You're Crying!"

Mary, the station exec in the control room when the cameras began recording Ruth's tearful outburst a few minutes before airtime, was shocked by Ruth's tears, but not because she thinks people do not cry at work.

Mary was shocked because she doesn't expect highly capable people to cry. "Successful people *don't* cry," she asserted firmly. She assumes that others like her—people at her professional level who make their own way in the "real" work world—simply don't cry on the job. If they ever had inclinations to shed workplace tears, she believes, "surely they learned to control those urges" early in their careers.

Mary equates work success with ambition, competence, and learning to control emotions. She believes this equation holds especially true in fields that have been traditionally open only or primarily to men. "Obviously you need excellent base line competence," she said. "But if your competence stands a chance of doing you any good, of getting you noticed, you've *got* to have firm control over your emotions. The real world is tough. People who want to get ahead *have* to show that they can withstand the shocks that are part and parcel of rising to the top."

When Mary realized that Ruth *was* crying, she struggled quickly to evaluate if she'd been wrong all along about Ruth's competence. Then she grew irritated about Ruth's tears. *Why is she doing that? Get it together, Ruth!* she fumed silently. And she was bewildered. *How can Ruth be doing this?*

Mary's response grew in part from a strong ideological belief that women who are successful have a special responsibility to behave in ways traditionally associated with success. They shouldn't ask for special consideration when it comes to traditionally "female" issues—like tears, or family needs, or any of those things. They should take the professional world on its own terms and make it on those terms. "To do anything else," she said, "is simply weak. At best, it demonstrates very poor judgment!" Mary is committed to the opinion that women in the professions aren't "weak." Like so many of the men who share her style—many of whom treat the issue of women's competence as a question rather than an assumption—Mary doesn't ask that the working world change its expectations of employees. She asks that women— and men—who enter that world and expect to succeed in it meet all its standards.

Mary's face-to-face reaction to Ruth's tears would not have been much different from her reaction at a distance. Had she been on the set with Ruth, she would have expressed her shock and disapproval, not loudly and derisively but clearly and firmly. She would have let Ruth know what she thought. She would *not* have moved in to comfort Ruth or to take care of her. "I *might* have tried to get her out of there," she offered. As Mary sees it, the tears were Ruth's problem. *Ruth* needed to get them under control. Mary, furthermore, did not assume that Ruth's tears came as a expression of a legitimate problem. "If Ruth's got a problem," she observed firmly, "she'd better learn to deal with it directly."

Although Mary sometimes has feelings about the tears she witnesses—she *may* feel moved by them—she believes strongly that they're inappropriate at work. She suppresses any personal emotional response to the weeping as quickly as she can. She feels qualms every now and again about having to suppress her responsive feelings, for in private life she believes that emotional expression and responses are natural and necessary. But she does not want to think about that at work.

Most "I can't *believe* you're crying!" people have a firm view of how the professional world works. Most are men, but there are many women who share this style, too. In general, they believe that those who have made it to the top have done so because they are very able, have learned the rules, and play by the rules. They believe that others who are capable—male and female—should make it playing by the rules. One of these rules is you don't cry on the job. Mary hasn't often or seriously considered whether it's a good rule, but she knows it exists. She believes that others who want to get ahead, like herself, should abide by that rule.

### Samuel: "I Wonder What She Wants"

Samuel, the evening news anchor, looked upon Ruth's tears with surprise, followed by condescension, and then with sympathy for his colleague Jack, who seemed to be the "target" of Ruth's tears. Finally, he viewed her tears with curiosity. "I just began to wonder what she was trying to get," he explained.

Unlike Mary, who was shocked by the tears, and Ed, who was dismayed by them, Samuel was not upset by Ruth's crying. "Tears are tears," he said. "I don't like 'em, but they're not the end of the world either." He maintained that he probably wouldn't have been very upset about her tears even if he'd been directly involved; "They're basically harmless. And usually not very effective!"

He has a "routine" for responding to tears, at home and at work. After ruling out any situational problem as cause for the crying (he didn't commit a gross error; the sky hadn't just fallen), he assumes that something must be wrong with the crier. "I figured Ruth had a problem," he said with a shrug of his shoulders. And he felt mostly curious then about what was going on. He didn't ask Ruth or anybody about the incident, though. He wouldn't have made those inquiries even if he'd been right there in front of her or been the "target" of her tears. In the absence of obvious, probable cause Samuel assumes that tears come from personal sources or are part of an indirect manipulative game. And he is not going to be the one to bring the game out into the open. "Ruth shed the tears," he said. "The next move is hers."

Samuel, however, was glad that he *wasn't* the "target" of the tears. Like his co-workers in the "Oh, help!" and "Why *me?*" categories, Samuel didn't want to respond to the tears. Tears make him feel awkward despite his best efforts to stay on top of the situation. He usually feels compelled to do something, though, if tears fall in his presence. He usually takes a relatively paternal approach, offering a pat on the back or some tissues. His "helpfulness," however, is less caring than Sophie's response, which is rooted in an earnest desire to help the crying person feel better. Samuel mostly wants to smooth over an awkward situation. He wants to look helpful, to appear as though he's not thrown by the crying, and to get it over with.

Samuel doesn't usually *begin* his response to workplace tears with the belief that the crier is trying to manipulate a situation. And "certainly," he said, "*men* don't cry to get their way!" But if there's no apparent reason for the tears and if there's no personal problem behind them that he can determine, he believes that "You're left with few options but to believe that she's crying to get something. It's too bad," he observed, "that it has to happen that way." People, and women in particular, he believes, should learn to get what they want by more direct means.

Most of Samuel's companions in this style category are men, although he has many female companions, too. As a group people with this response style believe pretty strongly that everyone would be better off if tears never saw the light of a workplace day. Crying can create such problems even when the tears are "innocent" or purely personal. And, as Samuel concluded, "They're simply not fair if they're used to get your way in a situation."

### Jack: "Well, We'd Better Figure This One Out"

Among the many who saw Ruth cry, Jack was the person who was most directly involved in the incident. His were the actions that led to Ruth's tears. Obviously other factors entered into the situation, too: the day had been full of irritations for Ruth, and it had certainly not been one of Jack's better days. The accumulation of events that morning had drawn heavily on the reservoir of good humor and equanimity that both usually brought with them to work. However, Jack's yelling at Ruth as she sat preparing to host the noon show was the specific event that precipitated her tears. Unlike the other observers—some of whom sought immediately to ascertain that *they* were not at fault in the weeping—Jack couldn't easily assume a "no fault" position. He knew that he'd "done it."

Because of his response style, however, Jack also knew that other issues—work-related and in addition to his yelling—were probably involved in the tears. "Tears," he said knowingly, "seldom come out of *one* bad exchange or experience!" The precipitating event, he believes, is sometimes "just the one that happens along when the problems have reached a critical stage." He knew he could have handled the whole thing better, and he felt a little guilt over it. But he didn't feel *much* guilt because he knew that he was angry at Ruth and he felt that yelling was a legitimate expression of that feeling (even though, he hastened to add, "I don't *prefer* yelling)." He believed that Ruth's tears, too, were a legitimate expression of feeling. In this case he assumed her feeling was anger. He also assumed that they'd work it out when she was through with the noon show. "I'd rather have dealt with it right then," he told us, "but that was impossible."

Jack is alone among his colleagues in that his reaction to tears can be characterized as "matter-of-fact." He saw the crying and quickly assumed that the tears were evidence of a problem he and Ruth needed to solve. "I'd had at least a small pile of evidence pointing in that direction already!" He laughed. But even if he'd not had the benefit of signs along the morning's way that he and Ruth were at odds over crew assignments, he would have assumed that her tears signaled a problem, probably a work-related problem.

He knows from experience that the needs expressed in tears are sometimes beyond the borders of someone else's ability to help, as, for example, when tearfulness springs from totally personal issues. "I can't fix someone else's divorce," he observed. But he knows, too, that tears in the office most often come from work-based problems that *can* be addressed, work-based problems that need to be solved.

Not that Jack doesn't experience a personal reaction to the tears. Like almost everyone else in the working world, he wishes that tears "weren't there; I could certainly do without them. But if somebody's crying, you've got to stop what you're doing and figure out what's wrong." He assumes that the problems underlying the tears *have* to be dealt with if productive work is going to continue over the long run.

Jack's first overt response to tears at work is usually to stop the action until the people involved can say what each wants. "I need to find out what the problem is," he said. "I'll wait if that's what's needed." And he'll support "taking a break if that's what's needed. If I agree to a break in the action, though, I make sure that we get back to it as soon as possible." The critical issue for Jack is getting to the "bottom of it."

Jack's response style category has relatively few members. Men and women are pretty evenly represented. People in this category are a little unusual in that they've learned—in growing up, at work, through hard experience (or somewhere somehow)—that tears at work are *not* the end of the world. Most people with this response style will tell you that tears are usually "a sign of something gone wrong." Some suggest that learning how to deal with problematic situations more directly would alleviate a lot of the tears, and the alleviation would be to the good. But people with this response style usually know that tears come for a variety of reasons. When they get to the underlying problems, if they involve work issues, they begin solving them.

## Thinking About Your Own Responses

Whatever your style of reacting to others' tears—whether you find yourself clearly in one category or mixed in your reactions—there are some very important things to keep in mind as you reflect on the importance of response style.

First, response styles are seldom tied directly to personality or to "position" within a workplace. People with personalities very different from those who represent the various styles described are often found within the same categories. For example, "I just want to help!" people like Sophie, may be warm, gregarious, parental, outgoing, and overtly protective. They may also be quiet, serious, careful, and almost professionally "distant" from the crier as they're helping. The thread that binds them together in the same response category is not composed of personal characteristics but of an orientation focused on making it better and fixing someone else's tears. Similarly, Samuel's "I wonder what she wants" style may be descriptive of people who have personal qualities and social orientations very different from his. Samuel is polished, concerned about appearances, and fairly condescending in his reaction to someone who cries, and he has a strong tendency to assume that a crier will always be a woman. Another "I wonder what she wants" person we interviewed is much more direct in her general approach to people, is much less concerned about the way she appears to others, and is committed to "changing some common misperceptions about women in the workplace." But her "gut-level" reaction to tears is to wonder what the crier wants, to wait for a bit and watch, "scoping it out," before she moves in with a direct inquiry (if she does). She's not particularly pleased with her response style, but she said quite matter-of-factly that's just the way she thinks about it at this point.

So people with very different personalities and attitudes may be companions within response style categories. So may people with varying positions within their workplace. Being the "boss" doesn't cause a person to be in one category and not in others. Nor does being the "new kid" in the firm, in the most junior position. Some styles are easier to implement if you're the boss and the crier is your subordinate; if the roles are reversed (you're the subordinate and your boss is crying), it may feel a little tricky, for example, to act out a "We'd better figure this one out" response or an "I just want to help" reaction. But in general, response styles don't emerge most directly from workplace position.

They do emerge from individual, personal experience with tears throughout life. They seem to be shaped primarily by personal history: how people have reacted to your tears, what you learned about crying when you were growing up, what responses you observed in others as you caught glimpses of tears in your home, and so on. And they seem to be shaped, too, by personal beliefs and attitudes about the meaning and function of tears in adult life. One who assumes that tears convey weakness is not likely to respond with a style that focuses on getting to the bottom of the problem causing the tears. One who believes that professional relationships should be characterized by cool, clear formality will not likely be found in the "I just want to help" or "Why *me*?" categories. This is true simply because the behaviors and basic attitudes that characterize those styles are not consistent with a strong belief in cool, clear formality.

One response style that we encountered in our interviews and analyses is not found in the descriptions above. It's not there because it appeared only rarely, not often enough to be considered a genuinely representative style. But it's a pattern of reacting that we grew to appreciate because it focuses on putting control of the situation into the hands of the crier. It allows the crier to identify the problems under the tears—the problems associated with the work at hand and those growing out of interpersonal processes attending the work. In putting majority control of the tearful situation into the hands of the crier, it addresses one of the most common problems that many observers have when someone cries at work: figuring out what the problem is and what to do about it. In tone and substance it is most like Jack's "We'd better figure this one out" approach, but it goes two steps beyond assuming that the problems at the root of the tears are necessarily linked to a work *task* issue and beyond assuming that the observer has primary responsibility for taking charge of the situation. It acknowledges that interpersonal issues surrounding the task may be problematic too. And it assumes that the *crier* has the responsibility and the right to take charge of the situation. The observer assumes that the crier is in control and waits until the crier has begun the process—which will become mutual—of problem definition and solution.

# 7

# Anxiety at Work

Stupidity is without anxiety

—JOHANN WOLFGANG VON GOETHE

TO A GREAT EXTENT the people we work with—and we ourselves—judge us on the basis of how well we do our jobs.
Being judged by one's job puts a lot of stress on a person.
And an important fact that exacerbates these natural stresses
is that how well we perform them is not always totally under our own
control.

Many people end up doing the work they do because they chose it.
Others got lucky and stumbled into the right jobs; still others were
pushed by someone into the wrong ones. Each of us has our own story.

There are many things we have not had complete control over: the
choice of bosses we work for and colleagues we work with; the kind of
equipment we must use; the clients, service personnel, production people, and administrators we interact with; and the offices and field sites
where we spend our time.

All these factors and a multitude of others directly and indirectly
influence how well we are able to do our jobs. Even during those times
when our work is largely under our own control, compatible with the
life-styles we choose to live, fulfilling, and financially rewarding, personal pressures at work can be substantial. It's natural for people to set
standards for themselves. When an important work-related goal is
achieved, it's likely that we'll set other, perhaps more difficult goals.
Relatively few working people really want just to "coast" these days.
If work is satisfactory, we want it to get good. If life is good, we want
it to get better. And we expect ourselves to create those realities—not
only for our own individual satisfactions but also for the well-being of
our families. Work is one of the most important tools we have for
creating the good life, however that life is personally defined. Considering the stakes, then, anxiety over work and work performance is often
inevitable.

The feeling of anxiety is very useful for charting progress toward goals. We define anxiety as the uneasiness, apprehension, and worry that may arise when we seem in danger of not achieving an important goal. We experience this emotion at work most often when we have concluded on the basis of some emerging data that what we desire may not occur. It looks as if the new boss is not going to be a fair person. Or the raise is not going to come through. Or the supply budget will be cut in half. Or the promotion isn't going to happen.

We get anxious as we anticipate the possibility that a work-related need or desire might be thwarted. When we use an anxious feeling to propel us into constructive action—into creating positive changes in some aspect of the situation—we use the anxiety wisely. Imagine what life would be like if we did not have anxious feelings! Many good opportunities would be missed, and many calamities would not be avoided.

*Anxiety prompts us to think,* to reconsider, to gather more information. Anxiety causes us to seek alternate approaches to a problem.

When we become apprehensive that something is not going to go the way we think it should, that feeling provides two important pieces of personal feedback. First, it lets us know that we indeed care about the issue, whatever it is. If we didn't feel strongly about the outcome, we wouldn't be so anxious about it. Second, the anxious feeling lets us know that we have evaluated what's currently going on and that things aren't looking all that good. Whether or not we have become consciously aware of it, we have been gathering and evaluating information that has led to the conclusion that the desired outcome may not occur. And for most of us anxiety usually stimulates this awareness far enough in advance of the outcome to have an opportunity to try to do something about it.

One of the most important things we can do with anxiety at work is to pay attention to it. Often a low level of anxiety appears when we have not been giving careful attention to what is going on around us. In these situations we have been picking up some cues, but we have not taken the time to evaluate key situations critically. We're just a little "bothered" during these occurrences. Something is not quite right, but we don't know what's wrong.

Anxiety prompts action in those who use it wisely. When we use it well, we review the situation and then either act differently in accord with the new facts or conclude that our most recent reasoning was incorrect and that things are still on target with respect to the goal. In either case the anxiety diminishes; the warning flags go down.

As we will see when we take a look at the anxiety styles below, useful anxiety at work is situation-specific. It emerges from concerns about particular goals. When anxiety at work is diffuse, when it is generalized to most components of the work experience, it is troublesome at best. At worst it can be completely debilitating.

People who experience anxiety at work on a rather constant basis often need to get some professional help in thinking through the personal issues involved. Or they may need to get other jobs that do not provide such a generalized level of stressful anxiety. Those courses of action are less necessary when the reasons for the chronic anxiety are obvious and not likely to last for an indefinite period of time. For example, as AT&T moved toward the court-mandated breakup in the early 1980s, many employees in that company experienced almost constant anxiety as it became clear that some personal and professional goals would not ever be achieved. If general anxiety results from company-induced transitional events like that one, then it is likely that most people will not suffer long-term harm from simply hanging in there until the uncomfortable events have passed.

There is much and sometimes severe anxiety to be found in many job settings these days. As external pressures and personal and corporate standards and expectations continue to rise, so do the levels of anxiety at work.

## Anxiety, Anger, Tears, and Caring

The relevance of anxiety to some of the other critical emotions and emotional expressions discussed in this book, such as anger, tears, and caring, cannot be overstressed. Anxiety is often the precipitating cause of angry outbursts and tearful moments. And anxiety is often the emotion that prevents positive feelings, like appreciation and caring, from reaching expression.

The presence of anxiety can be detected throughout the stories and styles represented in previous and later chapters. For many people who struggle with their own anger or that of a colleague, anxiety plays a role at several stages of the process. Some deal with their own anxiety over jeopardized goals by getting angry with others who are involved. It is not uncommon, considering the confrontational aspects of the situation, that in receiving anger at work, some people respond only or primarily with their own anxiety. Ella, the department store buyer, "froze" when one of her bosses raised her voice at her in a reception area. She, like many others, responds to anger outbursts at work with great apprehension. Of course, not all people become immobile when they feel anxious because others are getting angry with them. When provoked by anxiety, many others take action by walking out, trying to get more information, or yelling back.

Tears may flow when a person is overloaded with anxious feelings. Maria, the young researcher, cried out of frustration, anger, and anxiety over the responses of her colleagues to some of her innovations. It's also the case that anxiety is one of the most common feelings that people experience when they are confronted by someone else's tears at work. Many people respond like Ron, the cameraman who witnessed the noon show host's tears. They feel that they *should* know what to do in such a situation and become quite anxious as they realize they don't really know.

In Chapter Eight we will see that many working people keep to themselves their feelings of appreciation and caring for others because of anxious feelings arising from awkwardness at not knowing how to communicate positive feelings without being misunderstood or being seen as a little too "soft." Often personal anxiety prevents people from offering praise and support to those around them.

## The Importance of Anxiety at Work

Anxiety's presence in the workplace is very much acknowledged in public and private these days. The proliferation of books and workshops designed to help alleviate work-related stress and burnout is evidence of this acknowledgment. But to this point a sizable portion of these have emphasized the negative rather than positive aspects of the experience of anxiety at work.

We present below a few characteristic ways that many of us have of experiencing work-related anxiety. Since the positive contributions of anxiety to excellence on the job are so compelling, many of the conclusions drawn throughout this chapter rely heavily on the view that anxiety can be made a very useful personal tool for making positive changes at work.

So many people have been told that they should get rid of anxiety, make it go away, rather than make it useful. But eliminating apprehensive feelings without engaging in critical evaluation and action directed toward the problematic issues actually may interfere with the production of quality work. And it may increase the chances of action based on poor judgment and missing data.

Throughout this book we have suggested many times that effective management of feelings cannot result from denying their existence, for example, through suppression by alcohol and drugs or through excessive channeling of them into sports and physical fitness activities. Thus, you will find that we do not suggest in Chapter Ten (Strategies for Change) that anxiety be dealt with by engaging in a game of racquetball from time to time or even regularly. While fitness activities are critically important for health and well-being, they are used unwisely if they become an habitual substitute for directly dealing with the feelings that are such an important part of the process of working. Anxiety should be dealt with in a meaningful way within the situation that precipitates it. Anxious feelings are important for successful work. They should not be eliminated before they have been used to prompt evaluation and action within the environments that create them.

## Anxiety Styles in the Workplace

Capturing anxiety styles in the workplace is a bit tricky. It's often difficult, if not impossible, for an observer to recognize anxiety, for it frequently masquerades as other emotions. For example, quite a few people become angry when they get anxious, and their expressions of anger may take any of the forms described in Chapter Two. Some express apprehension through tears, as discussed in Chapter Five.

Two issues further complicate the difficulties associated with recognizing anxiety styles in the workplace. One is the fact that some people who recognize their anxiety do not want to admit it and deliberately cover it by a display of angry or uninterested behavior, for example. The second is that a substantial number of working people do not really seem to have any style of relating to their own anxiety at all. Rather, they simply react each time they feel apprehensive, and their reactions are usually controlled by the environment and the circumstances that precipitated their uncomfortable feelings. The result is that no particular pattern of responding emerges. The way they deal with their own anxiety at work one week may be remarkably different from their response pattern the next week.

In addition to those who channel work-based anxiety into other experiences and those who simply react to it in an erratic way, we have identified a third group of people who usually respond directly to their own apprehensions at work. They attempt to use their anxious feelings to improve the quality of their work or work environment.

## Styles of Channeling Work-Related Anxiety

If you are a person who suspects that you tend to channel anxiety into other emotional expressions, it would be wise for you to reread some of the styles described in Chapters Two, Three, Five, and Six. It may be that at least occasionally, you transform some of your anxious feelings into angry or tearful emotional expressions at work. We suggest that you pay particular attention in those chapters to the styles exemplified by the *deflectors, holders, and keepers.* The styles below depict the most common methods of channeling anxiety at work into experiences that are not anger- or tear-related.

### CLINTON: RUNNING ANXIOUS; ANXIOUSLY RUNNING

Clinton has a substantial amount of his own anxiety to deal with almost every workday. He owns and manages his own restaurant in Chicago and gets personally involved in every aspect of the business. In the beginning he even did a fair amount of the cooking himself.

Clinton tries to anticipate problems before they happen; he's often unsuccessful at that, and some days nothing goes right. He recalls one day when he had already dealt with three big problems before noon: A busload of senior citizens had arrived without notice for an early lunch, and they ate all the pies before the usual lunch crowd even arrived. The morning chicken delivery looked terrible, and he couldn't risk using it. The dishwasher had broken down at 11:00 A.M. Clinton was anxious.

Clinton usually deals with his anxiety by running. Every day, after the lunch rush has passed, he changes into running gear and does at least a three-mile sprint around the neighborhood where the restaurant is located. He said that when he returns, most of the anxieties that have built up throughout the morning are gone. He also finds that his afternoon run makes the evening meal preparations go more smoothly for him. "Afternoons and evenings are just better," he said. "It's the running that does it."

When asked if he knew other ways of responding to his anxieties, he just laughed. "Anxiety is just part of this kind of work. You've got a lot of things to orchestrate in the restaurant business, and you never have enough time to do everything that needs to get done."

Clinton doesn't make any strong connections between specific events and his apprehensions. "If I didn't get anxious over one thing in the morning, it would be something else," he said. We asked him about the spoiled chicken incident, wondering if his anxieties were associated with the problems he knew he would face in having to eliminate all the chicken items from the day's menu. He said, "No, not really. Or, rather, not exclusively. My chicken problems aren't new problems." Apparently Clinton's anxiety had been growing for about two weeks as he noticed that some of his daily deliveries contained insufficient quantities and that the quality of a piece or two was often a bit questionable. He had tried to get hold of the supplier once but never completed the call because his bartender distracted him with another issue. For about two weeks, each day that he was actually in the kitchen at the time of the chicken delivery, he felt some moments of anxiety as he worried over possible salmonella problems. Now that he had been forced to reject a delivery outright, he would spend much of the afternoon arranging for a new supplier, or a new menu, or both.

Clinton does not *use* his anxieties at work very much. He tries to eliminate them by going for a good run every day. It usually works for him.

Like many people, Clinton assumes that a certain amount of apprehension and worry comes with the territory at work. His aim is to make sure that the worries don't negatively influence his health or his personal relationships. Before he started running every day, he was having more trouble with his marriage than either his wife or he desired, and he always worried about "getting an ulcer or something." He blamed his work-related anxiety for the marital stress he was experiencing. He enjoys life more these days and worries less about his health. He and his wife are a lot happier than they used to be.

Clinton's style of managing his anxieties is a common one these days. In fact, it's a style that both men and women seem to be adopting in increasing numbers each year. The immediate physiological changes that accompany aerobic conditioning take a lot of anxiety-related pressures off the body and "clear" the mind as well. People who adopt this style are usually glad that they have discovered it. They feel better about themselves in general, and they seem to have more energy available for daily living.

Usually people like Clinton believe that worry and apprehension are inevitable at work. They have trouble connecting their anxieties to specific events. They can list any number of things that "have gone wrong" on any given day, but they rarely look upon anxiety as a signal that can provide specific information about a specific problem that needs attention.

### MARYBETH: DENYING AND DREAMING

Marybeth, a graphic illustrator, works under some tight deadlines and with some fairly demanding bosses and clients. She gets anxious as work comes due and when creative ideas won't emerge. She does not let the anxiety "get hold" of her, however. When she feels anxious, she gets "rid of it." She is one of those people who have considerable control over their feelings. Like so many others who are able to turn their feelings off on command, she controls them by monitoring what she says to herself.

When Marybeth starts feeling apprehensive and worried, she tells herself that the issues aren't really all that important, that anxiety does nothing to help the situation, that she is a person who has an amazing ability to control herself, that she's dismissed anxiety before and she can do it again, etc., etc.

If this self-talk strategy doesn't work, she turns to a kind of indirect, channeling technique that involves some daydreaming and creative visualization. Marybeth will attempt to remember, in vivid detail, something very pleasant, like a highlight of her last vacation or the expression on her toddler's face whenever the little girl sees chocolate cake. Sometimes she will take a few minutes to spin a daydream that involves her in a starring role and contains strong feelings of accomplishment, satisfaction, and peace.

Like Clinton, Marybeth believes that anxiety and other kinds of stress are inescapably part of the modern world. She said, "The best we can do is get control over our fears and anxieties. We need to remove these unnecessary pressures from ourselves. And we can!"

Marybeth's techniques are successful for her. If she is able to devote at least ten minutes directly to the task of anxiety management, it is rare that she cannot completely eliminate a fairly strong anxious feeling within twenty to thirty minutes of its appearance. She is reasonably good at connecting her apprehensions to specific events. However, she generally feels almost completely powerless to effect important changes in her environment that might reduce her anxiety levels. She believes that she has large amounts of control over her own feelings and actions. She *doesn't* believe that she has much control over her environment. She exercises the controls that she believes she has: She manages her thoughts, and they manage her anxious feelings when she desires that.

Quite a few people, men and women alike, use Marybeth's strategy for dealing with anxiety in the workplace. Each of them has a somewhat different way of accomplishing the task, but the goal is basically the same for all people in this style category: to eliminate the anxious feelings by getting intellectual control over them. These people don't just "will" anxiety away, however. Over the course of time they have carefully developed cognitive strategies that they kick into gear when anxious feelings come along.

### LUCIA: WHEN THE GOING GETS TOUGH, THE TOUGH GET GOING

Lucia is an account manager for a firm that designs office interiors. Her job requires her to pull together people, supplies, and designs. Most weeks are not anxiety-free as she worries that the furniture she encouraged the clients to buy for the reception area will actually be too large for that space. Or that the carpeting will come in the wrong shade of mauve. Or that the whole thing is going way over budget and she, rather than the client's buyer, who is authorizing the purchase orders, will receive the blame.

When Lucia feels pressured and anxious, she just works harder and longer. She does not necessarily attack the problems that are causing her the concern. Usually she just begins attacking the nearest pile of paper work on her desk. Or she begins to make telephone calls with fierce determination. Or she turns attention to a new room design she has been charged with producing for a client. Often Lucia loses track of time when she gets into these anxiety-motivated projects. When she eventually pulls away from her work, she is likely to feel an impressive amount of satisfaction. She has accomplished something that wasn't on the day's agenda, and she feels pretty good. In fact, her anxiety is usually greatly diminished or has disappeared altogether. She characterizes her way of dealing with the anxieties in her job with the well-worn sentence "When the going gets tough, the tough get going."

Lucia believes in channeling her work anxiety in productive ways. Like others who rely on this method of coping with anxiety, she substitutes a feeling of accomplishment for a nagging feeling of apprehension. And like most other people in this style category, her primary goal is to cope with the feeling of anxiety rather than to address issues that have precipitated those uncomfortable feelings. Later, she may or may not try to address the anxiety-provoking problem. Each case seems unique to her. "Some things I can change. Some I can't," she said. "What I *can* do something about is my own reaction to things. My own anxiety."

### HARRY: MOANING AND DITHERING

Harry runs a sports arena in a large southwestern city. "Needless to say," he said, "I worry a lot. I mean a *lot.*" The concessionaires drive him "crazy." The team owners "are out to bankrupt" him. There are "smooth-talking agents" who "try to pull a last-minute cancellation." The maintenance crews "don't even know where the mops are kept, much less how to use them."

Like others in this style category, Harry believes that work doesn't come without constant anxiety. Anxiety controls almost everyone and everything, he thinks. The most a person can do is try to keep up, "try to stay on top of things."

So Harry runs around—literally—checking up on the help, putting out "fires," delivering commands, and complaining about everything.

Harry doesn't even *try* to cope with his own anxious feelings. And he doesn't really attempt to anticipate or solve his problems. He just tries to get through the day. He would never describe himself as a person who channels his anxiety.

Nonetheless, he does. He channels anxiety into dithering, moaning, and groaning. He creates a constant verbal dialogue to deal with his apprehensions and worries. And he'll talk to himself if no one else is around. Harry channels his anxiety into a comic opera of sorts where he is the bedeviled hero who struggles to survive in a world of "crazy people and crazy ideas," as he phrases it.

He creates a constant, aggressive monologue with the world in an effort to get through the day without being completely overcome by his own anxieties.

"I've gotta get those floor lights *on,*" he says. "Don't people know how to find a blankety-blank light switch anymore? Even *I* can find a light switch and I can't even hardly *see;* I've been spending so much time trying to figure out the fine print this crowd of lawyers brings over here for me to try to read while they give me ten minutes to figure out whether I should sign it or not—and where *is* that blankety-blank [maintenance person] anyway? The fans can't cheer if they can't see. So what am I supposed to do? Ask 'em all to light a match so we can watch the game?"

While most people in this style category do not use these strategies as constantly as does Harry, they do tend to rely on them during anxious moments and days. They may spend a day or two dithering and moaning about everything, then return to a more calm and quiet demeanor for days or weeks after that until anxiety "strikes" again.

*Styles of Dealing with Work Anxiety Directly*

JOYCE: MAKING IT USEFUL

Joyce values her anxious feelings. As a head stewardess assigned to international flights for a major airline, she has her fair share of apprehensive moments. And she uses them to get her job done well. When Joyce gets an uncomfortable, anxious feeling while in flight, in preparation for takeoff, or in company meetings or workshops, she quickly asks herself where the feeling's coming from. "I wonder what I've been unconsciously noticing or figuring out while my attention has been focused on some other task I'm doing," she said. "I want to know what I'm worrying about. I trust my anxious feelings—whether I'm on the ground or in the air."

Joyce remembered a couple of examples from a flight she had been on recently. About two hours into the flight, after feeling mildly anxious for about a half hour for no particular reason she could put her finger on, she took a moment to glance casually around the cabin and then quickly realized that she had had a "funny" feeling about the passenger in 17C ever since he had boarded the plane. Looking at him now, with a cocktail in his hand, she realized that when she first saw him, the idea that he might already be drunk had flashed through her mind. Looking at him now again and realizing what she had been anxious about, she began to look for evidence that might confirm her hunch. After studying his behavior off and on for another twenty minutes or so and carefully attending to one or two slightly annoyed passengers around him, she realized she had been correct and moved into "automatic" as she began taking the steps that she has been trained to take in such situations.

The second noticeably anxious moment Joyce told us about occurred after this particular flight had arrived in New York and she entered the airline's administrative offices to file some paper work, check on the next week's flight schedule, and call a friend. As she came through the office door, the relatively new general administrative secretary responded to her exactly as she had on each of the other three occasions when they had met and spent a few minutes working on some routine paper work. The secretary was strangely "distant." Joyce became a little anxious. Something wasn't quite "right."

Several months earlier Joyce had requested special reassignment for the following month to a flight to Stockholm, not normally one of her destination cities. As the administrative secretary told her that final approval had not been received for that temporary change of assignment, Joyce felt her anxiety grow stronger. She really had no idea what cues she was using, but she knew that something about the way the assistant was reacting to her bothered her. She took the time, before she left the airport, to ask some questions of usually well-informed company colleagues and friends.

Her efforts were not wasted. Apparently a large misunderstanding had occurred involving Joyce and several people in the New York office. It was a matter that was easily handled, but it was an important one. She told us that if she had not acted on her anxieties that day, she probably would have been reassigned within the week to domestic duty. Things would have been straightened out eventually, but the communication processes and paper work would have taken so long to correct that she would have missed that flight to Stockholm, which was, in fact, her vacation flight.

Like other people with this style, Joyce hastens to remove her anxiety—but not until after she has used it. She wants her apprehension to diminish as a result of having dealt with the troubling situation that precipitated it. She doesn't want the anxiety simply to "go away," leaving her with some unsolved problem she's only half aware exists.

There are many men and women like Joyce in today's work force. Most share Joyce's positive attitudes toward anxiety. And most have unique ways of figuring out what the anxiety is all about and where it came from. Some move into moments of quiet reflection. Some talk it out with nearby colleagues. Others scan their recent memories for cues. Most people who adopt this style act rather quickly on the information they discover. They want to relieve themselves of the anxious feelings, and they know that can't happen until they have influenced and dealt with the issues that caused them.

### SAUL: SAVING THE ACTION TILL LATER

Saul is a professor in the economics department of a university. Like Joyce, he values his anxious feelings and uses them to improve the quality of his work. Unlike Joyce, however, he rarely deals with an anxious feeling when he first notices its presence. Saul lets his anxieties build up.

He hopes that some problems will take care of themselves. In fact, it's been his experience that a good many problems *will* straighten themselves out if he just gives the situations enough time to do so. So, when he feels apprehensive, he rather quickly makes the connection between his feeling and a problematic issue in his work life. Then he waits a bit to see what happens. His anxiety will come and go as he moves during his working day in and out of the situation that triggers it.

Eventually, if things don't straighten out by themselves, Saul will take action to achieve his goals. His personal anxiety strategy is one that causes him to take several initiatives every three to six weeks or so. During such a time period he's likely to become somewhat anxious over several work-related issues. He tends "to clean house" after he has lived with his anxious feelings for a few weeks and has identified those situations that will not take care of themselves and thus will need more direct action on his part. During his housecleaning phase he is likely to spend a few days devoting a considerable amount of time to allaying his anxieties by acting on the several issues that seem to demand his influence.

Like Saul, people who adopt this style have learned to live with their worries and apprehensions. They're aware of them, recognize what they're connected to, and watch them come and go as they move in and out of key situations. Unlike people who adopt Joyce's direct way of responding to anxiety, they seem to have a greater tolerance for absorbing it. They do not feel compelled to remove the anxious feelings as quickly as possible. People like Saul prefer not to be directly influential in situations if they don't absolutely have to be. Therefore, they usually wait to see what happens, knowing that they will have to pay the price of enduring their own anxiety for a longer period of time. When it seems necessary, they act.

There are many people like Saul in today's world of work. As is the case across all style categories discussed in this chapter, men and women seem to adopt this style in equal numbers.

### Just "Reacting" When the Anxiety Comes

A sizable number of people do not have a recognizable style of dealing with their worries and apprehensions at work. They don't channel them into other outlets all that often, and they don't deal with them directly with any regularity either. We have discovered that each of the people in this category reacts so differently that there is no single pattern of responding that can be described.

This category is best understood in terms of the factors that motivate people to deal with anxiety this way. There is a set of attitudes that accompanies this approach. These attitudes constitute the strongest motivating factors.

People who "react" to their own anxiety, adopting a different method of dealing with it each time, tend to think that their anxiety is controlled by circumstances. They say things like *"Nobody* could avoid getting anxious in a situation like this."

A second attitude, related to the first, is that to some extent the people or situations that have "caused" the anxiety bear major responsibility for its resolution. For example, one woman we spoke with who "reacts" to her own anxiety said, "The higher-ups around here are just going to have to live with the idea that they're going to get about a third less work out of me until they change the policy. I'm anxiety-ridden most of the time, and it's not going to get any better until they do something about this. It can't. Nobody can be relaxed under conditions like this."

A third attitude adopted by most people in this category is more difficult to capture but nonetheless equally important. This attitude holds that anxiety is clearly out of place at work. If anxiety is present, it's a good indication that the work environment is a poor one. Apprehension emerges when things aren't as they "should" be. If the "right" things were happening, people wouldn't be getting anxious at work.

This third attitude is based on the belief that a "quality life" does not contain anxiety. Anxiety is perceived as always debilitating and never useful. In fact, most of the people in this category tend to equate negative stress with anxiety. These two experiences are synonymous for them. While most people think of stress as a syndrome that involves being overextended and pressured while needed resources are unavailable (not enough money, time, energy, help, and so forth), people who "react" to anxiety seem to think that stress *is* anxiety.

In addition to these attitudes, one of the few shared characteristics of people who deal with their anxiety in this reactive way is a history of having not thought much about it. They may experience anxiety quite often and may dislike it intensely, but they really haven't given it much deliberate attention. When we asked such people to tell us about work anxiety and its functions, they most often reported not having given the subject much thought before. After considering the question for a few minutes, they were likely to say that their position on anxiety is a simple one. Anxiety is an uncomfortable thing, and people should have less of it in their work lives. People who have a tendency to respond to their own anxiety in this reactive way are often motivated to change dramatically once they have thought through what anxiety really is and how it might be useful for them.

If, after reading through the previous styles, you were unable to discover a style that you seem to use most often, and if you think of yourself as a person who has given the subject of anxiety very little attention over the course of your work history, it may be that you respond to your anxiety in this reactive way. If so, you will probably not be able to discover a pattern in your anxious responses. On one anxious occasion you may have become angry; on another you may have gone for a long walk or run; during a third event you may have denied that you were anxious and tried to suppress the feeling. Often in the past you may have ignored the anxiety, hoping that it would just go away, or that the situation might suddenly change, or that later on a brilliant solution to the problem might occur to you.

### Anxiety: Loosening Its Hold

As we talked with people, it became apparent that each of the styles we have just described—including the reactive approach—feels right for many of the people who use it. Clearly the level of comfort you experience with your own approach to anxiety depends in part upon the kind of person you are, your work-related goals, the setting you work in, and your attitudes toward the usefulness of anxiety.

Most of the people we talked with tended to combine two or more of the approaches identified above. They often responded using one method for dealing with certain problems, while relying on other methods for other kinds of difficulties. Generally people who identified several style tendencies that were dependent on a situation or role could single out one of these as being the most problematic and least satisfying or effective for them. This may be the case for you, too, and the way you use the change strategies in Chapter Ten may need to reflect this.

# 8

# The Upside of Emotions at Work

## Expressing Appreciation, Joy, Respect, and Caring

It is a sign of mediocrity to praise moderately.

—MARQUIS DE VAUVENARGUES

THOUSANDS OF PEOPLE across this country love their work. They're excited by their jobs and challenged by their responsibilities. They believe that work is an important part of their lives. They're not compulsive about work, nor are they workaholics. But time clocks do not close out their fascination with a problem on the verge of solution, the excitement of a project almost completed, a sale almost wrapped up.

Not that their jobs are perfect. Almost everyone who works in a hospital can tell you, for example, that no matter how good the specific facility, there are days when all the patients seem impatient and cranky, when complaints about everything bounce around the hallways. Many very successful salespeople can tell of days when the customer who stalled for months suddenly placed the order and demanded delivery to the regional office three thousand miles away in twenty-four hours— or forget it. There are days in a restaurant when the chef comes in late, the shrimp comes in rotten, and the two best servers don't come in at all.

But all things considered, their jobs are very good. And a great deal of what makes them so good is bound up in the way they feel about their jobs—the emotions they experience, the ways they express their feelings, and the emotional responses of others at work.

The good jobs, the good work settings, cultivate the upbeat, "positive" feelings. People like to be in these settings because they feel valued and rewarded; as a result, they are usually very committed. But people in the great work situations make positive use of the "negative" emotions, the ones that many people want to get away from, or ignore, or pummel into oblivion. In these job settings people use "negative" emotions—like anger, frustration, anxiety, or fear—to create positive and productive change.

We talked during our interviews with many people who had great jobs, people who were positive and enthusiastic about their work. The qualities that distinguished the cultures of their workplaces included a willingness to deal positively with problems as they emerge and an attitude of deep respect for colleagues and other employees in the firm. In no way were these job settings free of problems. Indeed, one production manager we spoke with laughed outright at the suggestion that he might consider his job great simply because the firm was so well financed and the work seemed to run so smoothly. "Having a lot of resources is a plus. There's no doubt about that," he said. "But I've been here when things were so tight that people worried about throwing away a paper clip. But even then the job was good. What made it good was that the people at the top listened to the rest of us. What we said mattered. When they made decisions, we knew about them, and we knew why. We had a feeling that we counted. They let us know that what we did was important. It sounds like simple stuff, but it made a big difference."

Simple things *can* make a big difference. The more we talked with people, the more impressed we became with the "simple stuff" that makes such a positive difference in employee attitudes toward work and personal commitment to the job. The keys to employee commitment and morale are to be found most often in the corporate culture, in prevailing attitudes and behaviors that convey four simple messages: What you are doing is valued; your thoughts on decisions related to your areas of work are valued; your input is respected; your efforts are important to the firm's success.

When these messages get through clearly and consistently, most people are a long way down the road toward the realization that their jobs are great. Issues of "fit" are obviously involved here—the great jobs usually make very good use of individuals' skills and expertise—but overall the critical factors seem to reside in attitudes and behaviors that convey respect for an employee and a valuing of his or her work.

That these attitudes and behaviors can reside alongside work pressures, intermittent work crises, and frequent heavy work loads is evident in many of the stories we heard from people with "great jobs." The ing good cheer about this ritual with ruthless straightforwardness about her evaluations of quality. In the midst of cheerful mouthfuls, offering up jokes about eating for a living, she's been known to hurl a piece of cherry pie or creamed cauliflower into a wastebasket, exclaiming loudly over the incredible gall it must take to put something like *that* into serious competition for a customer's consideration. She'll usually return from the trashing frenzy with a gallows-humor smile, asking calmly if there's anything better on tap or if they're through for this session.

New entrants to the firm sometimes wonder if Helen has always been like this. Older hands think she's gotten a little more outrageous over the last few years. But she's also more on top of it. And she's even more valuable to the company, as her bosses acknowledge by raises, kudos, quiet appreciation, and a lot of latitude to do her own thing, which she does so well.

Part of what she does so well is bound up in her insistence on quality in all aspects of the operation. Clients come quickly to recognize that they'll get the very best for their money when they work with Helen. If a client ever has a problem with food quality once the operation is under way, a call to Helen cures the difficulty. If not today, tomorrow. She takes her calls immediately. If she's in conference or at a client's operations, she returns the call within four hours. And she has the problem solved within the next twelve. If it takes longer, the client knows she's working on it because Helen is on the phone telling him or her that she's on it. She's been known to hold two phone lines at once, issuing calm assurances over one that the error will never be repeated and furiously lambasting a sales rep on the other for an offending shipment of fish that arrived partially thawed, mealy, and totally useless. She delivers final apologies and reassurances to the client with a smile on her face and a firmly confident voice. She hangs up that line calmly and in an instant is the very picture of wrath as she yells into the other line that an error like this will never (repeat, never!) happen again if the sales rep has any slim hope of ever getting another order from her.

Helen can be as rough on her colleagues—and subordinates and superiors on rare occasions—as she is on sales reps. She has clear and high standards for the company and the way things ought to be done. When those standards are contravened, her anger is quick to rise. And she's not shy about expressing it.

Not long ago one of her colleagues, Daryll—another division director in the firm—became angry with Helen's secretary on a day that had combination is also evident because many people who believe that ⸱ jobs are great are no strangers to negative emotions at work. Many ⸱ experienced anger, tears, frustration, and fears on the job. *But they also experienced problem solving and productive change when ⸱ negative emotions arrived on the scene.* To a person, they recou examples of times when things looked bad ("a time when I just ⸱ it," as one vice-president put it succinctly), but subsequent effor⸱ solve the offending problem succeeded in creating change and ir firming a fundamental respect for and valuing of the person.

## When Positive and Negative Emotions Mix
## to Produce Commitment and Success

Helen is the director of purchasing for a large corporation invo in in-service feeding for hospital, school, and corporate clients. Her ⸱ is growing, and Helen, who has been with the company for fifteen y⸱ is an important part of its success.

Helen entered her firm several years ago with an M.B.A. degree experience in the personnel and purchasing departments of a l⸱ regional restaurant chain. She shifted to corporate in-service after had finished her degree because she was looking for something ⸱ And she didn't think in all frankness that her former employer w⸱ make use of the degree or pay her well over the long run.

Helen is efficient, passionate, and determined about her work. employer affirms vigorously she is invaluable to the company. commitment to and enthusiasm for her job are evident in the way does the many things that are part of her work.

Helen is a strong person. In the midst of client conference⸱ negotiations on bids or contracts, she's the picture of no-nonsense, t commitment to the task at hand. She'll press on for hours, seel details about a client's feeding needs. Personnel, logistics, costs, spots in the budget or specifications, long-term goals, union contr⸱ transport modes and alternatives, characteristics of her client's clie short-term needs—all come under her probing eye. Prospective cli are impressed and persuaded by her diligence—her zeal and focus— they usually sign on.

Back in the office Helen is both a bear and a cheerleader. She m sales reps from a panoply of purveyors with enthusiasm and a ⸱ bottom line. She wants the best they can offer for the money her cli are paying. She eats her way through product-tasting sessions, com been particularly bad for him: his child in bed with a high fever, his wife in trouble with her boss for taking a sick-leave day to stay with the child, a three-car pileup and a thirty-minute delay on the bridge, an overbooked schedule for the day, and no delivery on a package of materials from Helen's office that had been promised for a ten o'clock meeting. The failure of delivery on the package of materials was the straw that broke Daryll's back, and he came roaring into Helen's suite, hot with anger. Helen, as he knew actually, was out at a client's. His anger poured forth on Helen's secretary, Lynn. It came in such a torrent that Lynn wound up in tears before he was through. She listened—and tried to respond—to his rapid-fire accusations of inefficiency, ineptitude, disorganization, and general incompetence. Then she told him, through quiet tears, that she *had* prepared the materials the previous day and had left them on her desk, intending to deliver them to him first thing in the morning. The materials had vanished from her desk when she arrived early that morning, and she assumed that he had picked them up. Somewhat mollified but still angry because he didn't have the materials, Daryll huffed off with a crack about hopeless disorganization and an order to have Helen call him the minute she came in.

Lynn was still red-eyed when Helen returned shortly thereafter. Helen asked her if something was wrong, if there was something she could do to help. Lynn told her what had happened, apologizing for the tears and for having "messed up" the delivery of the materials. It was Helen's turn for fury, but hers was directed at Daryll. Helen had picked up those materials herself from Lynn's desk late the previous day and taken them by Daryll's office so he could go over them that night, before the morning's meeting. He wasn't in when she went by, so she left the package on his desk chair. Apparently, she surmised, he hadn't come back in last evening, and apparently he hadn't gotten to his chair when he decided that Helen and her staff were guilty of gross incompetence. Helen assured Lynn, genuinely, that her work and organizational skills were excellent, as they always had been. She apologized for taking the materials without leaving her a note. And she told her vehemently that Daryll's behavior had been way out of line. With that said, Helen took off for her colleague's office.

He was leafing through the materials—having found them after returning from his angry outburst—when Helen stormed in. What happened next was the subject of office gossip later in the day. Suffice it to say that Helen yelled and stormed. She told her associate in no uncertain terms that he was way out of line, rude, and inconsiderate;

she added a few other choice descriptors for having treated her secretary as he had. "C'mon, Daryll," she stormed in conclusion, "if you need to pick a fight over a misunderstanding, at least pick it with *me,* so we can fight *fairly. Don't* jump all over my secretary!"

After somewhat more discussion Helen and Daryll worked their way through to a conclusion that was pretty acceptable to both of them. Daryll acknowledged that his behavior with the secretary had been poor and called Lynn to apologize. Helen wound up sympathizing over the cascade of irritants that had filled Daryll's morning and observed that she, too, would've been angry if promised materials had been missing.

Helen's behavior that morning was not at all unusual. Throughout most of her working life she's had a very direct approach to experiencing and expressing anger, which comes for her almost automatically when her personal or professional standards are violated. Newer for her, however, were her responses to her secretary, Lynn. For Helen had to learn on the job several of her specific behaviors toward Lynn that followed her colleague's tirade. She's now well known for the good rapport she maintains with all office staff, particularly those with whom she works closely. But it has not always been so.

Helen has an "expansive personality," as one of her colleagues puts it. It's always been easy for the people with whom she works to know where she stands on something. She's enthusiastic, outgoing, energetic, at home with letting people know what she's feeling and why. Helen pretty much grew up "just knowing that people know" how she feels—when she's upset about something, when she's positively impressed by something, and so on.

It was a startling awakening, then, one morning several years ago to walk into her office and find her secretary-receptionist, who was assigned to Helen and two other staff members, in tears. Helen looked at her in amazement, then shrugged her shoulders in awkwardness as much as anything, and mumbled, "Um, if I can do anything . . . let me know." She paused for an instant, heard nothing in response, and walked swiftly to her office. In the midst of wondering what, if anything, to do about the woman, Helen looked up to see the tearful secretary, Abby, walking into her office. She asked Helen if she had a minute. Helen nodded, thinking that she *didn't* have time to solve anyone else's problems that morning, but . . . She nodded again, and Abby sat down and began to specify what was wrong.

To Helen's amazement and chagrin it became evident quickly that what was wrong was located squarely on Helen's doorstep. Helen listened as her secretary told her that she was trying as hard as she could to do things right. Helen protested in genuine amazement, "Abby, I think your work is very good! Why in the world do you think I'm not satisfied with it?"

Abby responded simply, "Because you've never told me so."

"I have!" protested Helen. "You *know* I'm pleased with your work; I would've told you if I wasn't."

Abby persisted, shaking her head. "I *don't* know, though. You've never told me that my work is good. Sometimes you tell me to do something over. And then I think, *Maybe there are a lot of things I should do differently, and she's only telling me about the worst ones.* I'm really afraid you don't like it but won't tell me because you think I can't do any better. Or something like that," she finished weakly.

Helen and Abby had a long conversation. Helen learned many things that morning that she's never forgotten, things that have been particularly important in her relationships with colleagues and people who work for her. She concluded quickly after the discussion that she had neglected pretty completely to appreciate "out loud" the work that people did for her. Her outlook and attitude were basically positive, and she had assumed that people simply "knew" she was pleased with their work unless she told them differently. What she didn't realize was that many people, particularly people "below" her in the hierarchy, in reality had no way of knowing that she valued their work, that what they were producing was acceptable, good, or even wonderful unless she *told* them explicitly, especially early in a working relationship or early in a new set of tasks.

Helen learned well the "lessons" of that conversation. Her overtly expressed appreciation and valuing of the people with whom she works, the people whose effort makes *her* work possible, has been well known now for many years.

### WHAT MAKES IT WORK?

Overall Helen's emotions on the job have very positive consequences. They're a part of her style, a part of who she is, a part of how she gets things done and done so well. Helen uses her experience and expression of negative emotions (e.g., anger, frustration) and tears to create positive and useful change—in company policy, in personal interactions, in her own behaviors, in client satisfaction. Most important for our consideration at the moment, *she experiences and expresses positive feelings about those with whom she works.* She gives warranted praise freely. She communicates with her colleagues, superiors, and subordinates honestly and often. She listens with respect to their suggestions and has been known on several occasions to identify the "great idea Kerry [or whoever] gave me" as instrumental in bringing about successful change in her division's operations.

Helen does many specific, positive things to communicate her appreciation and respect for her co-workers. She does these things in her own inimitable style. But it's not her style or personal presence that is fundamental to making things go very well in her office. Others in her firm and in many other workplaces we've seen are also integrally involved in making things go very well, and they're very different people from Helen. Some are quiet; some are reserved; some are consistently amiable; some are quite serious.

What they and Helen share is a commitment to treating their co-workers as "real" people regardless of rank. What makes working with Helen and others like her so positive is not that they are always up, but that they appreciate those with whom they work and take the time to tell them so. The telling them so may mean giving praise and accolades; it may mean taking the time to listen; it may mean respecting individual circumstances and needs that on occasion contravene "normal" procedures. Whatever the specifics, Helen and those like her appreciate and care about those with whom they work. And they let them know it.

There are many different attitudes in today's workplaces about communicating concern, communicating a sense of caring, and giving positive feedback to those with whom one works. And there are many different styles of expressing joyful, caring, appreciative feelings.

## Styles of Expressing Concern, Care, and Positive Regard

Many qualities distinguish different approaches to expressing positive emotions toward others in the workplace. The most important of these qualities involves *attitudes* toward positive emotions at work. In most circumstances, characteristic *behaviors* follow from those attitudes. The styles described below represent those found most frequently in many workplaces today.

### Michael: "I Run a Business, Not a Charity!"

Michael is in his mid-forties, the executive director of a major art gallery with branches in several large cities. He's been in the business for about fifteen years. He came to it when he decided that his artistic ability was not strong enough to sustain the years of uncertainty and financial precariousness that often attend "serious" artists' efforts to become successful and self-supporting. His considerable technical knowledge and business acumen propelled him into one of the most prestigious firms, and he rose quickly through the ranks to his present position.

Michael is efficient, often described as "very sharp," and very much on top of his field. Michael can also be very difficult to get along with if you work for him. The issues in working with Michael go beyond those that people sometimes have with Helen's emotionally charged style; they also go beyond those associated with people who regularly have periodic trouble with anger or anxiety. Many people have worked for Michael and, by his own account, have left because they couldn't "take" him. People who currently work for Michael assert that the difficulty doesn't lie in his abilities related to art, art collection, or gallery management. Most are quick, in fact, to call him "brilliant," extremely capable, a real luminary in the field. They're also quick to acknowledge that the problems in working with Michael can be significant. *If* you can overlook them, working for him can be a stimulating and exciting process, they say. If you can't overlook them, you begin looking elsewhere fairly quickly.

Michael believes that the people who stay with him are the ones worth keeping. "The others," he says flatly, "I'm better off without." Michael knows that he loses people, sometimes good ones, because of this attitude. But he believes essentially that he's running a business and that a business is no place for the show of "weak, self-indulgent" emotion. "If people want to feel good," he expounds, "let them go home to get their hugs! Go to a movie or a touchy-feely shrink for all I care. But don't come in *here* to get your ups for the day. I run a business, not a charity!"

Michael believes that people, subordinates especially, will try to get away with things if you let them. If you want to run a real business, he believes, you have to keep a tight rein on things and on the people. He assumes that when he decides to hire people, they should know he thinks they're competent. "I wouldn't hire them if I thought otherwise!" he exploded. Once he's hired them, he expects that they'll concentrate on the job. If he has a problem with performance, he tells them about it quickly and in no uncertain terms. Until he does so, he believes they should assume that their work is meeting his demanding standards. He's concerned about appearing soft. "I'd be nowhere if my people thought they could get away with anything," he stated.

Asked for an example of a time when someone had "tried to get away with things," Michael said immediately and somewhat derisively, "I can give you a great example!" An assistant who had left his firm just a few months earlier had been hired away "by one of my toughest competitors," he said matter-of-factly. "I thought she was going to be really good. But in no time she was acting like a prima donna." The assistant, whom he'd hired two years earlier as "a real prize," was an extremely quick study; she had learned faster than anyone else he'd had in a comparable position. "Then," he said, "she asked for a vacation day, the week before a major opening. I thought she must be crazy. I told her no. She told me it was for her best friend's wedding. I thought, *She's really good, we can get everything done before that day, ahhh, what the heck!* I told her OK. Then she came to me a few days later and told me that she needed to leave two hours early the day *before* the vacation day, a change in schedule for the last afternoon plane or something like that. I thought, *What's going on?* and I told her no, there was no way. She looked shocked. I told her I didn't hire her to have her running off when I need her. She got quiet, and said all right. She took the day I'd agreed to, but she *didn't* leave early the previous day. Six weeks later she gave notice. She told me where she was going. Then she lit into me! Told me I ran the business like Scrooge. 'You spend money, but you sure don't spend anything else,' " he mimicked. "Complained that I never appreciate anything anyone does." He paused. "I don't have time for that. I hire people to do a job. I expect them to do it. If they can't, I'm better off without them."

Michael's attitudes underlie behaviors that are consistent and brusque. He focuses on—and only on—the business. By intention he shows minimal interest in anything having to do with an employee's personal life. He tends to be unilateral in his approach to problem solving; he tells people to "work it out" if they report a problem, or he works out the problem himself. He can be rude, and he knows it. He doesn't *try* to be rude, as he points out (and his co-workers who've been with him for a long time agree). It's just a consequence, he claims, of the fact that he's "all business" at work. Like the moderate number of men and women in today's workplaces who hold his style, Michael likes things that way because he believes success is linked to *his* "way of doing things." For Michael, and those who share his style, work satisfaction lies in the bottom line, in profits and individual skills, not in teamwork or any "good feelings" associated with "people issues." Michael doesn't thank employees, tell them he needs them, or deal with their troubles. He pays them to do what they've been hired to do, and he believes that's enough.

### Troy: Dr. Jekyll and Mr. Hyde

Troy, business manager for a major recording studio, is viewed by many as a comer in the business. He's had his eye on success for a long time, and he's made it to his current level within a relatively short time. Like many others who rise to prominence in their professions quickly, Troy's skills and abilities are evident to almost everyone who works with him. But depending on their position in the hierarchy of his firm, people hold very different perceptions of Troy's "way of getting things done."

It has been very important to Troy that those in a position to promote his skills and promote him see his talent in the best possible light. When he is with his superiors and when he is with colleagues he calculates may also be comers, he mixes his display of technical competence liberally with positive expressions of his regard for others' abilities, motivations, and interests. He is positive sometimes to the point of ingratiation but usually modulates his expressions "appropriately," as one of his bosses put it.

With his subordinates, however, Troy demonstrates very different behaviors. Many of his subordinates notice and resent his differential treatment. With them, and with others he decides have little to contribute to his success, he is indifferent and inattentive. He usually treats secretarial and clerical personnel on his staff with preoccupation ("at best!," as one receptionist said). Troy speaks to his subordinates when the need arises but often appears uninterested and can be quite rude if someone makes what he feels is an inappropriate or ill-timed request. Many notice and resent the variability in his treatment of people. Some of his subordinates say that there's little holding them to their jobs; if they could find another with the same benefits, they'd move in a minute.

Troy is aware of the ill will he generates at some levels. "I know some people have a hard time dealing with me," he said. "But I figure if they don't want to deal with me, they'll just have to move on. Frankly I don't have time to deal with it." Troy told of a secretary who'd been working on a major report for a week or so a couple of months ago. He had made many revisions in the report along the way and left them for her each morning along with new material. Toward the end of the week things backed up, and errors began slipping into the final version. He told her to get them corrected. When she told him she would and apologized for the mistakes, he commented that she must not be concentrating. She said back to him quickly, "I've been staying through lunch hours and staying late to get it done, and done right. I'm doing the best I can."

He immediately snapped, "You're *not* doing the best you can; the best you can do is *right!*" She started crying, and he left, irritated and disgusted. "It's her *job!*" he said emphatically. "Why should I have to hold her hand and tell her it's fine when it's not?"

Troy, like Michael, loses employees from time to time, when they decide they "just don't want to deal with the hassle anymore," as one employee, a week from leaving for another job, said. Troy's attitude sometimes precipitates concern among those above him in the company hierarchy—those who notice the differential treatment and find it contrary to their values. To some his skills make him worth keeping, although many of them believe life would be easier if Troy dispensed even a few more signs of appreciation for the work of those under his supervision. But appreciating his subordinates is clearly not something Troy values personally or professionally at this point in his career. He just doesn't see that it will get him ahead in the business, and so he does not spend time on it.

A moderate number of people in today's work force, men and women, hold Troy's attitudes and share his behavior. Often they are in the "upwardly mobile" phases of their careers, intent on impressing those above them. Some people with this style seem to grow more aware of its impact on others as they mature in their careers and may begin to initiate changes oriented toward developing a more "even" pattern of positive interactions with co-workers.

### Kim: "It Never Occurred to Me!"

Kim entered her present position as program developer for a state department of education after a very successful career as a high school science teacher. Her work as head of the science department in a large, comprehensive high school and her growing reputation for creative curriculum development brought her to the attention of the state secretary of education. Within a year Kim was working in a position created essentially for her. She loves the work and is excellent at it. She is frequently called on for consultation with education departments in other states and often presents papers at professional conferences. She has a reputation as a highly skilled professional in her field.

Kim's outlook on her co-workers and associates is positive. She values the people with whom she works and has long been aware that the "people factor" is a very important part of her attraction to the several jobs that she's held in the education profession. She "loved" her students when she was in the classroom and was popular with them and with their parents. Valuing other people, appreciating their companionship and abilities have been so central to her for so long that she—in some ways like Helen—simply assumes everyone with whom she works "knows it."

Kim's assumptions and attitudes have led her to a style of generally consistent positive emotional expression. "People know I value their work. We get along really well. They know, I'm sure, how much I like them. If anything ever *did* go wrong, I'd tell them; they know that." But something happened a few weeks before we talked to her a second time that called some of her assumptions into question. The questions raised by the event pointed to shortcomings in Kim's belief that everyone with whom she works "just knows" that she values them.

One of her assistants stopped her late one afternoon as Kim was rushing through the outer office on her way to a meeting. The assistant told her she "just had to know something." Kim suppressed a twinge of annoyance at the timing and stopped to say, "Sure. What is it?"

With a trembling voice the assistant replied, "Did you like the report I gave you last week? Was it OK?"

Kim was mystified. "Of course!" she exclaimed. "Rebecca, why do you think I wouldn't like it? Did someone say something to you to upset you?"

"No," responded Rebecca. "You just haven't said anything about it."

Kim was stunned. "I did. I must have," she replied slowly. "It was very good."

"No," Rebecca replied softly. "You haven't said anything to me about it."

Kim apologized and assured Rebecca that she really had been impressed with the report.

As she recounted the story, Kim was again thoughtful. "I just assumed she knew I liked it. I didn't return it to her. In fact, I used it just a couple of days later." She continued. "But she was right. I hadn't mentioned it to her. It just didn't occur to me that I'd need to point out to her that it was fine. I assumed she'd know."

Kim's assumption—that her co-workers will know that she values their work because she is consistently positive and upbeat when she is with them—is an assumption she has begun to question. A few months later she was making overt efforts to incorporate into her style more specific and explicit positive feedback to her co-workers, especially her subordinates.

Kim and others who share her style, men and women alike, believe that positive relationships are an important part of workplace success ("I knew that," she said, "after the first day I set foot in a classroom"). But she assumed that a "positive presence" is the primary requirement. Until her assistant called her attention to it, Kim didn't really think of *specific* positive feedback on others' work and performance as a significant, additional part of workplace appreciation. It simply didn't occur to her.

At present, it's "occurring" to her more often, and she's pleased with some of the changes. Many others with Kim's style, however, haven't yet experienced such a challenge. And for the most part many of them assume—only partially correctly—that their generally positive outlook and presence are creating a positive workplace environment.

Claire: "Everything Is Wonderful!"

Claire, like Kim, is described by most of the people with whom she works as a very positive person. Unlike Kim, however, Claire fairly "bubbles over" with positive emotion and positive responses to her co-workers' skills. Now in her early forties, she left the personnel and benefits department of a major auto manufacturer three years ago to open her own consulting firm to industry. Her specialty: the development of employee benefits packages that include significant attention to family-related benefits. She is particularly interested in the areas of employer-sponsored child care programs and family leave policies (for childbirth, sick child care, etc.). She enjoys her business very much now that the first uncertain years have passed. She was nervous about taking the "big step" but feels pretty secure and well established in the business right now. The demand for her services expanded a year ago to the point that she took in two new associates and expanded her staff of research assistants and clerical people.

Some of the people with whom she works describe Claire as "a ray of sunshine." It's a description that Claire is aware of and likes. She believes that workplace success is directly tied to positive employee morale, and she has worked hard in all her jobs to ensure that the people with whom she associates—subordinates and superiors alike—know her positive regard for them. Her beliefs that "everyone is wonderful" and "everyone needs a pat on the back" have caused her a few uncomfortable moments—as, for example, when a colleague is *not* wonderful or falls far short of expected work performance. But in general she moves ahead, trusting that the person will pick up the

negative feedback somewhere along the way and that things will somehow right themselves.

She is clear in her dislike of anything approaching confrontation.
As one of her colleagues noted, "She'd rather swallow a watermelon
whole than say no to anyone!" Claire was present for the comment and
agreed with it. "I just think it's really important," she said, "for people
to get along with everybody."

From time to time, though, Claire is aware of problems that don't
just automatically get better. And she feels stumped by that. Some of
her co-workers, who generally like her, pointed out to us that one
drawback of her sunny presence and her dislike of conflict is the fact
that some problems don't get solved. In fact, a few of them commented
that they sometimes take Claire's "sunniness" as most *un*helpful.
"When she comes across like Pollyanna," one co-worker said, "it's hard
to believe that she's real. And then I begin to wonder if her positive
evaluations of what I do are related to my work or if they're mostly
related to the fact that she won't say anything negative to anyone. It
feels sometimes as though *every*thing is superficial, that the praise isn't
really worth much."

Her colleagues identified a common problem that many co-workers
have in dealing with the relatively small number of people—more
women than men—who share Claire's style. Her style *is* positive, many
note with appreciation. But its invariably positive nature leads them to
wonder sometimes if there's any substance to it. And when they wonder
about the substance of Claire's style, many began to feel restive and
uncomfortable, as though her responses were automatic, containing no
more *real* positive evaluation than does a more negative style. Claire
is vaguely aware of the problem but doesn't know what to do about it.
The idea of "being negative" doesn't appeal to her at all, and she
envisions almost any change as a move toward negative outcomes and
conflict at work.

### Al: Polite and Perfunctory

Al, the executive director of a large metropolitan area charitable
giving campaign, has been with the organization for several years. He
has widespread grass-roots knowledge of the businesses in his community as well as the programs funded by the community giving campaign.
He keeps close tabs on their operating budgets and services; he's closely
attuned to the "political winds" and to the entry of new, potential donor
businesses in the community. He's efficient, businesslike, and pleasant.

He's at home with businesspeople and civic organizations, with university experts and direct-service providers. Many people agree that Al "knows his stuff." As one corporate president observed, "He's a good man to have at the helm of the campaign. You can trust him."

Part of Al's trustworthy style is his low-key manner of keeping tabs on everything and everybody in his organization. He knows what's going on; he's present for all decision-making sessions. In his interactions with associates and co-workers he's predictably polite and interested. He's concerned about the people with whom he works and with his broader "constituency." He's also concerned about appearances.

Appearances make a difference in his line of work; Al believes they make a difference in *any* line of work. In the interest of expressing concern and developing positive appearances, Al is very polite. Sometimes his polite style strikes co-workers as perfunctory or preoccupied.

At times Al's politeness appears to cause him to gloss over problems or issues of concern to his staff. Sometimes, he told us, he's aware of this, and it's deliberate. Really big problems—ones that might threaten the success of the campaign—he deals with thoroughly and well. But the others, the "little personal problems," as he called them, he'd really rather not touch.

Al wants to be positive around the people with whom he works, and he believes he is. To him being positive simply demands polite and brief responses. For many of his co-workers it's all right. But some are quick to point out that morale is "neutral." Employees' levels of commitment come from their belief in the importance of the work, not from Al's positive regard. For many his politeness seems more cover than real, and they perceive that it covers shallow regard. For the moderate number of people in today's workplaces who share his style—somewhat more men than women—a primary concern is "keeping things going smoothly." However, a primary problem that their style may engender is relatively low commitment and enthusiasm.

### Gerald: "I Just Don't Know How to Handle All That"

Gerald is manager of plant operations for a major regional grocery chain, a position to which he was promoted about two years ago. He can be very demanding and is a stickler for details. Both qualities have worked to the company's advantage as losses caused by spoilage, breakage, and loss have decreased significantly since he took over in this position.

For the most part the people who work with Gerald respect his competence and like working for him. Gerald is respectful in most of his interactions, and his sense of humor often dispels tension when time pressures or the almost inevitable mistakes in so large an operation create irritability and short tempers. "Things get hassled in here a lot," he said, "but that's part of the game at this end of the operation. For the most part things go pretty well. Our losses have gone down. The guys in the front office always like that."

When we asked how he manages the large and varied staff he supervises, Gerald thought for a few moments and then said, "Well, for one thing I know that most of them know what they're doing. In fact, that was one of the first things I worked on when I got over here. I let a few people go pretty quickly and talked with a few others whose performance was marginal. Once people were used to me, things were smoother. But the main thing is I assume that my people know what they're doing. If they come to me with a request to do something differently or if they tell me they need something else to get the job done well, I listen. I figure they're in the best position to know some of the details, and I ought to pay attention. It usually works well."

Gerald's style is characterized by respect for the people with whom he works. He views the personnel management parts of his job as important, but important primarily in the service of getting the job done, of cutting losses, of increasing efficiency. He appreciates his employees and colleagues because he knows they're the backbone of his operation.

The one significant problem he identified with his management style was centered squarely in the area of appreciation and positive feedback to employees. Several of his employees agreed with his assessment independently. Like the moderate number of people who share his style—more men than women—Gerald knows that specific positive feedback and expressions of appreciation are important. But he has a very hard time "getting them out."

One of the people who work for Gerald, Linda, recounted a time when she had spent several late nights getting a reorganization plan prepared for presentation. It involved writing, organizing, and recategorizing some of the many materials Gerald had given her, designing graphics for the presentation, and, of course, the revisions. "I worked hard on it," Linda said. "It was stuff I like to do, so that part was no big deal. But it was a rush job. If I'd known at the beginning how much was going to be involved, I would never have estimated just a week to get it done. But I poured it on and got it done. It was good, too. But I never heard that from Gerald. I heard it from someone else who was at the meeting when he made the presentation. He got several compliments on it. I'm glad it all went well, don't get me wrong. But it would have been nice to know directly from him that it was good, that he appreciated all that extra effort."

When we asked Gerald about this, he knew immediately what we were talking about, both the specific incident and the general problem. "I wanted to tell her more than thanks, but I didn't know how. I wish I *could* pass out more compliments," he said, shaking his head. "It's not that I don't think the work is good. When you've got good people, you get good work. But I just never know what to say. It all sounds so corny. Then I think, *What if they get the wrong idea?* I can't imagine what to say that's not going to feel awkward. So I usually don't say much of anything. Just 'thanks,' and then things go on."

The fact that Gerald is generally very respectful of people works strongly to his advantage. His employees tend to know that he regards them and their work positively, so the absence of specific positive appreciation doesn't grate, as it does for many who work for people with styles like Michael's or Troy's. But some of the people with whom Gerald works, and Gerald himself, would be more satisfied with their jobs if he knew how to "speak out" the appreciation that he feels for their work. Unlike Kim, who doesn't think about expressing her appreciation specifically, Gerald does think about it. But generally he feels embarrassed about complimenting people's work. He gets "all tied up," wondering if it's appropriate ("After all, it's their *job,*" he said. "Maybe it's insulting to tell them, 'Great work!' ") and wondering what he's supposed to do *after* he passes the compliment ("what if the person gets embarrassed, and . . ." and on and on). He thinks that he doesn't know how to compliment "smoothly," and so he doesn't, relying instead on the goodwill that his competence and general respectfulness create.

### Ben: The Caring Comes Through

Ben is vice-president for development at a major insurance company. Over the years he has developed a reputation as a person skilled not only in the substance of his work but also in managing people. He often receives inquiries from employees in other divisions of the firm about opportunities for transfer into his "shop."

Ben assumes that his people *want* to do their jobs well. In this respect he is like Kim and Gerald. But unlike Kim, Ben *thinks* about the need to express his appreciation and positive feedback in direct, specific ways; it "occurs" to him that his co-workers need and appreciate that feedback. And unlike Gerald, who's very uncomfortable expressing his appreciation directly, Ben has developed ways of giving critical feedback and appreciation in ways that feel appropriate for him, his co-workers, and his firm.

He told of a time when he had asked one of his staffers to prepare an important progress report for a meeting of division chiefs. The person he assigned to the task was very good; it was one of the reasons Ben assigned him the task in the first place. Ben was under pressure and wanted a very good first draft quickly, with specific data organized into relatively complex categories. He gave the assignment and asked to have it back three days later. His staffer accepted it, saying that it would be tight because of other things that had piled up but that he'd have it done at the appointed hour. What Ben received at the appointed hour was a well-written report that spoke in global terms about the issues; some of the desired data were included in appendices, but nothing about the draft report fitted the categorical structure that he'd asked for.

"I was furious," he said, "and I called him in immediately. I told him that it wasn't what I asked for and asked him what had gone wrong and what we needed to do to get it done right. I told him it was well written would have been fine for more general distribution, but it wasn't what I'd asked for. He said he knew it wasn't and apologized. Things had gotten backed up for him, and he'd decided to go with the more general report—hoping that would do for a while—rather than ask for more time. I asked him what he needed to get it done right within twenty-four hours. He thought for a bit, told me, and we juggled another project to make the space. I told him I'd asked him to do it because I knew he'd do it well. And I still thought so. But it had to be right the next time." He paused and added, "It was."

Like the staffer who "blew" the assignment and recovered, almost all of Ben's people view him very positively. They articulate well the sense of respect and positive regard that he works to create. "He gives praise when it's due," said one. "When you've done a good job, you know it. You know when you haven't, too, but you also know usually that you can repair the problem and get back on track."

In many ways, Ben's style is like Helen's. It's honest, respectful, direct. He doesn't share Helen's intensity, but he shares her sense of fairness and caring. His characteristic behaviors are unlike Michael's "I run a business" style (where people assume that positive regard isn't really necessary in a business relationship) and unlike Claire's "Everything is wonderful!" style (where people assume that being positive about everything meets all interpersonal needs). Ben and Helen, and the moderate number of men and women who share their style, assume that appreciation and feedback—and praise and correction—need to be explicitly conveyed, and often, *frequently* conveyed. And unlike Troy ("Dr. Jekyll and Mr. Hyde"), who differentiates between co-workers above him and below him in the company hierarchy, Ben and Helen are convinced that position is largely irrelevant when it comes to positive human interactions. People in all aspects of office operations need positive, honest feedback, they assert. The company needs it because the company needs its employees' productivity for the bottom line. People know where Ben stands, and they know that he cares about them. He cares about them in ways that convey a positive sense of their professional competence. His people usually grow in competence and confidence—much to his benefit, theirs, and the company's.

Many things go into creating a "great employee" and a "great job." A basic requirement is an excellent fit between an individual's skills and interests, on the one hand, and the job tasks and responsibilities required on the other. However, excellent employees in great jobs are also characterized by commitment to doing their work well.

In job settings where people feel appreciated and valued, where there is clear communication of positive regard for an individual and his or her work, people tend to believe that their jobs are great. And employers usually reap the benefits of committed, actively engaged employees.

Just as there are different ways of expressing negative emotions in the workplace, so are there more and less effective ways of expressing joy, positive regard, caring, and appreciation at work. The development of increasingly committed and productive employees depends in large part on individual commitment to consistent, effective expression of appreciation for others and the work that they do.

# 9

# Differences That Make
a Difference

The number of potential differences is infinite but very few of
them become effective differences

— GREGORY BATESON

HEALTHY ADULT PERSONALITIES are quite plastic; they adapt
relatively easily from situation to situation, revealing amazing
behavioral flexibility. As evidence of the versatility most of us
have, you have only to recall the last time you surprised yourself by doing, saying, or thinking something that was unexpected.
Chances are that occasion was not too long ago since most of us are
capable of experiencing that kind of moment on a relatively frequent
basis. Similarly many of us experience sometimes surprising differences
between our behavior in one setting (e.g., at home) and our typical
behavior in another (e.g., at work). What makes the difference? What
factors influence our reactions and choices? *Why* do we tend to say and
do certain things in some circumstances while behaving quite differently in others?

The *systems* you're part of create some of the crucial differences. At
the moment you cross the threshold into a new work environment, you
are entering a system whose characteristics will profoundly influence
you and your behavior. You bring the potentials. Your work environment evokes some of them but not others. It encourages you to display
some particular attitudes and behaviors and to conceal the rest. It's a
transaction.

Now, certainly work environments don't *control* your behavior in
a deterministic sense. Rather, they *influence* which parts of yourself
you will feel comfortable in showing and sharing and which new behaviors you're likely to risk developing. This is particularly true of your
emotions.

Another set of crucial factors that make a difference has to do with "circumstances" of birth, or demographic characteristics, such as geographic location and gender. For example, Americans tend to think differently on some matters from Europeans, and people on the East Coast tend to do things differently from people on the West Coast. And surely (!) most of us are aware that men are importantly different in some respects from women. Geographic and gender differences can have substantial influence over our feelings and the ways we express them.

The influence of system and demographic characteristics over emotions in the workplace is as powerful as that of individual style. And there are some specific system and demographic factors that have influence over the kinds of emotions each of us experiences and expresses during our workaday lives—the differences that make a difference. Two of the most influential variables are gender and the culture of the organization we work in. The interaction of sex role socialization, corporate culture, and personal style results in the characteristic ways you have of dealing with your own and other people's emotions at work.

### Men, Women, and Emotional Differences at Work

At thirty-eight, T. A. Logan and Terry Johnson were on their way to the top. Graduates of well-respected programs, they had entered a prestigious manufacturing firm several years ago. Both had taken risks that paid off and—by anybody's standards—had achieved success on the job. T.A. had advanced to the highest mid-management level. He expected a significant promotion within the next few months and was well prepared to take advantage of a recent offer to jump to a competitor if he didn't get it. Terry had done equally well in a comparable division, and it was widely anticipated that the division chief's retirement in six months would result in her swift promotion to that position.

At midyear the chief executive officer called a meeting of all division chiefs and associates to discuss changes in the corporation's priorities. As they prepared for this major meeting, Terry and T.A.—as was true of almost everyone in the office—felt the pressure building. In general, though, they both worked with characteristic efficiency and enjoyed seeing others rely on their own obvious competence. Both calculated privately that the situation was probably working to their advantage in clinching their anticipated promotions.

Palpable tension filled the office when the day of the conference arrived. At the appointed hour the top executives gathered, putting papers in place, taking coffee or water, making jokes and anxious small talk as they waited to get going. Soon the last of the participants rushed in. As he slipped into the room, a secretary pulled the large doors closed. Those in the outer office heard little from behind the imposing doors as the morning progressed.

As lunchtime approached, the doors swung open, and the sounds of scattered conversation, scraping chairs, and shuffling papers filled the reception area. People spilled from the room, walking in pairs or proceeding singly toward various destinations. Some were animated and gesturing. Others were preoccupied. A few seemed to be determined—and hurrying.

T.A. was among those who emerged quickly from the room. He walked with long strides down the hall to his office. He turned sharply inside, and a few moments later colleagues in the hallway could hear him yelling into his phone, "You *told* me those figures had been checked! Can I trust *any*thing you do? Get those spread sheets to me *now!*"

He slammed down the phone, raised his eyes to the ceiling, ran his hand through his hair, and let out a loud sigh. He jerked up from his chair, and it careened into the wall behind the desk. T.A. glared at it, then kicked it, really jamming it into the wall. He paced to the window and stood there, scowling at the street below. He pounded his fist against the wall, oblivious of the quick, curious stares of colleagues passing by his open door. He turned suddenly and went swiftly into the hallway. "Where *is* he?" he muttered loudly as he scanned the corridor. He ignored—or never heard—a colleague's friendly "Hey, T.A., how's it going?" His scowl deepened. He wheeled furiously back into his office, yanked up the phone receiver, and punched the intercom number. "Where *is* he?" he demanded of no one in particular as the phone rang on, unanswered. He jammed the receiver back down and strode furiously to the door as the sound of hurried footsteps resounded down the hall. "What's *taken* you so long?" he yelled angrily as he gathered up the spread sheets from his associate. "Well, come in, come in," he demanded in a somewhat mollified tone as he strode toward his desk and began leafing through the data.

Terry, too, had emerged from the conference room in a hurry. "Later!" she yelled out preemptorily to a colleague trying to catch up with her. Without glancing back, she pressed on at an even faster pace. She turned left at her corridor, moved swiftly into her office, and slammed the door shut behind her. She jumped guiltily as the noise reverberated against the walls. She took a deep breath and began walking to her desk, then wheeled around abruptly and defiantly jammed in the lock button on the door handle. She picked up the phone, and she punched in the first three digits of an intercom number but stopped and slammed the receiver back onto the unit. She stared up at the ceiling intently and blinked her eyes. Suddenly, with one urgent motion, she fell into her chair, crossed her arms on her desk, dropped her head, and began sobbing. Shaking with anger at her boss—and furious with herself for crying instead of calling him—she let the tears flow. Long before comfort might have come, she jerked her head upright, searching with horrified anticipation for smudges of mascara on her suit jacket sleeves. Relieved that there were no telltale signs, she struggled to bring the tears under control as she groped for her purse, hoping she'd find a tissue inside.

She spoke softly but vehemently to herself between tears and clenched teeth, "No one will *ever* get to me like this again!" She drew in her breath, shook her head as she wiped her eyes, and looked blankly out the window. "I can't *believe* he asked me to justify that recommendation," she whispered through the tears. "He *knows* how strongly I argued against it. He's more ready for retirement than I thought!" She paused, then cautioned herself grimly, "I'd better get that rationale in order. I'm sure they can hardly *wait* to hear what I come up with, given my big production over how easy it would be to pull the data together over the lunch hour." She rummaged through the files on her desk and sighed angrily as a quick search yielded nothing. She wiped her eyes once more and checked her appearance in a small hand mirror. She picked up the phone again, grateful that she hadn't broken it earlier, and punched in a different number. "Jim?" she said. "Bring me those spread sheets on the old divisional accounts, will you? I need them. Drop what you're doing and get them over here now. Thanks." She sighed, returned the phone to its cradle, and gazed out the window. "Now, *Mr.* Sullivan, how am I going to deal with you about blindsiding me in that meeting?"

She turned to the phone and lifted the receiver but replaced it as she remembered the locked door. She got up, smoothed her hair, and turned the handle to release the lock. She felt her composure settling back in as she opened the door quietly and looked out in the hallway at the sound of Jim's approaching footsteps. In a sudden panic she looked surreptitiously down at her sleeves again for telltale signs of tears. Relieved, she returned her attention to Jim's approach. As they went inside her office, she smiled vaguely at him and thanked him for coming down.

Terry got the data she needed, as did T.A.. Both made convincing recoveries from the embarrassments of the morning. Appearing with near-customary poise and confidence, each responded in the afternoon session to the separate requests that had caught them so off guard. They had been friends for a long time, and they exchanged rueful opinions about the meeting much later in the day. They observed that neither seemed seriously injured by the whole affair, but neither ever wanted to be caught so short again. They didn't share with each other some lingering anxieties over the day's events. T.A. was very troubled over two caustic comments about "yelling all over the office" that had been thrown his way after the meeting was over. Terry was disturbed by her knowledge that she had been "reduced to tears," even if in the privacy of her own office. Both were perplexed and anxious about their behaviors. T.A. had never imagined himself as one to slam chairs into walls. Terry had never envisioned herself "breaking down" in the office or avoiding a confrontation, either. Each wondered where these emotional intrusions had come from. Had they observed both of their responses to the provoking events, they might have wondered also why each had reacted so differently to the same event.

T.A. had yelled, and Terry had cried. T.A. left his door open and was apparently oblivious of—or didn't care about—the reactions of his colleagues. Terry had shut her door immediately and locked it; before she let anyone in, she checked to make sure she looked all right. T.A. shouted out his anger, but Terry didn't express her anger directly. To all appearances, T.A. didn't care at that moment how he was perceived. Terry seemed to feel guilty about her behaviors, almost as soon as they occurred.

The reasons for their different responses are many. Some are related to their personalities. Some come from unique features of their own histories. Some—perhaps most—of the differences are related to traditional socialization practices for children in the United States, which often dictate that emotions and their expression should vary by gender. Boys should be tough and girls should be tender; boys should be strong and girls should be caring. And on and on, through countless examples that each of us could add to the list.

Some of the unwritten rules for the ways men and women should behave in their emotional lives are changing. But even as some parents try to raise their girls to be caring *and* independent, their boys to be strong as well as nurturant, cultural beliefs about appropriate male and female behaviors are still strongly in evidence. A few moments in a toy store are all that is needed to discern the obvious differences between "girls' toys"—Barbie dolls, playhouses, tea sets, pink ponies, and makeup kits—and "boys' toys"—cars that roar, weapons that blast, GI Joe, Superman, He-Man, and Rambo.

Many of these gender differences have functioned well—or have been assumed to function well—in family life, where complementary roles and responsibilities are characteristic of many productive and caring interactions. But they have raised questions, confusion, and misunderstanding in the work world.

The sources of the gender differences are many. Some are pretty well documented. An example is the strong tendency of many adults to treat boys and girls in very different ways throughout childhood. Even early in infancy, when male and female babies tend to look pretty much alike, adults frequently describe girls as soft and fine-featured, boys as vigorous and strong. In childhood parents often keep girls closer to themselves, physically and psychologically, and give boys more latitude and independence. Parents early tend to allow girls to express their fears, seek protection from others, and, on occasion, shed tears. Just as early, parents usually encourage boys to shed their fears and suppress incipient tears.

School experiences support these different expectations for boys' and girls' attitudes and behaviors, as do their friends. Many a little boy close to tears has been stung into stoic suppression and fisticuffs by a well-aimed rendition of "Cry, baby, cry!" Many a little girl has been told firmly to suppress her expressions of anger and behave like a "young lady."

The "modeling" that parents and other important adults provide for children is also heavily implicated in girls' and boys' learning that there are some clear standards for how one *ought* to behave as an adult woman or man. Children watch many of the men in their lives freely expressing anger, aggression, and strength in conversations and in the physical give-and-take of contact sports. Just as often they watch many of the women in their lives talking things through, nurturing, and perhaps on occasion crying. Children also frequently experience different kinds of interactions with their parents, depending on their sex. When disagreements over responsibilities or behavior are at issue, girls and their parents tend to negotiate, while boys and their parents tend to confront.

These contributors to sex role socialization often lead by adolescence to clear differences in many boys' and girls' interests, behaviors, emotions, and ways of expressing feelings. A brief look at Terry and T.A. during the high school years they spent together highlights some typical differences.

Leaving study hall together one afternoon during their Sophomore year, T.A. had told Terry that football cuts were coming up next week. He was sure he'd make the team. But he also wished it weren't taking so long. Terry commiserated. Her tryouts for a part in *Swan Lake* were the next day, and she was unabashedly nervous.

"I want it so much," she said as they walked along, "I'll *die* if I don't get it. It's such an *incredible* chance." She shook her head. "But I think Shelly's going for it, too."

"So?" asked T.A. after a pause. "Other guys are trying out for my position, but *I'm* going to get it."

Terry stopped and looked at him quizzically. "How do you know that? How can you be so sure? I want the part, but I don't *know* I'm going to get it."

"You've got a problem, Terry!" He laughed. Then he said seriously, "You just need to go in thinking that you'll get it. And you'll get it. You have to get mad and fight for it. If you fight, you'll get it."

Terry's expression remained unchanged. "I *don't* understand you, T.A. Isn't Tom going out for 'your' position? Isn't he your best friend? How can you go out there and get mad at him and fight for it? Don't you *worry* about that?"

It was T.A.'s turn to look puzzled. "No," he said, "I don't. It's just part of the way you play the game. If you don't play it that way, you wind up losing, and who wants to be a loser?"

Terry shook her head. "Clearly not you!" She smiled. "But I don't know, T.A. I really don't. . . ."

"Well, let me put it this way." He grinned. "How are you going to feel if you *don't* get the part in *Swan Lake?*"

"That's easy," she said. "I'll be furious. I'll die; I'll cry buckets; I'll leave dancing forever. And I'll probably start practicing again tomorrow."

It was T.A.'s turn to look perplexed. "Girls!" was all he could manage as Terry waved and headed for the parking lot.

Like T.A., most boys have learned by adolescence that men suppress any "soft" emotions, that they argue and "go at it" with each other. Like Terry, most adolescent girls have learned that women often feel that friendship and competition are mutually exclusive ideas; they shouldn't let many kinds of strong feelings "out" because they contradict the nurturing behavior commonly expected of women. And like Terry, most girls have learned by adolescence that tears are an acceptable way to express feelings, at least on occasion.

Along with countless other adults, Terry and T.A. entered the world of work with lifetimes of socialization that told them how they should behave in life, what emotions they should feel, and how they should express them. So the fact that their emotional responses were very different on the day of the big meeting in their thirty-eighth year was not surprising. They both felt emotion because they had a lot invested in their careers, were committed to their jobs, and were working hard for promotions. The events of the morning's meeting threatened all those things. Both dug in to meet the challenge. But some aspects of their responses were different because they had spent a lifetime learning different things about the ways they should feel and ways they should express their feelings.

A problem with this reality is that many workplace cultures value one approach to emotions and emotional expression and devalue many others. This singularity of approach confounds productive activity on the part of many very competent men and women.

### Corporate Cultures and Corporate Emotional Standards

When Terrence E. Deal and Allan A. Kennedy wrote *Corporate Cultures* early in the 1980s, the role of emotions in the workplace had not yet been scrutinized or culturally recognized. However, it is clear that Deal and Kennedy had an intuitive appreciation of the role of human emotions in the development of corporate cultures, even though their book gives little formal attention to the importance of emotional standards for the evolution of a distinct corporate culture.

Interestingly, many scholars who have written about the nature of work over the last century have specifically denied or overlooked the role and functions of emotions in the workplace. Sociologist Max Weber, for example, whose thinking about bureaucracies was influential in shaping the culture and practices of many businesses during this century, pointed to rationality and efficiency as critical for the success of organizations. Frederick Taylor, focusing on time and motion studies, was similarly influential in promoting a strong cultural belief that organizational efficiency is paramount and that such efficiency is purchased through the development of cool, considered, rational patterns of work activity. Emotions, positive or negative, have little place in this orientation toward reasoned, consistent, rule-governed work settings.

In the subsequent era of William Whyte's *The Organization Man* and Sloan Wilson's *The Man in the Gray Flannel Suit,* personal control at work and organizational control in general were at a premium. And personal control, it was assumed, clearly precluded emotional displays. Many in the culture "bought" the notion that emotions and rational thinking are mutually exclusive. Many accepted the conclusion that the military model of a hierarchical, goal-directed disciplined machine is the best way to run any work setting.

As many more contemporary observers of productive management practices have noted, however, emotions and reason do in fact work very well together in successful businesses. Thomas Peters and Robert Waterman's consideration of the conditions of excellent performance in successful organizations involves numerous references to the role of personal emotional factors, such as commitment, zeal, and enthusiasm in workplace success. And of course, Deal and Kennedy's work alludes to the varied and sometimes strong emotional qualities found in many contemporary work cultures.

In what quickly became a classic in the corporate organization literature, Deal and Kennedy point out that all companies have a distinctive "style," a recognizable culture. The characteristics that define each corporation include specific values, symbols, rituals, and communication patterns. While these authors did not specifically note the fact, many of the symbols and rituals found in corporate life are geared directly toward the management of work-based emotions. It is also relatively easy to see that each company culture contains a specific set of attitudes toward the *kinds* of emotional expressions that are encouraged, discouraged, or tolerated in the employees who work within that culture. "The way we do things around here" refers to the behaviors people engage in at work but also reflects assumptions about emotions at work.

Some corporate cultures tolerate (and even expect) that people will express anger—as they feel it and to the degree they feel it. The "tough-guy, macho culture" described by Deal and Kennedy contains much license for anger display. In this type of corporate culture, people take many risks, feedback is quick, and much temperamental behavior is accommodated as long as individuals produce.

One supervisor we talked with in a software development company described his work culture in terms that evoked strong images of a "macho" orientation. The people in this firm believe that they're on the "cutting edge" of their field. "We have to think that," he said, "or we'd go under in a minute." The firm is far from going under, but it is also far from calm, cool, and collected. Many people in that company work long hours, and most claim to enjoy the excitement and pace of the work. There is obvious pressure to produce, but the environment is not overly time-pressured. There are project due dates, but there are not constant, day-to-day deadlines. The needed resources are available, and everyone with whom we spoke there felt that his or her work is usually valued. The culture of this company, nonetheless, is intense and emotional. And the emotions expressed are not usually positive—at least on the surface.

"We do a lot of teamwork," the supervisor said, "with different guys working on different parts of a major project. Sometimes we develop competing approaches to a project, then fight it out among ourselves to come out with the best final product. Tempers and emotions often fly."

People in the suite where he works frequently emerge from their private offices yelling, gesturing, and calling each other obscene names. This vehement and obvious anger can continue for a long time, and others occasionally arrive to join in. "It really is a melee sometimes," he said. "It sounds like a major-league manager yelling at the ump, magnified ten times over."

New entrants into the firm learn quickly that this behavior is normal, and it's part of the way things get done. They also learn that it doesn't lead to permanent interpersonal rifts or destroyed projects. On the contrary, in this company's culture these behaviors have become part of a productive work routine. They're so integral to the work processes that our informant observed that he had a hard time trusting someone who *doesn't* participate in these expressive, raucous corporate rituals. As he said of one person who'd recently left the firm, "He never was one of us; he never entered in. I don't know if he thought he was above it all, or what. He was pretty good at what he did, but he just never caught on."

Many people, we suspect, would have a hard time entering this culture. But it is a culture that "works" for the participants and the company. And it is a culture with clear rules governing the expression and function of emotions at work. As sociologists Peter Berger and Thomas Luckmann have argued so convincingly, realities are socially constructed. And the construction of cultural reality in this corporation is based in part on a strong belief in the usefulness of vehement emotional expression. Those who participate and succeed in this culture accept this assumption and act on it. Their own emotional expressions are influenced by the company's cultural norms.

In contrast, there are corporate and institutional cultures that require all employees to behave conservatively—especially in expressing emotions. Displays of joy and camaraderie are discouraged, even when they are directly related to workplace activities and successes. If you're a member of such a work culture and you want to celebrate a great new deal, you and your colleagues will probably by instinct choose someplace other than company property.

Recently a senior executive with a national reputation in his field was vigorously sought after by a competing firm. He decided to make the move and has been operating within his new culture for several months now. He talks about his new corporate culture in terms that reveal how very strange it still "feels" to him.

At his last company informality was an unstated but strong norm. People came into the office in the morning, greeted each other, caught up on the latest ball game, and engaged in time-limited but off-task conversation for ten to fifteen minutes each day. Everyone joined in. "It was simply expected—and comfortable," he said. "You kind of get to know people that way, and it makes working with them easier, more productive sometimes." During the course of the working day it was not unusual for colleagues to drop into each other's offices, cups of coffee in hand. If invited in, they'd stay a few minutes and "shoot the breeze," sometimes about work, sometimes not. "We got a heck of a lot done," he said. "And some of that off-task talking contributed a lot to getting it all done."

But in his new corporation formality and distance are the cultural bywords. "No one says, 'Hey, how're you doing?'" he said, "No one! I do, and they tolerate it from me; but I've really eased up on it, I can tell you that. I miss it. I frankly don't think people are as productive here as they think they are. But there's a real intense assumption that work is serious, and we're all *serious* about our work."

Seriousness about work—which is highly valued in his new firm—is demonstrated according to this culture's rules by walking directly into one's own office in the morning, coming out only for a good reason, and moving quietly about the firm purposefully when out of one's own office. "I'm telling 'em"—he laughed—"that there's a better way to do it. But I'm getting used to their ways, too."

### Learning the Rules

As is the case with so many of the established attitudes and behaviors that form a cultural style the assumptions about appropriate emotional expression are rarely verbalized and hardly ever written down.

In fact, when company rules governing emotions and their expression *are* written down—in office manuals, employee handbooks, and the like—there is probably a move afoot somewhere in the administrative hierarchy to counteract a prevailing or emerging norm.

Most employees learn the rules the way they learn any other cultural standard: through observation and through trial and error. We pick things up by paying attention to what goes on around us and by being particularly sensitive to feedback concerning our own behavior. One insurance executive we interviewed, who recently made a lateral transfer to another agency, felt a few tears forming in her eyes after learning that the biggest corporate deal she had ever put together had fallen through at the last minute. As they passed in the hall, one of her new colleagues whispered to her that "the last person who cried around here—over anything—was back peddling auto insurance within the week." That's an example of company enculturation in action.

After taking a new job with a major recording label, another executive was told that failing to stand behind his new proposal for increased marketing visibility would result in a fairly quick corporate exit or demotion. "If you don't get excited about this thing, if you don't swear a little as you defend it, they're going to think you're a wimp," one helpful colleague confided. "People have to get some emotion behind their stuff around here, or they just don't make it." That message, too, is corporate emotional enculturation in action.

Most often enculturation messages are much less direct than that. An astonished comment might be made about an employee in "the office down the hall" who "actually yelled at one of the secretaries." Or a junior employee begins to notice that it's a routine practice in the company for people to shout out their glee when a deal goes through or someone gets hold of a crucial piece of information. The methods of communication may be subtle, but the messages are quite clear. These messages let you know which feelings are OK to express and where and when those expressions will be endorsed by the corporate culture.

In some cases those messages convey information not only about what feelings are OK to *express* but also which ones are OK to *feel*. For example, in some work cultures it's considered a sign of weakness to feel "attacked" when your work is disparaged in public. The norm requires people in such companies to feel self-confidence at all times. If your work is criticized, you are expected *not* to feel anxious or hurt. If you do, you will have to entertain the notion that you're not really a good fit with the company. You're not made of the kind of "stuff" that the corporate culture needs and admires. This kind of message is geared toward the *management of the feelings themselves.* To feel hurt and to act nonchalant about it are not enough. The culture expects the actual feeling to be consonant with the behavior.

Delivering something as potentially benign as a heartfelt thank-you message is also determined to some extent by the corporate culture. Some companies encourage their people to express feelings of gratitude and dependence on other employees. In other companies people rarely or never hear an expression such as "Thanks! I couldn't get along around here without you." In this latter kind of environment, expressions of need and gratefulness may be thought, for example, to undermine a prevailing cultural norm that encourages independence, self-sufficiency, or formality.

Often corporate cultures have different standards for the emotional behavior of men and women. For example, one company we know expects its male executives to react with assertive anger when that is "appropriate," but the company's female executives dare not do likewise. Interestingly, in a company headquartered just across the street, both men and women executives are expected to assert their emotions. The unwritten rules there state that assertion of personal qualities of all sorts is in the best interests of the company as it jockeys for its share of the market.

## Work Environment Characteristics That Provoke Uncomfortable Feelings

Over and over again, as we talked with people in many different occupations across the country, we heard comments to the effect that "people who have jobs in industries (or professions) like this one get angry and tearful more often than people who have other kinds of jobs. Feelings like anger come with the territory around here." Certain kinds of work situations do tend to contribute to the creation of certain kinds of emotions in people. Uncomfortable experiences like anger, anxiety, and weeping occur more often in three recognizable kinds of settings: time-pressured, undersupplied, and undervaluing.

Time-pressured settings require that important decisions and actions consistently occur at specific times. Media-related environments, like newspapers and television, some stockbrokerage settings, and the production departments of many businesses constitute good examples. The need to keep an eye constantly on the clock is relentless. The demands of these work environments include the necessity for several people to work together to make sure a specific thing happens at a very specific time. A functional kind of dependency on co-workers and on the clock is critical.

In these environments it is much more likely that anxieties will build and tempers will flare. When someone does something that seems to constitute "dropping the ball," others don't have time to pick up the slack, but they become part of the resulting failure even if they did not directly contribute to the error. It's not unusual for anger or sometimes weeping to follow these failures. Some occupations, like those we have mentioned, provide opportunities for this kind of experience on an hourly or daily basis. Others provide such opportunities only occasionally—for example, when the report needs to get out, when the big decision must be made. If you work in a setting that creates this kind of climate constantly or just at times, it is helpful to be aware that your own way of experiencing and expressing emotions may be altered or intensified as a result of the situational variables.

A second environment that often creates unpleasant feelings can be found wherever resources are in short supply. When there are not enough staff members, computers, adequate offices (or even paper clips!), frustration builds, and bad feelings more often result. While it is not inevitable, sometimes lack of funds for adequate salaries also creates this kind of environment.

While the dynamics in time-pressured situations create opportunities for failure and blame because the work environments require so much dependency on the competencies of specific other people, in undersupplied environments blame may also contribute to the production of uncomfortable emotions, but the blame is much more diffuse. People become angry at the "administration" or the "CEO," or the "secretary," or whatever. Often the objects of anxiety and anger are unclear or unavailable. Nonetheless, bad feelings emerge.

The third kind of work environment that occasions many unpleasant feelings fosters a sense that its inhabitants and the work they produce are not valued. There may be few time pressures, and there may be more than adequate supplies, yet anxiety and anger are almost constantly present in these settings, and tears more easily result as well. Usually the people in charge of the resources in these environments believe that the workers aren't doing enough, or aren't doing it well, or aren't interested in and committed to the "right" products or processes. Sometimes they simply don't know how to communicate positive feedback. Negative messages are frequent, and little praise—public or private—is forthcoming. A lot of diffuse blaming occurs in these environments. Self-blame is common, too, as people try to figure out why praise and other positive reinforcements don't come their way. In this kind of environment, both stresses and bad feelings multiply.

Paying attention to the characteristics of the environments you work in will help you see that certain feelings arise from encounters with specific people and in specific circumstances. It's possible, for example, that your typical emotional styles are evoked only in some kinds of jobs or only at certain times during a particular work cycle, when the demand characteristics of the work are particularly high.

There are major differences among companies in the ways that pressures affect employees. For example, some emerging companies have developed a work culture that makes it possible for people to feel good about themselves and their work even though because of cash flow difficulties, basic supplies are not as plentiful as they should be. The company culture in such cases emphasizes working for the future and encourages an esprit de corps that makes it enjoyable to come to work despite the lack of resources. Likewise, many time-pressured situations are found within companies containing cultures that have developed rewarding rituals which accompany the worst of the time-pressured moments. We know of several science departments in one eastern university that "break out the champagne" as soon as a difficult and lengthy research grant application has been placed in the hands of an overnight express carrier. The work culture in that setting expects people to repress any negative emotions until the job is done. As soon as the champagne appears, people can holler for joy or begin complaining about an aspect of the process that might have gone more smoothly if so-and-so had changed his or her attitudes or routine in a major way. The cultural norms dictate that most feelings are appropriate for expression after the preparation process is over, as long as the champagne bottles are in sight. When the champagne bottles disappear, so does the open expression of feelings—until the next time.

So the idiosyncratic nature of corporate expectations affects the kinds of feelings people have and the way they may express them in the workplace. While certain environmental characteristics tend to elicit bad feelings, they don't necessarily *have* to elicit them. Moreover, the general culture that pervades each work environment is far more important than any single characteristic. While individual differences in emotional style are critical, the culture of the particular work environment in which you labor has a lot to do with the aspects of your style that you will display and develop.

## *Putting It All Together*

What happens when a person with a well-defined style of experiencing and expressing a specific emotion enters a work culture with a well-defined set of expectations regarding that emotion? And within that setting what difference does it make if the employee is a man or a woman? Here is an example of what we might expect.

Recall Ken, one of many people in today's work force who report that they don't get angry, they get even. Ken doesn't go out of his way to get revenge. He waits until an opportunity presents itself to withdraw support, share his true opinions, or withhold rewards of some sort. The intensity of his angry feelings diminishes almost as soon as he has the thought that vindication will eventually come his way.

We expect men to "stand up for themselves," and many people assume that placing oneself in the position of "dealing out justice" is a male-appropriate thing to do. That is why somewhat more men than women adopt this style. More important, it's why more men than women are able to recognize and admit that they use this style as a way of dealing with their anger. A man is likely to believe that asserting himself on behalf of his emotional well-being is praiseworthy.

People who adopt this approach prefer to be less confrontational than direct dealing usually requires. Getting even rather than angry allows the offended person to be assertive yet indirect. As one man who deals with his anger at work in this way confided, "Why should I make myself miserable by feeling angry or hurt? Better just to get back at the guy. And I usually do."

In light of our general cultural expectations, then, it's not surprising to find that very few women who rely on this way of dealing with their anger are quick to admit it. Picture a woman standing with a group of colleagues announcing that she's going to get even with someone who has just been offensive and that she prefers to get even rather than make herself uncomfortable with angry feelings. Likely the picture is just a little out of focus as you try to imagine it. If you do achieve clarity with this image, you probably also will associate other assertive or aggressive characteristics with this woman. Often people imagine such a woman to be less feminine when they begin to picture her using this way of dealing with her own anger.

So the sex-related cultural messages are clear. If you are a man, this way of dealing with anger at work is frequently accepted as long as you don't go out of your way to plan or create misfortune for your offender.

It's even OK for you to let others know that this is your chosen style. Letting others know puts them on notice, and that's a respectable way for a man to behave.

If you are a woman, getting even instead of angry won't be so positively sanctioned. "What kind of woman behaves that way?" many will ask. Further, what kind of woman would let others *know* that she has chosen this way of dealing with her anger? *Thus, a style that lets us know where a man stands serves to create confusion where a woman is concerned.* We seem to know less about what to expect from her. Our general culture has not prepared us to understand her very easily.

But what kinds of work cultures can accommodate this style whether it's owned by a man *or* a woman? The macho culture that Deal and Kennedy have described is well equipped not only to tolerate this kind of style but also to encourage it—from women as well as men. This kind of corporate culture relies on individual personalities and achievements to meet corporate goals. Success is the ultimate criterion against which most behaviors are measured. If the style "works," then it's sanctioned by the culture without much fuss.

But what happens when a man like Ken, who has been using this style for years within a macho corporate culture, transfers to a company that is far more conservative and rewards such things as teamwork and strong emotional control? In that setting the messages may be mixed. On the one hand, the work culture does not want him to express his anger directly, so the more indirect way of dealing with those feelings might seem, on the surface, to fit. But it probably won't fit at all. In all likelihood, since the culture values cooperation and conservative approaches to problems, this company will not want Ken to "lie in wait" for opportunities to get even after someone on the team has offended him in some way.

It's also possible that he may keep his approach to himself in this setting, rather than make it known, as he did in his former place of employment. He might "go underground" with it for a while as he collects information—probably at an unconscious level—on the approaches that people in this culture have for dealing with their anger. If one or another of these ways seems to fit for him, he may adopt it. In all likelihood, if his current work culture's approach is to be effective for *him,* it will have to be one that encourages assertion. People who have adopted the "I don't get mad, I just get even" style tend to need to use an assertive *action* of some sort in order to deal with their anger.

If the current corporate culture doesn't seem to contain options that fit for Ken, he may have to adopt one of the very indirect approaches we have described. Perhaps he'll be able to cultivate an approach that permits him to take his anger home to share with his wife, as does Martin, the federal court bailiff. Or maybe like Richard, the political campaign manager, he will stifle the anger and will eventually experience its presence through a physical ailment such as a chronic "nervous" stomach. If he can't find a suitable substitute for his former approach to personal anger, he may have to consider the possibility that he's badly placed within this corporation. If there are other important areas of misfit, he may have to consider moving.

On the other hand, some people choose in such a circumstance to hang on to their former styles. If so, they risk an uncomfortable clash with the work culture that may result in their firing or quitting. It is also possible that the clash may contribute to a change in the cultural norm. If others respond positively to seeing this kind of style appear in their work environment and they begin to use it from time to time, the culture will change. This is one way cultures evolve. Individuals change them by providing alternate approaches to institutionalized attitudes, feelings, and behaviors.

# 10

# Strategies for Change

All things are possible until they are proved impossible—and
even the impossible may only be so, as of now.

—PEARL S. BUCK

SHOULD YOU DECIDE that your usual way of dealing with your
emotions or responding to those of others is hindering your
performance at work, you may want to think seriously about
changing your style—or at least some aspects of it. Chances
are, your problems with anger, anxiety, gratitude, and tears are similar
to those we heard so often when talking with people about their histories with work-based emotions.

## Methods for Developing Strategies for Change

Each time we talked with someone about emotions in the workplace
we asked about the major advantages and disadvantages associated
with the particular styles that he or she had developed over the years.
The change strategies that follow were developed to address the problems that we often heard people express as they outlined their characteristic approaches and styles.

Because our emotions are dependent upon our personal interpretations of situations, many of the suggestions that follow are designed to
provide opportunities for altering cognitive "tapes," those habitual
comments we make to ourselves as we observe and evaluate the daily
situations in which we participate. A related strategy we suggest is
called image rehearsal, a technique that provides the opportunity to
visualize yourself behaving and feeling in new ways within old situations. A third principle involves conscious commitment to change.
Deliberate declarations to the self are a valuable part of any change
process. Identification of specific periods of practice time is also important. Like each of the other principles we rely on, this helps bring old

habits and attitudes to conscious attention where you can then modify or discard them.

## Anger: Making It Less of a Problem

### Problem No. 1: Getting Angrier Than the Situation Seems to Require

Some people feel anger at work that seems way out of proportion to the offense. They get angry over "nothing at all." Despite their recognition that this happens every once in a while, they feel at a loss to control it. And they don't understand why they do it.

Discomfort results, of course, when we feel or do something that "doesn't make sense," something that seems unjustified. Nobody likes to violate his or her own standards. However, many people who have this problem probably aren't violating their own standards at all. Rather, they simply need a bit more explicit insight into what those standards are.

People with this problem are slow to feel their own anger and don't realize that it builds within them over time. They become involved in a *process* of anger buildup, getting angrier and angrier at a particular person over the course of several days, weeks, or months, but since the experience hasn't reached an "awareness threshold," they don't label the feeling as anger until, at a seemingly sudden moment and possibly over a relatively minor infraction, they realize that they're furious. This style causes its owners to think they're tinderbox people, even though they're not.

Carla, the software package creator whose style we presented in talking about the various approaches to expressing anger, shares this problem with Daniel, the slow-burning production foreman, and with many other people. Recall that when Carla approached her boss's door, at some level of cloudy consciousness she knew she was going to receive the bad news she had been anticipating with annoyance for weeks. As she approached the meeting with Bea, she was *already angry but did not realize it.* Her snappish retort and quick exit resulted in large part because she had built up a powerful load of anger before she became involved in the specific situation that she believed triggered it. But that incident hadn't triggered the response at all. Rather, the anger had grown across the weeks when Carla developed her anticipation that Bea would reject her work. She had many an imaginary conversation with Bea during those days and didn't really realize it. She had made lots of anger-provoking statements to herself long before the actual anger-provoking incident occurred. The strength of her "quick" response puzzled her, and she was distressed as she wondered if others thought she had actually slammed her boss's office door. People like Carla and Daniel don't realize that they have been getting angry over time and that they are reacting to the "final straw that broke the camel's back." So they are surprised both at the feeling and at the dramatic nature of their behavior.

Learning to recognize their angry feelings much earlier in the process will help solve a lot of problems for people who experience undetected anger build up as well as for those who are around them and feel their wrath from time to time. People on the receiving end of this problem endure a lot of discomfort since they don't know why Mr. Smith or Ms. Jones is getting angry over such a little thing or why the problematic issue, even if it is somewhat substantial, deserves such a strong and dramatic response. As we have seen, *people who find themselves overreacting are generally reacting to the past rather than the present.*

So, how does someone like Carla or Daniel learn to recognize her or his own angry feelings much earlier in the process? We suggest the following steps:

• For a week or two, at the end of each day, spend a few minutes asking yourself if you have been annoyed or irritated that day.

• Be sure to search for occasions when you might have been anticipating irritating behavior on the part of a colleague at work. Recall the times when you were guessing that so-and-so would probably do such-and-such and were feeling annoyed merely at the thought.

• Look for patterns at the end of the week. If you notice that you became irritated two or three times with the same person or in the same situation, try to figure out what issues were common to all the episodes.

• Do not wait for more than four or five instances involving the same person or situation to accumulate before you attempt to change things so that they are more agreeable to you. That is, don't *let* your anger build up. Start letting your difficulties be known to the person who precipitates them long before you are actually angry. (See Problems No. 6 and No. 11 for specific ways of improving communication.)

• After you have used this approach for several weeks, you should be able to slack off a bit, requiring yourself to reflect on daily irritations only twice per week or perhaps only once, at the end of the week. After using this strategy for six months or so, you should find that you have become much more spontaneously aware of your feelings or irritations while at work, and the time needed for review of the day's or week's activities should be unnecessary.

### *Problem No. 2: When the Anger Comes Too Slowly*

Many people feel disadvantaged in certain work-related situations because their anger does not arrive until long after the precipitating incident is over. For some it never comes at all. When anger does emerge, many are surprised to discover they're angry.

While it may seem that this problem is very similar to the one we just described, it isn't. People who have difficulty with Problem No. 1 are usually capable of feeling and expressing anger. They may have felt irritated, frustrated, tired, or tearful on many previous occasions but were unaware that these responses were masking a growing anger directed toward a particular person or situation. In contrast, the people we are concerned with here find it difficult to *experience* anger (or irritation or frustration) at all—whether as a result of one serious incident or several such incidents. And often they are equally slow to communicate their anger should they experience it. While the people discussed earlier feel many negative things in substitution for anger, the people we're concerned with here tend to feel nothing at all.

Sometimes people with this problem regret the seemingly lost opportunity to have expressed anger. Many slow burners later and privately can manufacture awesome retorts that they might have delivered—if only they had known they were angry at the time. Lots of reveries have been devoted by slow burners to scenes that depict their quick assessment of all the emotional and intellectual aspects of a situation and the stunning remarks they hurl to halt any further comments from their adversaries.

While many of those we talked with about this issue found their slow-burning or cool-customer ways to be troublesome, others didn't. Elizabeth, the real estate salesperson who had to give up part of her commission, is a good example of a slow burner who is comfortable with her approach. Meredith, the computer store manager, is a cool customer who thinks that others may take advantage of her occasionally because she severely limits her feelings of anger at work. She occasionally tries to let her anger rise but has mostly been unsuccessful at that since she tends to value emotional control more highly than she values emotional expression.

Many people wish they could slow their anger down, but a sizable number think that feeling anger more often might serve them better than their current approach does. They suspect that the ability to feel angry would provide them with more options. But how do you experience your own anger at work when you've had years of experience coming to it slowly or not at all?

SUGGESTIONS

The key to change here is privacy. Most slow burners and cool customers just aren't used to or don't choose to feel a strong emotion like anger in the presence of other people—especially within more emotionally distant relationships such as those found at work. In order to feel anger, these people need to be off somewhere by themselves, allowing idle thoughts to emerge as they will.

If anger is to occur, attention must be given to the specific statements that you make to yourself during the offensive moment or very shortly thereafter. Within a day or two of the event it's important that regular, focused attention be directed toward those self-statements in some private location.

• Go to a private place on a regular basis every once in a while for several weeks. For example, you might plan a private lunch on Tuesdays or a walk around your neighborhood on Fridays after work.

• Review work situations that have occurred during the previous few days. Just let your mind wander, as it will, from incident to incident.

• Recall *what you were thinking* during each incident. Look for negative thoughts present during those situations that might have provided opportunities for anger.

• After reviewing a specific uncomfortable incident, always ask yourself the questions, Were the people involved in that situation behaving fairly toward me and my work? Might someone else have been justifiably irritated or angry over that?

• Do nothing differently at work during the weeks you've set aside for these reviews. Just follow the first steps on a regular basis.

• At the end of a few weeks you will probably notice that there are some patterns to the statements you have been making to yourself in certain uncomfortable situations. For example, you may notice that you think certain people may be taking advantage of you by being habitually late with promised assignments. Or you may have noticed that the negative events you have repeatedly focused on always involve someone's interrupting you in mid-sentence. You will probably have experienced at least mild irritation over these memories. Your identification of the actual statements you made to yourself will provide earlier access to the feelings in the future.

• After a few weeks have passed, look for occasions at work when you catch yourself saying the kinds of things to yourself that you discovered were part of the pattern of negative statements that are usually implicated when you have feelings of anger or irritation potentially available. As you catch yourself thinking these things, you will be actively focusing on them *in the moment* and any possible irritation or anger will have a greater opportunity to be realized. The key is recognizing the emotion-inducing potential of the interpretive statement you make to yourself.

• Continue to schedule regular private time for reflection on work situations for several more weeks. Consult other problems and suggestion lists below if you could use some assistance with developing new ways of expressing anger.

### *Problem No. 3: When Guilt Accompanies Angry Feelings*

For some, just *feeling* angry causes guilty feelings even if the anger is not expressed. In addition to feeling the discomfort that is so associated with the angry emotion itself, many people feel the discomfort that results from guilt. All in all, coming to anger can result in some pretty miserable moments for those who feel guilty as soon as they feel angry.

Matthew, the zookeeper who feels anger quickly, and Hazel, the anger deflector who was disappointed by her dishonest dress shop manager, represent people who have serious difficulties feeling OK about getting angry. Both Matthew and Hazel, and many others like them, are very good at providing excuses for those who offend them or malign their work. They are "understanding" people who are able to see many sides of an issue and believe that if they were in the other person's position, they might behave in a similar way.

Mark, the slow-burning director of advertising, also has this problem. Unlike Matthew and Hazel, however, he tends to feel guilty over his angry feelings almost exclusively as a result of his expectation that he should have had more control over the whole situation so that no one's anger would have been necessary. He also believes that mature adults simply do not get angry at work. They should be "above" it.

An important part of this problem is that people like Matthew, Hazel, and Mark don't have to express anger in order to feel guilty.

They merely have to experience it. Often the people in their environments do not know what these three people are feeling. And they certainly don't routinely harm their offenders with inappropriate displays of angry aggression. Rather, people who have this problem tend to have much more control over whether or not they come to anger than whether or not they experience the guilt!

SUGGESTIONS

The feelings of people who experience this problem will change when some important attitudes change. As we empathize with the positions of others, when we conclude that their behavior makes sense in view of the circumstance, we either change attitudes or values of our own or do not. When we change what we *think,* feelings change. In a disagreeable situation, when the other person's position or reality is not persuasive enough to influence change on our part, a valid anger remains, an anger that functions as it should, in connection with our principles. If you understand another's motivations in a way that allows you to change your own opinions about things, you simply won't feel angry. If you don't change your attitudes, if empathy doesn't emerge, you're probably going to feel anger—a justifiable anger. The anger you are potentially able to feel can be useful for both you and the people you work for and with. Feeling guilty about anger in these situations is not only unnecessary but counterproductive and painful as well.

Another fundamental attitude is that angry feelings are not harmful, nor are they childish. Since anger functions as a support for the meanings that we attach to our experience, it is appropriate in mature adults for anger to accompany violations of important values. *The feeling of anger never hurt anyone else. It's what we do with anger that can cause pain and damage.*

• Spend some time remembering times when you *might* have been potentially angry but understood another's point of view and motivations very well and had empathy, even when the other person had offended or harmed you in some way. Pay attention to the values inherent in each situation. Reconsider what feelings and behaviors might have been justified.

• For a few weeks during ordinary conversations throughout the day be alert for references to angry feelings so that you can see how others separate anger and guilt.

• Talk to people. Attitudes toward guilt are often best changed through discussion with people whose opinions you value. For several weeks make it a point to ask others about their experiences with anger and their positions on feeling guilty for feeling angry.

• Over the course of a couple of months take note of the times when you are feeling guilty as well as angry at work. Do not attempt to change your responses.

• After six or eight weeks have passed, identify a subsequent period of time as one when *you will not express anger at all.* Instead, allow yourself simply to feel it rather fully, stressing to yourself, during and after the experience, that simply feeling anger is certainly nothing to be ashamed of or to feel guilty about. If you do not feel significantly less guilty at the end of this stage, repeat it for another month or so.

• Return to expressing anger at work if you choose to do so. If you want to develop alternate ways of expressing your anger, consult suggestions in other sections of this chapter.

### Problem No. 4: When Direct Anger Results in Hurting Others

Some people express their anger directly toward its source and do so in the most caustic and demeaning ways they can manage. Usually these people feel justified in the vehemence of their anger because they—and what they believe in—have been so badly offended. They think their responses are appropriate. This kind of anger expression can be a problem for everyone concerned—the sender, the receiver, and the innocent bystanders. If there are any immature aspects involved in the anger experience at work, they involve the name-calling (which is under consideration here) and the silent punishing and huffing that are never transformed into direct expressions of feeling and expectations (which are considered in other sections).

Some of those we talked with who have adopted this style *do* find it to be a problem. They have noticed that relationships are undermined or destroyed with aggressive verbal attacks, and although they would like to continue to express their anger directly, they would like to do so in less volatile and harmful ways.

Recall Stan, the dry goods importer who told his customer off when the man reneged on a verbal deal. Stan went a whole lot farther than most of us would think necessary or appropriate. He didn't care what the man thought of him; of greatest importance to him right then was what *he* thought of the customer. That attitude is a reasonably effective one to have in times of great emotional stress when a major offense against you has occurred. But it isn't a complete response, and generally it isn't a very useful one.

Aggressive displays of anger that carry attacks on issues and personal characteristics that are not involved in the dispute are almost always harmful. As we pointed out in earlier chapters, negative emotions at work can be extraordinarily useful, contributing to productivity and self-respect, as long as they are not transformed into attacks on the offender's entire person. Anger that is directed toward what someone *does* can be effective. Anger that is directed toward what someone *is* can be harmful.

If he were to practice the strategies that follow, we suspect that Stan could learn to express anger effectively toward *all* kinds of people who make him angry—even women. Because he doesn't know how a woman might respond to his direct and aggressive style, he keeps his angry feelings tightly controlled when a female is involved in a problem at work. Much of the ambiguity and fear associated with expressing anger directly toward groups of people whom we perceive to be different from us can be eliminated if a reasonable, nonaggressive method of direct expression is developed.

SUGGESTIONS

People who share Stan's style and want to change some aspects of it will probably feel much better if they not only direct their anger toward its source but also *direct its expression toward the specific offense.* Kevin, the food store manager who becomes furious and spells out exactly why he's angry, provides a good model for people who wish to transform a style like Stan's into one that is less harmful. This is one of the easiest styles to change in a positive direction because the person already has a strong sense of his or her own values, is willing to express a strong angry feeling directly, and is usually not burdened with extraneous feelings (like guilt) that confuse the issues at hand. Change, however, does require some willingness to do some fairly uncomfortable soul-searching. But once the decision has been made to change, it can happen rather rapidly.

This style is one of the most important ones to change because it is one that has given the whole idea of anger at work a bad name. When people equate anger with aggression, it is this style they are usually thinking of.

• Spend some time recalling the occasions when you have told someone off. Remember the exact words and gestures you used. Imagine for a few moments what your own feelings might be if you had been on the receiving end of your own anger. Pay particular attention to the specific aspects of the person that you attacked. Note that some of these were probably not relevant to the specific offense and may have been attacked because you guessed that by addressing them, you could give back to the person some of the hurt you had experienced at his or her hands.

• Within the next week or so get off by yourself somewhere, pick out two of the angry episodes you have recalled, and rewrite the scripts. Picture yourself focusing *solely* on what the person has done that was unacceptable. As you imagine the situations, tell the person in great detail just *exactly* what he or she did wrong and why it was inappropriate. Tell the person with as much vehemence as you would like how you feel about his or her actions. That is, say you're furious and can barely "see straight" because of it. Turn as much as you can of the power behind your reaction to a description of the strength and reasons behind your feeling, omitting entirely any references to extraneous issues. (If you need some assistance in creating these images, consult the description of Kevin's style in Chapter Two.)

• Notice how different you feel about yourself and the other person in these new scenarios of old episodes. If you're not feeling enough satisfaction in these images, you are probably limiting the strength of your feelings—needlessly. It doesn't cause nearly as much harm to yell about how darn angry you are as it does to yell about what a fool someone is.

• Decide that for the next few weeks you will limit all angry expressions at work to a description of the exact offense and your emotional responses to it. Commit to the idea.


*Problem No. 5: When Indirectness Doesn't Satisfy*

For many people, like Kirsten, the bank officer, the indirect approach is the preferable one. They do not let the transgressor know clearly and unequivocally what incident has displeased them and how angry they are about it. Rather, they use subtle communication techniques. Often these strategies rely heavily on the withholding of certain things. Work proceeds slowly. Cooperation is restricted. Now and then an indirect verbal statement is made within earshot of the offender in order to reinforce the message, and it may be directed ostensibly toward no one in particular. Yet there is the intent to register displeasure and anger without confrontation.

Many people who engage in indirect methods of communication with those who have violated their standards and provoked anger have a bit of trouble with this style. Anger stays with them longer than they want it to remain. Unlike those people who get angry directly, often getting it over with quickly, many indirect people stay steamed for a longer period of time. This may be due to the fact that any deep satisfaction that is associated with expressing oneself and being heard is not available for those who adopt the indirect style. In the case of indirect messages the sender never knows exactly *when* the information is received. In fact, he or she can never be sure that it really *was received.* Further, it's quite unclear most of the time whether the messages will precipitate change. When anger is expressed directly, the person who sends the message is aware of influencing his or her world. People stop what they're doing, and they listen. When communication is good, the angry message helps change behavior—not only the offender's behavior but often that of the angry person.

Perhaps most important, the *feeling* of anger often remains when indirect approaches are exclusively relied upon. Rather than sending energy outward, an indirect approach tends to result in a retention of energy and thus a retention of the anger for a while.

Many people have reported that the anger just eventually goes away, usually when some competing emotion takes possession. And often this new emotion may be totally unrelated to the events that precipitated the angry feelings. For example, you may send strong, communicative, indirect messages but remain angry at your boss for days. Then comes news that the owner of a house has accepted the contract you offered and the house is yours! All of a sudden the anger toward your boss is gone. There's no room for it now since your emotions are invested elsewhere. For many people this often is not a fully satisfying solution, however. For one thing, they have learned that this solution is usually only temporary. They would really prefer to express the anger and get it over with. But how?

### SUGGESTIONS

There are two approaches to this problem that can be effective. Your choice of which to use depends on whether you want to move from an indirect approach to a more direct one or on whether you would prefer to retain a basically indirect style but would like to develop its effectiveness in communicating your feelings and needs. It is likely that adoption of some direct style strategies will result in shortening the length of time anger is experienced. If that is an important goal for you, then we suggest that you use the first set of strategies that are outlined below. If you prefer to maintain an indirect approach but would like to learn to use it more effectively—i.e., to improve your ability to *communicate* through indirect messages—then you will probably be more interested in the second set of strategies presented below.

STRATEGIES FOR CHANGING TO A MORE DIRECT APPROACH

• Start by committing to a change process that will probably take several months. Indirect styles do not change as quickly as others. (But they definitely can be changed.) At the start of your personal change process be sure you clearly understand that it will probably take about three focused months before you will begin to see marked developments in your style.

• During a two- or three-week preparation period talk to as many people as you can about the ways they express anger at work. Find out what people like best and worst about their personal styles. It will provide you with ideas about alternative behaviors and will help you get accustomed to some of the risks that sometimes pay off for people and sometimes don't. Do nothing differently at work relative to anger during these weeks.

• During the next week take some private time to recall two or three occasions when you were very angry at work and found that your indirect ways of dealing with it were unsatisfactory to you. Carefully identify exactly what you did to let the transgressor know what you thought and felt. Be sure to identify "passive resistance" kinds of behavior if they were present. These behaviors are a little more difficult to "see" since they involve the absence of something, rather than presence. (For example, you might have withheld a greeting or smile or neglected to do an elective task you usually do.)

• Reconstruct one or two of the above events in your mind. Replay the script, giving yourself a direct role. Imagine telling your offender what happened that you didn't like. Imagine saying that you are angry. Practice asking the offender how things might be changed so that this kind of thing won't happen again.

• Some people have found it useful to involve one or two people in the work environment who are respected and work close by. If you decide to do this, tell them that you are attempting to become more direct in expressing your irritations and angers at work and ask them what they would think of your practicing with them from time to time. Give them a glimpse of your former style, and share with them your hopes for how you will respond to offenses in the future.

• During the two or three weeks that follow, become especially familiar with the strategies outlined earlier in Problem No. 4. The parts that will be important for you are those that describe anger expressions that are focused on exactly what the transgressor has done and how you feel about that.

Commit to this strategy. That is, be sure to recognize that you deliberately decided to behave indirectly, have identified the most [impor]tant things that need to be communicated, have overdetermined [m]essage by delivering it in several ways, and have identified a [specifi]c length of time during which the process will spin itself out. [W]hen the time for this process is concluded, conclude the process. [Typ]ically comment to yourself, *It's over now.* You have done as much [a you] could. Hanging on to your anger any longer will most likely be [se]lf-defeating rather than effective.

### Problem No. 6: When Your Anger Hits the Wrong Target

[M]any people do not get angry either directly or indirectly with the [perso]n who caused them harm. Yet they don't keep their anger com[pletel]y to themselves either. Recall Marianne, the publishing house [edito]r who let her colleagues know she was angry, but never the people [who c]aused her anger. Or Martin, the federal court bailiff who lets no [one a]t work know he's angry but has been known to keep his wife up [half t]he night while he lets off steam.

[F]arley, the stockbroker who blamed fitness proponents when he [spill]ed over his boss's briefcase, presents a special case of the kind of [prob]lem we're concerned with here. Unlike Marianne, Martin, and [many] others who share the discomforts associated with this problem, [peop]le like Farley are unaware that they are really angry with someone [othe]r than the person or situation they are currently blaming. They [caus]e even more problems for others than do such people as Marianne [and] Martin. And creating problems for others is the major problem [expe]rienced by most people who do not direct their anger toward its [sour]ce or who keep it to themselves but choose to express it to others [who] have had no hand at all in creating the offensive incidents.

[F]arley's version of this approach is one that is not commonly used. [Mos]t of us have displaced our anger onto a "safer" object at some time [in o]ur history, but few people use this way of dealing with anger almost [excl]usively, as does Farley. While strategies for dealing with the prob[lem]s created by Marianne's and Martin's styles are reasonably easy to [dev]elop and use, Farley's difficulties are more complex. People who are [ha]bitually unaware of what has motivated their feelings are out of touch [wit]h themselves in ways that often cause them many interpersonal [diffi]culties and much personal pain. Usually psychotherapy can help [pro]vide insight and strategies for change.

[ ]When people such as Marianne and Martin are aware of who has

• Take another private hour to reflect or
during the previous weeks about anger in gene
of dealing with it, and your own behavior as y
strategies. In an imaginary situation involvin
has offended you and your standards, try to i
might behave more directly. You may have to
*feeling* of anger is a valuable feeling and tha
express it in ways that are effective and not ha

• Make the next month or so a trial period c
yourself to respect your anger, express it towarc
dered it, and learn from the experience whether
or uncomfortably.

• You may need to recycle some of the pre
of that time there should be a noticeable chang
of responding to your frustrations, irritations,

### STRATEGIES FOR IMPROVING INDIRECT COM

• When you get angry and decide that ar
preferable, identify for yourself *exactly* what yc
as detailed in your description as you possibly

• Identify those portions of your message t
receive if change is to happen. Remind yourself i
deliberate approach to this particular problem
anger. You are indeed doing something about it.
what happens next.

• Decide what indirect methods will convey
that you intend to deliver. *Be sure to put time*
*strategies.* For example, if you intend to stop fie
problems for a while decide that you will disengage
for exactly two days, or two weeks, or whatever.
because when things drag on, it is more difficu
subside or disappear.

• Be sure to use two or three methods to conv
You will need to overdetermine your reaction. Sir
circuitous, you will have much more confidence
having been clearly received if you send it in your
in two or three different ways. For example, you
withhold a service, such as routine troubleshooting,
comment that identifies the thing you value, and (
gressor the loan of a magazine article that is releva
some way.

• Take another private hour to reflect on what you have learned during the previous weeks about anger in general, the ways others have of dealing with it, and your own behavior as you began to use different strategies. In an imaginary situation involving someone at work who has offended you and your standards, try to imagine clearly how you might behave more directly. You may have to remind yourself that the *feeling* of anger is a valuable feeling and that you intend to learn to express it in ways that are effective and not harmful for you or others.

• Make the next month or so a trial period during which you permit yourself to respect your anger, express it toward those who have engendered it, and learn from the experience whether it turns out successfully or uncomfortably.

• You may need to recycle some of the previous steps. At the end of that time there should be a noticeable change in your habitual ways of responding to your frustrations, irritations, and anger at work.

### STRATEGIES FOR IMPROVING INDIRECT COMMUNICATION

• When you get angry and decide that an indirect approach is preferable, identify for yourself *exactly* what you are angry about. Be as detailed in your description as you possibly can.

• Identify those portions of your message that the offender must receive if change is to happen. Remind yourself at this point that your deliberate approach to this particular problem is in service of your anger. You are indeed doing something about it. You are in control of what happens next.

• Decide what indirect methods will convey the specific feedback that you intend to deliver. *Be sure to put time limits on withholding strategies.* For example, if you intend to stop fielding someone else's problems for a while decide that you will disengage from those activities for exactly two days, or two weeks, or whatever. This is a crucial step because when things drag on, it is more difficult for your anger to subside or disappear.

• Be sure to use two or three methods to convey a single message. You will need to overdetermine your reaction. Since your approach is circuitous, you will have much more confidence in your feedback's having been clearly received if you send it in your offender's direction in two or three different ways. For example, you may decide to (a) withhold a service, such as routine troubleshooting, (b) deliver a general comment that identifies the thing you value, and (c) offer your transgressor the loan of a magazine article that is relevant to your issue in some way.

• Commit to this strategy. That is, be sure to recognize that you have deliberately decided to behave indirectly, have identified the most important things that need to be communicated, have overdetermined the message by delivering it in several ways, and have identified a specific length of time during which the process will spin itself out.

• When the time for this process is concluded, conclude the process. Specifically comment to yourself, *It's over now.* You have done as much as you could. Hanging on to your anger any longer will most likely be self-defeating rather than effective.

### Problem No. 6: When Your Anger Hits the Wrong Target

Many people do not get angry either directly or indirectly with the person who caused them harm. Yet they don't keep their anger completely to themselves either. Recall Marianne, the publishing house editor who let her colleagues know she was angry, but never the people who caused her anger. Or Martin, the federal court bailiff who lets no one at work know he's angry but has been known to keep his wife up half the night while he lets off steam.

Farley, the stockbroker who blamed fitness proponents when he tripped over his boss's briefcase, presents a special case of the kind of problem we're concerned with here. Unlike Marianne, Martin, and most others who share the discomforts associated with this problem, people like Farley are unaware that they are really angry with someone other than the person or situation they are currently blaming. They create even more problems for others than do such people as Marianne and Martin. And creating problems for others is the major problem experienced by most people who do not direct their anger toward its source or who keep it to themselves but choose to express it to others who have had no hand at all in creating the offensive incidents.

Farley's version of this approach is one that is not commonly used. Most of us have displaced our anger onto a "safer" object at some time in our history, but few people use this way of dealing with anger almost exclusively, as does Farley. While strategies for dealing with the problems created by Marianne's and Martin's styles are reasonably easy to develop and use, Farley's difficulties are more complex. People who are habitually unaware of what has motivated their feelings are out of touch with themselves in ways that often cause them many interpersonal difficulties and much personal pain. Usually psychotherapy can help provide insight and strategies for change.

When people such as Marianne and Martin are aware of who has offended them and instigated their anger but habitually choose to deal with it by sharing it with confidants rather than express it to the offenders, they often keep their anger for a longer period of time than do others, and they may alienate their listeners as well. Marianne, for example, feels that her colleagues at work probably refer to her angry outbursts as griping. They become weary of hearing about her anger at her boss and wish she would put the anger where it belongs—in her boss's office. But Marianne is reluctant to do that. Why? And what can she do to change?

SUGGESTIONS

Most of this problem is located within the interactions between the offended person and the friends and relatives who support his or her style. Some spouses, for example, agree that dealing with work frustrations within their marriage is one of the important benefits that marriage provides. When this is the case, there is no problem for the person who brings anger home. At work some colleagues become good friends and are more than willing to absorb one another's anger because that makes it possible for both persons to manage in difficult times and circumstances on the job. So this style constitutes a problem only if an angry person's listeners get weary of hearing or if the offended person hangs on to anger too long because there was really no satisfaction gained through sharing with noninvolved co-workers, friends, or family members. Unfortunately in some cases the angry person doesn't get enough feedback to know that the griping can become offensive.

• Take some time to consider the reasons why you are reluctant to let your transgressor know you are angry and what the violation has been. Look for patterns across the past few years. Have you always operated this way, or is this approach one that you use only with a particular person who offends you at work or a particular *kind* of person? Make a list of all those things you think you gain and lose by not sharing your opinions and anger with the offending person. Evaluate the list.

• Read through the descriptions of work-related anger styles in Chapter Two. Decide which styles you might prefer over the one you now rely on.

• Think about those times in your work history when you may have displayed behaviors that are associated with the style in Chapter Two that seems most preferable in your opinion. Later during this time imagine yourself behaving in that way on the job with a specific person who has offended your values or work in the past. Be as detailed in constructing your picture of yourself as you possibly can.

• Commit to using the strategies you have chosen for two or three weeks. At the end of the initial period review your results. Decide what your greatest successes were and in what ways you need to refine your developing strategies if you are to make the style you have chosen a habitual one. Try another period of practice.

• Recycle through the previous steps until you have a style that satisfies you.

### Problem No. 7: When Keeping Anger Makes You Sick

A number of people keep anger to themselves so habitually that physical ailments result from time to time. Richard, the political public relations expert who believed that his job required him to stifle his angry feelings, became susceptible over the years to recurrent gastric ailments. Both he and his physician became convinced that his methods of dealing with work-related anger (and anxiety and fear) were at least implicated, if not causal.

People like Richard come to the conclusion that a few aches and pains from time to time are an acceptable price to pay for the privilege of continuing to create, achieve, manage, and earn. The only serious doubts they may have occur when their stomachs actually hurt, or their heads pound, or their sides ache. When the pain subsides, so does the motivation to do things at work a little differently. Most people who absorb their anger through physical symptoms aren't delighted with the arrangement; they just don't know how to go about making changes.

Some of those who suppress their anger find it hard to believe that the way they deal with anger at work has anything to do with their physical symptoms. The idea that emotions can have that kind of influence on bodily symptoms is a foreign one.

How can people who have developed this style reduce the negative influence of their approach on their physical well-being?

#### SUGGESTIONS

Making the connection between physical ailments and anger is absolutely necessary if any change in this style is to occur. People who absorb their own anger in this way need to develop an understanding of just how powerful emotions can be and how their own emotions are currently affecting their bodies. Without this kind of insight the habits of a lifetime will probably prevail.

• If you are giving some serious attention to the description of this problem, it may be that you have already made the first and most important step: a beginning recognition of the relationship between anger and physical well-being in your own life.

• Identify the next few weeks as a period of time when you offer yourself a short course in mind-body linkages. Go to a bookstore or library, and withdraw several books from the psychology, medical, fitness, and self-help sections that discuss in detail the intricate ways in which the emotions and body influence one another. Be sure to read from several sources, rather than a single book since it's usually helpful to get more than one perspective on this issue.

• Visit your family physician or health specialist. Ask him or her about the potential relationship between significant unexpressed anger and any particular physical ailments you might have.

• Review your anger history at work. Pay careful attention to what you *do* immediately after experiencing your own anger. Chart your responses to your own anger across the week following an angry experience on the job. Then identify some physical problems that you are already experiencing that could be associated with not expressing work-related anger.

• Spend the next few weeks carefully observing the connections between the feeling of anger and the physical symptoms you have targeted. Notice how much time elapses after an irritating or angry episode before a given symptom appears. See if you can discover connections between a particular symptom and a particular kind of irritation at work. Look for physical symptoms that occur after tense exchanges with one or two specific persons with whom you work. It will work best if you set aside time for this kind of analysis at the end of each workday for the full trial period. Often a ten- to twenty-minute block of time will be sufficient. The length of time is not quite as important as the regularity of the time.

• Do nothing differently at all at work during the above two stages. Do not try to change your style.

• At the end of the assessment period you should know quite a bit about what situations tend to influence your particular physical ailments. At this point you might sit down with a trusted friend, relative, or colleague who can spend an hour or two with you thinking through how you might approach your work life in general in a different way. This step is not absolutely necessary, but it can be very helpful since it provides access to a different perspective on the issues.

• Decide which style you would like to develop. Consult those problem descriptions in this chapter that will provide you with step-by-step assistance in learning to develop that style. Be sure to add those steps at the end of the process just outlined. Your particular style requires a longer diagnosis stage than some of the others. Discovering what actually goes on before you attempt to change things is crucial for success.

*Problem No. 8: When You Miss Indirect Cues*
*or Too Often Choose to Ignore Them*

One of the major problems with sending messages via indirect cues is that many people can't read subtle signs. Others choose to ignore them. If you are a person who has trouble receiving indirect messages or know that you tend to ignore subtle messages more often than you should, this problem may be one that you wish to focus on. Ignoring or missing anger cues can be very problematic in work situations because irritations and angers build up, and extreme actions are sometimes then taken in order to get the message across. Responses that are way out of proportion to the original offensive events can emerge.

Recall Jed, the auto dealership manager who originally could not pick up on indirect signals. Once Jed's skill in this area had improved, he still did not respond to this type of message because he thought it was a waste of time to communicate anger so circuitously. Jed is not afraid of confrontation and he doesn't really understand the goals and motivations of those who are. Therefore, he now routinely ignores any criticism that is not put to him directly. Some people who share Jed's current approach still wish they wouldn't go quite so far with it. They would prefer to have more response options available to them when confronted with other people's anger at work.

SUGGESTIONS

The steps outlined below are divided into two sets. The first set has been designed to help those who wish to develop their skill in picking up on indirect messages. The second set is provided for those who are fairly good at reading indirect cues but want to get better at responding to them.

RECEIVING INDIRECT MESSAGES

1) Spend a couple of weeks developing an appreciation for the positive consequences of choosing this method—rather than a more direct approach—for communicating angry feelings. This step will help you a great deal in learning to pick up on this kind of signal. Ask some

people whom you respect who tend to use this style *why* they prefer it and how they would prefer people to respond to their indirect strategies.

2) During this same time period reread those sections in Chapters Two and Three that describe various approaches to an indirect style. Notice what specific methods people use to get their angry points across.

3) Identify a period of time for beginning to work on the development of your skills in this area. During these weeks watch for indirect messages of the type your friends have described and of the type illustrated in previous chapters in this book. When you suspect that a circuitous message has been aimed in your direction, ask the person if your suspicions are correct. Many people find that the resulting conversations will elicit important feedback about the accuracy of the guesses and contribute to overall better communication at work in general.

4) During this period review the events of the workday each evening. Scan the day for evidence that someone might have been trying to communicate with you indirectly.

5) During the following few weeks proceed at work on the basis of what you have learned. By this time it should not be necessary to be as tentative as you were during the previous weeks. You probably won't have to solicit as much feedback about the accuracy of your interpretations. Assume that you have a reasonably good emerging ability to grasp the indirect message. The decisions you make concerning how you want to *respond* to indirect messages are, of course, not at issue here.

Remember, many indirect messages are ineffective because people are not particularly good at sending them. If you fail to receive one, the fault may lie with the other person's inability to get the message across, or it may be a shared responsibility.

---

STRATEGIES FOR DEVELOPING
RESPONSES TO INDIRECT ANGER

---

1) Learn to appreciate better the advantages of an indirect approach in some situations. Talk to people you respect who use this approach at work. Find out what they gain from avoiding confrontation. Most will say that an indirect approach requires more time and that additional time itself often eases a situation.

2) Use two or three weeks as a practice period. Use the image of dancing as you observe an indirect message and offer an indirect response in return. Pay attention to the rhythm that is created by two people who are mutually involved in sending indirect messages.

3) The key to developing flexibility in this area lies in developing an appreciation for this method of communication—at least in some circumstances or with some kinds of people. You may find the appreciation does not emerge, at which point you can decide whether or not this strategy is for you.

### Problem No. 9: When You Respond to Anger with Aggression

Some people are outraged when someone directly expresses anger at work. Recall Nancy, the head nurse who tends to react strongly when people send angry messages that they are displeased with her. Like Nancy, many people have short fuses when someone confronts them at work.

A large number of people tend to react this way, and the basis of their reaction is often surprise and confusion. These people assume that the workplace is for best efforts and best dispositions. They believe that the negative aspects of people's emotions and behaviors belong at home. Added to this assumption is their understanding that they are competent and respected employees. They do not *expect* to do anything at work that is bad enough to merit anger on the part of someone in the work setting, and they are surprised when it happens. Therefore, they wonder, why is someone falsely accusing them?

#### SUGGESTIONS

The key to easing this problem lies in the development of the understanding that no one is expected to be perfect at work and that anger is a normal human reaction to a violation of personal standards and values. At times carefully listening to the reasons why someone has become angry at you will find you understanding and agreeing that you did not do as well in retrospect as you might have done in a given situation. At other times this understanding will not come because you possess somewhat different values from your accuser.

In either of these cases permanent damage to the relationship need not result. Since only a communication "problem" may exist between the two of you, the issues may not be critical. Even if you messed up badly, you deserve forgiveness and a second chance. We all do—no less necessarily at work than anywhere else. Finding out what people are angry about will provide good' information from which everyone involved can benefit.

• Go to the psychology and self-help sections of your local library or bookstore. Choose two or three books that discuss the need to be easier on yourself, to understand that messing up from time to time is normal and acceptable.

• In order to begin the change process, decide that for two or three weeks at work you will not respond directly and assertively to either indirect or direct messages of anger.

• Reread the section in Chapter Two that describes David's open and empathic responses to anger. His style allows him to listen to his accuser without becoming defensive in return. Consider adopting some of David's strategies for responding to anger, and add some of those that particularly appealed to you as you read through other descriptions in Chapter Two or elsewhere in this book.

You may have to *control* your anger in order to allow yourself the opportunity to experience other ways of responding. Simply acknowledge to yourself that you are doing that. You have chosen to do so in order to learn something new.

• Identify the next three or four weeks as a period when you will be flexible in your responses to others' anger at work. At times you may wish to respond assertively with angry feelings of your own. At other moments you may wish to respond more passively. You should now have enough flexibility in your behavioral repertoire to consider the merits of each situation and to choose a course of behavior that seems best to you.

### Problem No. 10: When Pulling Out of the Situation
### Just Doesn't Help

The most common method of dealing with personal feelings of anger at work involves just plain exiting the situation or at times huffing off. An overwhelming majority of people in today's work force who feel anger on the job rely on this strategy at least half the time. And just about everybody has experienced this problem at least once during his or her work history. Thus, *the most popular method for dealing with work-related anger seems to be not to deal with it at all,* at least not within the relationship that precipitated it at the moment it's experienced. Like Carla, the software package creator, most people said that they rely on this strategy as frequently as they do because they *just don't know anything else to do at the time.*

As much as anything, most of us use this strategy because we're afraid of the results of our own anger. We would rather stifle our own feelings than risk an aggressive response and the consequences it might engender. So in many situations large numbers of people will decide on a hasty exit so that the anger won't burst through.

Sometimes self-righteous thoughts supported by strong feelings transform a simple exit into something we think of as huffing off. This version of the angry exit is somewhat like putting some effective spin on a tennis serve. We're not simply leaving; we're also intending to make a somewhat aggressive point. But whether or not there's a bit of huff involved in the parting, a predictable set of consequences follows an abrupt exit in response to the emergence of personal anger.

*When we pull out of an angry incident prematurely and abruptly, the other person is left to imagine rather than to understand.* It is difficult to reconnect. Anger seems to hang on longer. And perhaps most important for the goals at work, communication suffers. Time and time again people have commented to us that their worst moments with anger at work occurred when they just left rather than stayed to talk it through. Only a few people said they gained a lot by stalking off. In some cases people reported that the leaving let their offenders know that they thought so little of them that they weren't even worth the energy it might take to give them a piece of their mind. However, most of these people then noted that they did regret having missed the opportunity to make a point, set things straight, clear the air, solve the problem, and so forth. Along with all the others who frequently pull out when angry, they complained that relations between them and their offenders were sometimes strained for days or weeks afterward, with everyone involved acting out of tension and anxiety. Perhaps most unfortunate of all, most people reported that no visible progress on the issues that provoked the anger was made. The best they could manage after the incident was over was a firm promise to themselves never to get angry at work again and to figure out some way to go around their offenders when they were next in the position of having to deal with the same issues.

### SUGGESTIONS

Most people don't like the results of abrupt exits. They just don't know anything else to do in those situations. The most effective approach to this problem is to start imagining yourself behaving in other ways during those confrontations from which you typically exit when your anger rises.

• You might begin by listing those work-related occasions when you left or huffed off when you started to get angry. Carefully note how the issues were resolved during subsequent days and weeks. Make a list of all those consequences you thought were good and all you thought were bad.

• It may help to reread those descriptions in Chapter Two of approaches that you particularly admired or that you thought were uniquely adaptable to your own style.

• Decide how an ideal you might react when angry at work. Picture yourself acting differently from your typical behavior during an angry episode. Carefully attend to exactly what you would say and do as you construct your image of the situation. Compare your image of yourself, as you are now, with the ideal self that you have decided upon. Do nothing differently at work during this image rehearsal stage.

• Identify a period of several weeks or so when you commit to *not* walking out at work if you get angry. You should put a time limit on the episodes. For example, you could commit to not leaving an angry situation for five minutes, allowing yourself that time to practice your newly emerging strategies.

• Commit to reconnecting with your offender within thirty-six hours following an angry episode. You could simply say to the other party, "I think there are some issues we didn't get into the other day that are important; let's decide when the best time to get back into this might be."

• About twice a week for the duration of the trial period take a few minutes to imagine yourself behaving in the way you desire to behave in the future.

• Decide that during the following three or four weeks you will stay with an angry episode as long as need be for things to arrive at the best possible conclusion. Some situations have greater potential than others, depending upon who else is involved, the work environment, and a host of other factors. Remember, your goal is not to solve all anger-related problems at work to your great satisfaction. Rather, it is to conduct yourself in a way that makes you feel better about how you handle your anger.

*Problem No. 11: You Don't Know What Else to Do,*
*So You Do Nothing*

Lots of people just don't know what to do when someone confronts them with anger. Ella, the department store executive, just freezes, often giving her accuser the false impression that she is disdainful of the attack. Clark, and many others like him, do nothing for a while, then eventually just leave. The vast majority of people like Clark and

Ella would much rather do something other than what they are accustomed to doing when someone at work gets angry at them. However, they have no image at all of any other way they might behave.

As we pointed out earlier, most people have not thought about how they *respond* to anger at work. While a fair number of us have given thought to our usual methods of expressing anger, most of us have given our typical responses to anger no attention whatsoever. Occasionally you will hear someone say, "I am not the kind of person to let someone get *to* me." Remarkably remarks such as that are very representative of the entire pool of statements that people come to work prepared to use if someone turns a hot temper in their direction. Most people simply react. Each time someone gets angry, it's probably a surprise. Amazingly, despite their knowledge of human nature and their own experiences to the contrary, most people do not expect others to get angry with them at work—either indirectly or directly.

SUGGESTIONS

Image rehearsal will provide a fairly quick and easy solution to this problem for many people. Since most people have not spent much time thinking through how they would like to respond to angry outbursts or indirect messages at work, simply beginning this process will help a great deal.

• Consider the various ways that one might respond to direct and indirect anger in the workplace. Which of the styles described in previous chapters are most appealing to you and are likely to fit in with your general way of being at work?

• Decide which style might work best for you. Take some additional time to imagine yourself behaving this way in uncomfortable situations at work. Recall an occasion or two in the past when you responded to anger in a way that displeased you. Replay the scenes with you now behaving in a way that fits your desired approach. Be sure to concentrate on images of you responding to indirect as well as direct messages. You will probably need to adopt more than one set of response strategies, depending on the method the angry person chooses to convey his or her feelings to you.

• Over a specific period of time at work respond to indirect and direct anger with new approaches. At the end of this time it is likely you will have developed a much wider range of behaviors that will be available to you in the future as you are met with other people's annoyance and anger on the job.

### Problem No. 12: When Tears Take the Place of Anger

Because we have commented so much on this phenomenon earlier, we simply take the opportunity here to note that this experience is common and problematic for many people. Specific strategies for change are considered later in this chapter.

### Problem No. 13: Special Work Situations
### That Help Create Angry Feelings

In Chapter Nine we talked about time-pressured, undersupplied, and undervaluing work settings, pointing out that environments such as these have more than an average amount of expressed and unexpressed anger. When people must work closely together as they move toward a deadline, emotions are felt and released much more often than they are when things move along more slowly and people work more independently. Frustration and anger also appear more often when there aren't enough critical supplies to go around and when the work and the workers aren't valued by those who control the resources and rewards. Each person's unique style is stressed in environments like these.

No satisfactory solution to the variety of problems found in such settings can be designed for an individual's use. These problems are *system problems,* and it takes a lot of people working together to change things. Solutions can be found, but since they need to be geared toward a system rather than an individual, they are beyond the scope of this book. We suggest, however, that if you work on a daily basis in an environment such as these, it can help to pay careful attention to your typical ways of feeling, expressing, and receiving anger. It may not be possible to adopt strategies that will allow you to function with maximum vitality and dignity in your workplace as a result of the system's problems over which you have little control as an individual. However, developing more effective anger strategies is vitally important for preserving personal health and well-being. These are the situations that can result in burnout if personal needs are consistently ignored.

### A Final Comment on Anger

During the past seventy years or so we have been so concerned about controlling anger in the workplace that we have lost many opportunities to profit from the good things that can flow from healthy anger experiences during the workday. Many people have even lost access to the feeling itself. They feel anxiety, guilt, depression, and even a host of physical ailments, but rarely the anger that can be normally expected to occur in light of the pressures of work in our stressful society.

When expressions of anger hurt people—the senders or the receivers—it is anger gone awry. Usually harm results from anger only when someone's character is attacked, name-calling erupts, or punishing withdrawals of efficiency and good cheer become standard operating procedure. Anger that provokes good communication can clear the air, create understanding, develop creativity, and result in people feeling better—about themselves and those with whom they work. And importantly, the *feeling* of anger itself never hurt anyone else. Only the methods of expressing it have that capability.

## Transforming Tears and Confusion

The primary problem with tears in the workplace is not that they exist but that most people respond to them—their own and those of others—by stopping the action and focusing on the tears. When we take tears as a signal that work-related problems need to be addressed, then the tears themselves are not the problem. Rather, they point to problems that may be interfering with work, blocking personal productivity, interfering with the sense of satisfaction that's central to good employee morale and just possibly the workplace bottom line. In fact, the most common liability people pointed to in discussing the shortcomings of their own styles of crying or responding to workplace tears was that they ended up feeling blocked from effective, personal expression of their own positions on the work issues at hand.

### Problem No. 1: When Tears Take the Place of Direct Communication

Many people we've talked to easily identified a major problem with their own workplace tears: They cry instead of saying what's on their minds. In the midst of work situations with important issues at hand, they find themselves suddenly "reduced" to tears. They may have been groping for words to express their positions or their feelings. They may feel heightened tension because of the importance of the issues or because they perceive their own performances or positions to be "on the line." But as they reach for the words to craft persuasive verbal responses, their feelings—about some or all of the issues involved—rush in and seem to flood out the possibility of coherent verbal statements. They feel "beyond words," as tears well up in expression of the emotions that will not be denied. They often report in retrospect that they came suddenly to assume—in view of the immediately preceding actions or the situation in general—that *whatever* they could find to say was going to be inadequate to the task of conveying what they meant. They assumed that whatever they could say would not be heard, would not be understood.

Frustration often precedes tears that threaten to fill the spaces a crier wanted to fill with persuasive, compelling speech: frustration over a host of small things gone wrong, frustration over the way a situation is moving, frustration over perceived inability to control a torrent of events that are going inexorably along a "wrong" path, in clear contravention of everything that seems sensible to the crier.

For example, Sandy, the youth minister at a large urban church, found herself fighting off tears when her senior minister began the second half of her annual performance evaluation ("Now for the bad news," he had said). She felt her tears coming as a sense of anger and injustice and anxiety rose to the fore.

Sandy was angry because she felt that the criticisms of her performance—she wasn't doing enough liaison work, she was being (perhaps) too much of a "lone wolf" in her job—struck her as particularly unfair. They felt unfair because she had been hired to work with the youth, and she had done that—and well. She'd succeeded in that effort because she had committed all her work time to the "kids." And now, suddenly it seemed to her, new expectations had been added to the mix. No one had told her explicitly about these expectations. But several people appeared to be holding her accountable for not having met them. Her feelings that the expectations themselves were unfair ("Do they want me to add another twenty hours to my work week?") rose up on an urge to cry. She could find no words at that moment to express the combination of feelings swirling inside her. She was supposed to be listening to her senior minister and what he was continuing to tell her after all. But the urge to respond, to cry pressed forward, and she shifted her attention from his words to holding back her tears. The "conversation" went on, filling the room outside her mind. Inside, she raced with conflicting thoughts and strong feelings. She felt guilty over having some of those feelings in the first place; she "shouldn't" be feeling anger after all. And she felt doubt. Maybe they *had* told her about the expectations, and she just hadn't paid attention.

Sandy held her tears back and saved them for later. But her efforts to control them took all her energy during the remainder of the evaluation session.

Sandy now believes she would have been much better off if she'd gone straight to the point right then and asked simply where these expectations had come from. She could have worked then with her senior minister to develop a way of incorporating the new expectations into a manageable work load or eliminating them altogether.

Sandy, of course, is not the only one who has found direct expression of position or feeling held back by a sensation of choking up, a frantic effort to hold back tears, or a flood of weeping. Tom Jeffreys, the health firm executive, found his rationale for saving his old friend and mentor Len from enforced early retirement foundering on a sea of feelings that he couldn't adequately express. In his effort of will to suppress his feelings, to keep threatening tears at bay, he did not say what he wanted to say—about Len or about the ongoing process, in which Patricia and her caustic verbal knife, in Tom's view, were adding unnecessary pressure to an already strained situation.

Like countless thousands of other women and men who've dealt with their own tears at work, Sandy and Tom both found tears crowding forward to take the place of directly expressed feelings and positions.

SUGGESTIONS

In many circumstances tears come to take the place of direct statements of position because so many (often conflicting) feelings about an issue have developed over time. And in the moment that tears threaten, it seems virtually impossible to reduce all those feelings to a simple, succinct statement of position.

• The critical first step for many people in dealing with this problem lies in identifying and expressing positions and feelings "earlier in the game," as they come up, rather than hold them, in effect, for one big moment.

• Take some private time to think through situations in which you've done any form of crying. Remember work situations that have brought you to (or close to) tears. Analyze carefully all the feelings you were experiencing. What was going on in the situation: overload, undervaluing, time pressure, external stress, etc.? Why did tears, rather than statements about your position or feelings, come to the fore? What are the things you wish you had done rather than cry?

• During the next three to five weeks plan to pay careful attention to *all* your feelings at work. It may be that you are experiencing emotions such as anger and anxiety more frequently at work than you suspect. If so, you could be quite susceptible to feeling overloaded if you suddenly find yourself in an unexpected situation that contains strong criticism, rejection of your work, or the imposition of additional demands.

• After identifying which emotions might be implicated in your tearful times, work to establish strategies for dealing more directly with the precipitating feelings. For example, if you have discovered that anger or anxiety is often involved, consult the strategies for change in handling these emotions identified in this chapter. Developing ways of coping with the feelings that lead to tears reduces the likelihood that tears will become a problem for you at work. If precipitating feelings are dealt with more directly and your communication patterns at work have been changed, it is likely that fewer situations will result in tears for you.

• Another critical intervention step is centered in the process of image rehearsal. Many people who find tears taking the place of direct communication get into that spot because they haven't envisioned or planned for any alternative responses. For example, they can't imagine saying, "I'm really angry about this! From my perspective . . ." and going on to state their position. They may know, as did Tom Jeffreys, that things are building up and "getting tight." But they usually simply hope they'll be able to pull it off, to explain their position without letting their feelings show. They may hope that the situation will get better or at least won't come to a head before they've had a chance to get their act together.

Tom didn't envision choking up. But he didn't envision, either, how he *might* deal with the potential for strong opposition to his recommendation about Len. He simply hoped it would go through. When it didn't, he found himself unable to express his many feelings and thoughts about the issue. He choked up. Unlike some people whose tears take over, Tom *was* able to get out a brief statement about his position. But it was not accomplished with the clarity or the persuasiveness that he'd intended. He certainly didn't feel very effective in the delivery of his weak rationale. It was the best he could muster under the circumstances. But if he'd done a little image rehearsal—if he'd planned out for what *might* happen and how he *might* respond to this tricky, emotionally sensitive issue—he would not have found himself without any alternative ways of playing the scene.

• Preparing alternative responses for use in potentially difficult situations is always a good strategy. The next time you have a particularly demanding event coming up, play the upcoming scene(s) over in your mind. Imagine that the decisions you least desire will occur. Then imagine yourself behaving in specific ways that you *want* to, given the negative circumstances.

• It's also a good idea to develop a few general responses for use in problematic situations that may emerge quickly. If you have a repertoire of effective responses for use in such situations, you will be much better able to avoid having your tears take the place of direct communication. For example, you might take some private time to imagine yourself saying out loud in a tense and awkward situation, "I need to check on some things related to this issue; let's get back to this in ten or fifteen minutes." This kind of response allows you to take a few minutes to develop more composure and prepare a more effective response to the issues. You also might imagine yourself saying, "I want to return to this issue later." Or you might tell your colleague that right at that moment you have a stronger need to discuss another set of factors or problems that the two of you have in common.

• The general strategies that you imagine yourself using in situations that catch you by surprise will serve you best if they enable you to gain some control over the situation. When we are struggling to gain control over ourselves—for example, in situations that could provoke tears—almost always we feel we have lost influence over the situations. The sense of being almost out of control does little to help us regain composure. Therefore, make sure that the strategies you imagine using are ones that will help you regain or maintain influence in problematic situations.

• A final response step for this problem focuses on learning that tears do not mean an end to one's ability to speak. Talking through tears, as they're falling and after they've fallen, is a very important skill for anyone who's cried (even one time too many!) and found communication blocked by an assumption that tears preclude discussion. Because being at a loss for words is so common an element of workplace tears—from both the crier's and the observer's perspective—we treat the issue separately below. Tears and coherent communication may be unexpected partners, but they can go together pretty well once you've learned how.

*Problem No. 2: "When I Can't Talk for the Tears
or the Choking Up"*

If you're going to cry, many of us assume, surely you can't talk. It's not only the more obvious criers who've experienced the apparent and uncomfortable truth of this belief. People who merely feel a lump in the throat may know all too well the sensation that incipient tears have just rendered them speechless.

Jennings, the "teddy bear" of a gruff pediatrician, traced part of his decision never to cry to an implicit assumption that he'd be rendered speechless if he ever cried. If he were rendered speechless, he continued logically, he couldn't carry out a very important part of his job: reassuring both his patients and their parents in times of stress. He assumed, as do many people, that the emergence of tears makes an entire situation uncertain, uncomfortable, and out of control. For Jennings, being out of control—even giving the appearance of being out of control—is simply untenable, considering his beliefs about the way he should behave on the job.

Susan, the public relations firm president who dislikes her own tears so intensely, assumes that tears mean she's not "on top of it." As she believes, so she behaves. She struggles to suppress her tears (or at the least to keep them out of sight) because she doesn't want to give anyone the impression that she's not in firm control of her feelings and the situation.

One thing that Susan and Jennings have not considered, though, is that they might cry *and* stay on top of it. They might cry and talk sensibly at the same time. There is nothing inherent in tears that mandates stopping the action.

Criers aren't the only ones who sometimes assume too quickly that crying means you can't discuss an issue reasonably, with care and concern. Kyle, for example, with the disdain that a denier can sometimes muster, disregards tears and tearful people because he assumes that anyone who cries is incapable of saying what's wrong. If someone has a problem, he believes the least he or she could do is "tell you about it instead of blubbering all over the place!" Some of Kyle's disregard for criers may come from the efforts he's made in his own life to suppress "weak" emotions. His opinion of office criers certainly didn't seem to be affected by any reflection on his part about the causes and meaning of his own choking up.

For Kyle, one of the central problems with workplace tears is the fact (as he calls it) that they block productive action. They block productive action in Kyle's experience because the people who've cried in his office haven't *talked* about the problems precipitating the tears, not then and not to him anyway. But Kyle seldom imagines that a problem "reduced" to tears can—or should—be resurrected in speech. He doesn't think that a legitimate office problem might reside under those tears.

Almost always, when people feel speechless around their own or others' tears, it's partly because of an assumption that the tears are *not* an integral part of the ongoing interaction. People assume, rather, that the tears are something to be fought, stopped, and quickly forgotten.

But tears, taken as part of a discussion of problematic issues, can increase productive work involvement. Before that can happen, however, those who believe that speech is blocked by tears (present or threatened) must begin to rethink the relationship between tears and talking.

They need to rethink that relationship as did Anne, the newspaper editor, who finally decided that tears were simply bound to fall during some of her working days. She decided subsequently that if tears were going to fall, they'd create much less confusion, attention, and work stoppage if she developed the habit of excusing herself briefly—by turning around or leaving—and returning almost immediately to the situation with as much explanation of the tears as she deemed necessary. She learned to talk through her tears, to identify her feelings, to the extent that they were relevant to the business transaction at hand, and to state what, if anything, she wanted from the others involved. Sometimes what she wants is simply the resumption of business; at other times it involves a change in direction or decision. By learning to talk through and around her tears, she got the benefit of some tension release as tears spilled and the benefit of behaving true to her own style—and the benefit of continued work.

Anne learned to do this by following a series of steps that involved reassessing some of her attitudes toward office tears and developing some new behaviors. Her process included the steps below.

### SUGGESTIONS

Some of the strategies presented below have been designed by acting coaches who teach people how to talk while crying when they are onstage. These techniques can be useful for all people who want to continue communicating even though they are shedding tears on the job.

• Analyze the situations you've been in when tears threatened or actually fell. Did you leave the situation and cut off talk? Did you apologize for the tears or try to cover them up? Discern what your most common attitudinal and behavioral response to your own tears is. Know which crying style you most commonly use (see Chapter Five). Have you tended to assume that tears preclude talking? Do you behave in ways that lower the possibility of talking about the issues underlying the tears?

• Think about the proposition that tears can be a useful and accept-able sign of a problem that needs to be solved. Spend some time discuss-ing this position and the specific issue with friends and colleagues.

• Imagine removing the focus from yourself if you become tearful at work. In other words, imagine that you are not concerned about how "awful" you might look as you cry. Imagine that the observer is not particularly concerned with how you appear at that moment. As you practice these images, imagine that the focus of the interaction is *not* on your appearance as you cry and is *not* on your tears but, rather, is directed toward the important *issues* under discussion. The most im-portant thing occurring is not your tears. The issues are much more important than the tears. They are certainly much more important than your appearance at that particular moment.

• When you next find yourself on the verge of tears at work, do a quick inventory of your feelings that seem to produce the urge to cry. Similarly, produce a quick inventory of the *issues* that are motivating your tearful feelings the next time tears threaten at work. Choose one feeling or one issue to begin talking about during the tearful interaction. Which issue or feeling you choose is not critical. What matters is that you focus the interaction *off* your (incipient) tears and on to the work-related matters of importance.

• If necessary, take this discussion in stages. Suggest to the others involved that you take a break from the discussion for a while, with a fixed point of return to continue consideration of the issues or problems.

• Think about the fact that speaking while feeling tearful is not impossible. Many people, notably actors and actresses, accomplish this on a regular basis. Many of their techniques are adapted below.

• In the beginning it will be best to affirm that you *can and want* to talk through the tears. Remind yourself that the tears do not mean that you are out of control or that the situation has gotten beyond you. Tell yourself quickly and firmly that you *can and want to continue the interaction through the tears.*

• Take a deep, diaphragmatic breath, more than one if needed. When you breathe deeply into the diaphragm and then expel the air, you literally quiet the quivering of your vocal cords. You make it physically possible to speak. One of the reasons many people perceive that they cannot speak when they're crying or choked up is that the tension they're experiencing is manifested in the vocal cords. When the vocal cords tense and quiver, speaking becomes very difficult, if not impossible. Take a deep breath all the way into the diaphragm, and then expel the air. When you do this fully, you'll reap the double advantage of releasing some of the tension and quieting the vocal cords.

• Focus your attention on identifying and then performing one or more quick physical actions. These actions should be very simple and involve specific movements. Tell yourself, for example, to stand up, and then stand up deliberately. Or tell yourself, "Open the drawer, and take out the file on this issue," and then, again deliberately, do so. Or tell yourself, "Walk to the window," and do so. Or say, "Take a notepad out of your briefcase and write," and then do so. The point is to focus your attention on a simple physical action that is somewhat related to the ongoing interaction and that you can accomplish easily. The action should be simple because all your attention at that moment should be centered on directing yourself to do the specific physical action and then doing it. This simple sequence of giving yourself an order to move and then moving to do it has at least four beneficial consequences. It takes your attention away momentarily from your tears and your distress. It orients your attention outward to a very specific, immediate, achievable goal. It affirms for you—and you are your most important audience at this moment—that you are maintaining a share of influence and control in the situation. And it provides time for developing your second quick-action step.

• Focus your attention next on identifying one element (and *only* one!) of the problem situation that you will speak about first. This short step is different from the physical-action step above but is equally critical. Many people find themselves choking up or in tears because issues have built to a point where they feel overwhelmed. The tears come as response to the perception that the situation has become too complicated for words. The point here is to identify just *one* of the several issues or feeling that may be involved. Begin your talking by stating that point. Remind yourself that you don't have to solve the whole problem immediately. Remind yourself that you don't have to explain your position fully with the first five words out of your mouth. Identify a place to begin the talking, and begin.

• Most people will probably alternate physical-action steps with talking steps as they continue discussion of the problem(s) that precipitated their tears. And of course, taking slow, deep diaphragmatic breaths as needed may continue throughout the process, too. Your choices will depend largely on various aspects of your situation and your own decisions about pacing yourself through the discussion. The important point is to take these short action steps in the ways—in whatever number and in whatever order—that best enhance your ability to continue, through the tears.

• Image rehearsal, of course, can make an important contribution here, too. Playing out in your own mind—in advance of a potentially tense and tearful situation—what actions you *might* take will be immensely helpful if and when you find yourself in such a situation. One older manager said that he realized, after he quit smoking, how often he had used the smoking ritual as an intermission, a brief and culturally acceptable time out from tense situations. He recounted that he would pull out the pack of cigarettes from his pocket, pull out one cigarette, pull out a pack of matches, light the cigarette, smoke, and exhale (all with a thoughtful expression on his face!) before he really had to say something about the issues at hand. On more than one occasion, he told us, he had used that break time to regain control, to formulate a response. In these days of escalating awareness that the health risks of smoking probably outweigh the intermission benefits, this manager (and, we suspect, thousands of others like him in workplaces across the country) found himself looking for other ways of making time and space for collecting his thoughts in tense situations. Image rehearsal— thinking of and then mentally practicing simple physical actions and statements appropriate for you and your work setting—can go a long way toward giving yourself a repertoire of resources on which to draw for those occasional (or even frequent!) times when tension threatens your speaking voice and draws you into tears.

Think of tears as a beginning, not as an end—as a sign of commitment and investment, not as weakness. Imagine yourself *talking* about the work-related problem that precipitated your emotional reaction, rather than focusing on the tears and apologizing for them.

### Problem No. 3: When Control of the Situation Seems "Gone with the Tears"

Susan, president of her own public relations firm, had a strong and earnest desire never to cry at work. You may recall that her denier style saw her shedding workplace tears on a few, but very memorable, occasions. She has cried at work, and she hates it. She never lets people know about these tears or see them, if she can help it. And usually she can help it. ("It's one of the advantages of being the boss," she said with a smile when we asked her about it.)

In her early years on the job Susan saw others cry on occasion but never saw any good come of the tears. Workplace tears, she grew to believe, are fundamentally opposed to success in her line of work or most lines of work for that matter. If you cry, "you might as well write yourself out of the picture," she told us.

In many ways Susan's problem with tears—a problem she shares with many, many workplace criers—does not lie in a belief that she's incapacitated by the tears. She *knows* that she gets the work out, that her tears are really a small aside, an incidental event, even when they do fall. Her problem lies rather in her belief that tears wash away her chances of retaining or sharing control in a situation. She assumes that tears automatically put someone else in charge. Without even thinking about it, Susan and others like her assume that in shedding tears, they become "babies"—small, helpless, out of control. They don't challenge the assumption but allow it to take over. Not wanting to be seen as weak, "like a baby," they fight off the tears, they send others away, they beat hasty retreats to the nearest rest rooms. They do not want to be out of control, and they don't want to be *seen* as giving up control. And so they turn their attention to the tears and struggle to suppress the presumptive evidence.

But do tears automatically wash control and influence right out of a crier's life? Not if the person who's struggling with tears does not *give it away.*

SUGGESTIONS

The first key to solving this problem lies in imagining and then practicing the belief that tears are another, valid expression of emotion. A second key involves acknowledging that *if* you shed tears, you also need to tell the other people involved in the interaction what you want—what the problem is and what you want them to do in the immediate situation.

• Putting all your energy into efforts to control your tears is often disastrous. When people are focusing on themselves, they usually find it very difficult to have any influence over the rest of the situation. If you find yourself facing tears on a future occasion at work, focus your energy not on your tears but on the *situation,* including the issues at hand. Let the tears fill your eyes if necessary. Let the tears fall if need be. Your task should be to get on with the work. And usually, in order for quality work to proceed, good communication must take place. You will need to let the other person know your emotional and "rational" position at that moment. If you stay in the interaction, you will be maintaining influence.

• Be sure to tell the observer(s) what issues need to be on the agenda as far as you are concerned. Whenever possible, enumerate these issues—i.e., let your listener know that there are three basic problems (or two, or whatever) that have resulted in your strong reaction. Make sure that each of the problems gets some "airtime" in subsequent discussion.

• Let the observer know whether you can be assisted by something he or she might offer—e.g., a tissue or a few moments to collect your thoughts. Make sure that whatever assistance you accept from someone else is comfortable for you. If the offering is not suitable (e.g., if you don't want to take a break "until you feel better" or don't want pats on the back), be sure to say so. But then be sure also to say what you *do* want. The latter step, of course, will be much easier if you've thought in advance of the ways an observer of your tears might be helpful.

• If you conclude that your observer is having a great deal of trouble allowing you to maintain influence and control in the situation, comment on that fact. Tell the observer that *your tears are taking care of you in their own way and that you prefer to ignore them.* You might also suggest that the conversation be postponed until the observer's awkwardness over your tears has subsided. Avoid letting another person's inability to react effectively to your tears control the entire situation. If you break from the interaction, schedule another meeting before leaving that encounter.

• Again, image rehearsal is an especially effective tool for this kind of tear-related problem. Take some private time to imagine yourself retaining control of a situation *while* you let your body react physiologically through the release of tears. Imagine yourself focusing on the issue at hand rather than on yourself or your tears. If your observer displays genuine awkwardness or confusion or offers to assist you, visualize yourself responding in such a way as to refocus the event away from your tears and back to problems at hand. Avoid the tendency to be overly concerned with the other person's response or with the tears themselves. Imagine yourself assuming that the tears are a positive event, one that indicates commitment and investment and reveals a need to repair damaged lines of communication.

### Problem No. 4: "When I Want to Feel More Accepting of My Tears at Work"

Some employees can and do take advantage of an ability to save their emotions until later. When they feel a situation pressing them toward tears, they seem able to turn on a hold-it button, which keeps the tears at bay. Other employees for a variety of reasons cannot hold their tears back once they've formed. Their tears simply come forth wherever they are, sometimes despite earnest and frantic efforts to hold them back.

Several people from both groups—those who feel they can and those who feel they can't suppress tears until later—expressed a wish to be "less hung up on the silly things," in the words of one person. She shared her opinion that her tears weren't nearly as bad, probably, as all the effort and attention she focused on trying to stop them, or apologizing for them, or scurrying around to "smooth things over" after they came. It seemed to her, she told us, that if she could just let her tears come and then get on with things, her life and the lives of others who happen to be around when her tears come would be much easier.

Her sentiments were certainly shared by Carol, the fashion buyer who had moved over the years from profound shock and embarrassment about her every-now-and-again tears to a point of accepting them. She worked on accepting them after it had become obvious to her that crying was simply something she does every now and again and that going into a prolonged escape routine every time tears came to her eyes was going to necessitate more time, struggle, and logistical effort than she wanted to spend on essentially nonproductive action.

Larry, the department store manager who found himself in private-office tears after a bitter encounter with a new superior in his firm, observed with surprise some weeks after our initial interview that if the tears hadn't "waited" until he was alone, he "would've had to do something about them right then." He didn't want to be embarrassed by any tears, that was for certain. But when he realized that some people—who are competent and on top of things—find tears coming in public, he said, "I guess they just have to accept them. And then get on with things." He added, "I'd better figure out how to do that if I ever need to!"

SUGGESTIONS

Since so much of the problem is centered in *attitudes* toward crying, identification of the desire to become more accepting of one's work-based tears provides an important first step in the process. As soon as you develop the *desire* to become more accepting of occasional workplace tears, that acceptance has already begun to occur.

Looking tearful or crying does not necessarily mean the loss of influence or the end of a career. The tears are not what matters. What *does* matter is what *one does with the tearful experience.* Heretofore many who have shed tears at work have invested tearful behavior with far more meaning than it has. If a crier invests tears with a great deal of meaning, the observer often sees an open invitation to make more of the tears, too. Simple acceptance of the tears, combined with strategies for using the emotional moment to work on the important work-related issues involved, will often result in more positive outcomes. These positive outcomes, in turn, are likely to promote change in desired and productive directions. The adage "Nothing succeeds like success" will be particularly true for those who have decided they want to become more accepting of their occasional tearful experiences at work. In order to get to the stage of experiencing "success" in the face of tears—in this case the ultimate strategy for improvement—we suggest the following specific steps.

• Talk to people who share an interest in this important work-related issue. (There may be many more of these people around than you originally suspect!) Find out what their attitudes are toward their own tears at work as well as their attitudes toward the tears they observe. There are numerous competent people in today's work force who occasionally weep at work. As you discover firsthand that many people you respect have had experiences similar to yours, you're likely to become more accepting of your experiences. This may be a difficult step for you to take if you're unaccustomed to discussing "private" issues with others at work. If so, and if you want to try it, select one person whom you trust well for your first efforts in this direction.

• Read through the strategies enumerated in the discussions of other problem areas in this chapter. Many of them will help you develop ways to improve communication when you feel choked up or tearful. Developing these strategies will be very helpful in meeting your goal of attitude change because they will allow you to avoid many of the common negative consequences of tears at work.

• Image rehearsal will be very valuable. Picture yourself retaining influence while in a situation that might produce tears. Imagine yourself telling an observer that your tears are not the important thing to concentrate on at the moment. Imagine yourself focusing on the *issues* rather than the tears. Imagine you and the observer being relatively unconcerned with the tears or looking upon them as a sign of commitment and vitality. If you take your tears as a sign of commitment rather than a suggestion of incompetence, you'll have come a long way toward accepting and dealing productivity with workplace tears.

### Problem No. 5: *"When I Absolutely Don't Want to Cry"*

Throughout our discussion of workplace tears we've emphasized the importance of understanding tears and understanding where they come from. We've emphasized, too, the importance of treating tears as signs of issues that need to be resolved if optimally productive and satisfying work is to continue. We formulated this position after our discussions with our original research participants several years ago, and we've continued to find support for it in more recent interviews, almost all of which have pointed with striking similarity to two basic ideas.

First, tears rarely, if ever, come "for no reason" at all. They emerge or threaten to flow at work when problems block the smooth and expected flow of productive activity. Some people we spoke with had shed workplace tears over personal issues (e.g., critical illness in the family), but even then they experienced at least some of the tears as coming from frustration and worry about getting the work out in the face of powerful distractions.

The second observation—not made quite as frequently but significant for its implications—was that many highly competent and professionally well-regarded people have experienced workplace tears that "just came." They felt tears forming on a tide of strong emotional investment, commitment, and concern. And suddenly their tears were out in the open.

As a consequence, much of our focus in this chapter on problems has centered not on suppressing tears but on dealing productively with them if and when they come. We have not emphasized suppressing tears, or putting them down, or turning them off at all costs. We have not emphasized suppression strategies because we have come to conclude that in most cases suppression efforts are counterproductive since energy is directed from the work to one's self.

Nonetheless, there are times—even for those who accept and deal well with workplace tears—when we just don't want any tears around. Deborah, for example, the police detective who accepts her tears, was adamant that she did not and would not let tears spill when she's with the "public." And Vernon, the postal supervisor, had very strong beliefs about not letting tears show when he was with employees or customers.

In other words, in some circumstances *not* crying may feel like a highly desirable course of action—even if you're committed to dealing more openly with emotions and the tears that sometimes accompany them than most of us have traditionally thought possible.

So we offer suggestions here for keeping tears down during those times. In all circumstances, however, we strongly encourage you to evaluate quickly whether any given situation is really one in which you *should* suppress your tears. If it is such a situation, and if you're among those who can hold tears back, the suggestions for increasing your control over the settings and timing of incipient workplace tears may be helpful.

Most of these suggestions are geared toward urging you to make situational decisions quickly. Eliminating an emerging physiological response is not easy; it requires deliberate and prompt intellectual intervention. The suggestions below provide you with simple techniques for achieving a goal: the elimination of the urge to cry.

• As you experience the possibility of your own tears at work, ask yourself if you want to put your energy into controlling your tears (i.e., eliminating them) *or* into dealing with the situation that has precipitated your emotional response. *It is very unlikely that you can give energy to both.* Many people who try to do both report having failed at both; the issues are not dealt with, and the tears come anyway. Preparation for change involves planning to ask yourself this question each time you are on the verge of choking up: Do you want to concentrate your energy on the problem *or* on controlling your tears?

If you are not dealing with the problem that precipitated your tearful feelings when you first feel the tears coming, the answer is probably an easy one: You'll likely want to control the tears. For example, you may be in your next meeting and discover that the full impact of a previous event is beginning to hit you, and you realize that you're choking up. If the precipitating problem is not an issue in the present meeting, you may well quickly decide to put your energy into stopping the tears, into "controlling yourself."

Whatever you decide and for whatever reasons you arrive at that decision, go with it. It is usually very difficult to change strategies midway during emotionally precarious moments. This is true no matter what emotion is involved (e.g., anger or anxiety), and it is almost always true when tears at work are involved.

• Many people we have talked with reported that these strategies "work" for them. All involve shifting your attention from your tears to something else in order to eliminate the urge to cry.

a) Focus your attention on an object in the room. Examine it methodically and intensely. Begin to free-associate with that object: Name for yourself all the objects you associate with that one.

b) Call up a powerful and pleasant memory, and concentrate on it for a few moments. Have a store of a few such memories ready for just such occasions.

c) Engage in some private, pain-inducing actions—like digging your shoe heel into your foot, biting your tongue, digging your nails into your palms—in order to get your mind off the potential tears. Needless to say, we have many qualms about recommending that you engage in pain-producing techniques in order to eliminate the desire to cry. However, many people have reported to us that they engage in these activities in order to prevent tears, and they find this kind of strategy can be effective.

• Work to cut down the number of times you find yourself close to tears because your feelings have grown too intense for words or because too many feelings have piled up on one another before you expressed them and tried to solve the offending circumstances. This will involve identifying your emotions earlier in the process and expressing them earlier, when they're not yet so intense or complex.

• Escape strategies are effective for some. Excuse yourself for a specified period of time (preferably brief) and then return.

a) If the interruption can be only a short one and if you have a suitable space available, you might go to the most private place you can find and scream as loud as you can! This can be especially helpful if anger underlies your urge to cry. However, most people don't have such a soundproof private spot. If you can get to a private place even without soundproofing, you might go through the motions of screaming and gesturing (frantically if you want to). We recommend these strategies for occasions when you only have a brief respite from the situation because they are likely to be effective considering that they involve active and dramatic use of your body and thus permit quick energy drainoff. If you have only a few minutes in your break, it's usually best not to let the tears begin to come. For many people a minute or two for tears is simply not enough time.

b) If you have a longer period of intermission available to you, seek a private location and allow the tears to do what they can do well: cleanse, release, and clarify.

*Problem No. 6: When Everyone in the Office Has Seen the Tears*

During our interviews, especially among people who work in relatively open "public" office spaces, there emerged a problem that had little to do (on the surface anyway) with the crier or the immediate responder. As one journalist explained in a voice heavy with weariness and feeling, "*I* could do just fine with my tears. I think my editor could, too, to tell you the truth, even though I know he doesn't like them very much. What I *can't* handle is the fact that twenty other people see whatever goes on when I'm talking with my editor. And forty more people hear about it, if it involves anything 'unusual.' And you can bet that tears are hot items on the grapevine! This is such a public place," she continued, "you can't do *anything* without everyone else knowing about it, and then talking about it, and then trying to find out 'what really happened.'"

Much of what we seem to fear here is the idea that those with whom we work will evaluate our performance and worth in much less favorable terms once they've seen us shedding those compromising tears. One person recounted in detail the mortification she experienced during a meeting when her voice wavered and trembled as she began a speech intended to "win one" for her position in a department meeting. She just knew, she told us, that everyone present realized how weak and vulnerable and close to out of control she felt at that very moment.

### SUGGESTIONS

In many ways solutions to this problem lie as much in the crier's attitudes toward his or her tears—and the behaviors that those attitudes precipitate—as they do in the reactions of the observers. And equally to the point, one's own attitudes and behaviors are usually more amenable to personal control than are the behaviors of others. The critical issue in dealing with this problem lies in what you think about your tears and how you treat them—when they come and after the fact.

• Take some time to assess your own behavior in tearful episodes. If you're a hider, it may be that your very attempts at secrecy are giving your office grapevine special impetus. If your tears are going to be seen no matter what you do, trying to hide them is probably going to be no more than an exercise in frustration and embarrassment for you. And it may give your unwelcome observers the impression that much more happened than actually went on.

• If you've never acknowledged your tears before and if you've consistently tried to hide them, experiment with carrying your handkerchief conspicuously after a tearful event has occurred, and talk matter-of-factly about the obvious fact that you cried (e.g., "I really felt strongly about that one, strong enough to be worth tears!").

• If you have let your tears be known and still feel that there's too much gossip and speculation about them and the precipitating events, consider letting more information out to various colleagues. By all means, however, don't make a big deal over the tears. Instead, demonstrate by your willingness to be open about them that there's really not so much to them after all. The important point here is not that you fill everyone in on the details but that gossiping often slows considerably when the object of the gossip gets directly involved in providing information.

• Be sure that you follow up on any issues flowing from the episode. This is generally a critically important rule for the productive handling of tears. And it may be especially important if your tears are "everyone's business." Let others know, as you choose to, of your follow-up activity. The point to make with them: Your tears aren't the end of the process. You and the others directly involved used them in a process of problem solving.

• Gossip usually comes and goes. Many people say a lot of things about many of us in our daily lives and work, and we have little control over those thoughts and comments. The important goal for most of us is consistently capable performance. Infrequent episodes of tears, even if they're noted by others, aren't likely to wreak much havoc in most careers, especially if the person who cries moves on—with others in the workplace as appropriate—to deal with the problems that led to the tears.

### Problem No. 7: "When I Have NO Idea What to Do About Someone Else's Tears"

Ron, the television studio technician standing near talk show host Ruth Carden as she burst into tears, felt paralyzed by her weeping. Literally. He knew he should respond and do something, but the right "something" completely eluded him. He struggled with a vague but insistent sense that he should "take care of her"; he was, after all, a man, and men are supposed to help women who cry. But that script, growing out of his adolescence and family history, felt very wrong in this situation. Ruth was not his wife, nor was she his sister. She was a famous television personality, a co-worker, to be sure, but someone he knew only through work. They had no personal relationship on which to base a purely personal response. What he might do in responding to his sister, he decided very quickly, definitely would not work here. He was embarrassed even to think about the reactions of his colleagues if he actually went over to her, put his arm around her, and told her that it was going to be OK. But to stand there and watch her seemed so callous. Worse, it made him feel like a voyeur. But what would those farther removed from the scene think of him if he stood like a bump on a log (*An interpersonal idiot!* he thought desperately), doing nothing in the face of obvious need?

ιys call for personal, nurturing responses. This *may* be true within
:onfines of family and personal life. But tears shed at work are most
uently shed over work-based issues. And work-based problems do
often, if ever, need nurturing as a first line of response. To be sure,
/eying concern and care may be a fine accompaniment to a more
tantive response to workplace tears. But the substance of a work-
e response must lie not in simple comfort but in *identifying and
ng the underlying problems.*

• Assume that the crier is expressing something about a work-based
»lem through the tears. The crier probably does not want you as the
rver to engage in a guessing game about the problem any more than
r she needs you to offer a hug as your first and last response to the
»de. The crier often most needs to hear the question What is the
»lem here, and how can we get to the bottom of it? And then the
· needs time, during a break or while you wait, to formulate the
ines of the problem.

Give both these ideas some thought. Allow them to replace the
»n unconscious) assumption that you need first and only to take care
ιe tears and then the crier. Envision past times of observing tears.
/ would you have changed your response behaviors if you had
med that *problem solving,* rather than taking care of the crier, was
»roper focus? Envision and practice responding to tears by saying
ζs that reflect these principles (e.g., "I can tell that you're invested
ιis issue. It looks like we've got a problem to solve here. How can
»egin to figure it out?).

• Develop alternative plans for your own specific responsive actions
ι someone at work cries in front of you. These may be as varied
fering to get the crier a tissue, asking the crier if you can get back
ther in five minutes to discuss the problems at hand, or simply
ιg what, if anything, the crier wants you to do right then. The
»rtant point here is to feel personally comfortable with your initial
»nse behaviors and to facilitate the process of problem solving.
al imagery and rehearsal around putting these responses into prac-
will be helpful.

• Work to give at least half the control in the situation to the person
's crying. Remember, the tears are his or her expression of strong
ιgs. It's not up to you to know or to guess what the feelings and
· source are. If the crier is going to keep up his or her end of the
·action, the crier must retain some power in the situation. Putting
»nsibility for the next step—beginning further discussion of the
lem at hand—into the hands of the crier will go a long way toward
:ing this goal,

Ron's inability to think of something to do ~~d~~
fact that no possibilities had entered his mind.
"knew" for tears felt completely inappropriate i~~n~~
didn't know what *would* fit. Ron, like many peo
spoken, dislikes workplace tears in large part bec~~a~~
and inept when confronted with them.

SUGGESTIONS

The critical issue for Ron and for anyone wit
understanding—and accepting—the reality that t~~a~~
is not the observer's problem. Participating in the
tions to the problem that precipitated the tear
purview of the observer's responsibilities. But eve
not the party responsible for "taking care of the t~~e~~
of" the crier either.

There is a big difference between taking care
ticipating in the development of solutions to a pro
crier are the signal of a problem. The observer's
lies in helping identify the problem that needs to b
sibility for the "uninvolved" observer may beg~~i~~
simple question to the observer: "Is there someth
Or "Is there something you want me to do?" Th
that the observer *wants* to help out in some way
want to help, the best course of action for the u
probably to stay uninvolved. Turn attention else~~w~~
for further action from the crier. A person crying
or wants a personal response that begins and ends
from co-workers who aren't also close friends.

If you're one who is more directly involved i
your responsibility as an observer usually lies
suggested for an uninvolved observer ("Is there s
help?") and then, importantly, in committing t
solving process if the tears grow out of work issue~~s~~
that may be helpful in breaking through the sens
idea what to do" include the following:

• Take some time to rethink your attitudes a~~t~~
Remember that some people express emotions th
people rarely turn them on to make a point. Do t~~h~~
tions with friends and colleagues as well as in y

• One of the attitudes most commonly under
grounded in the erroneous assumption that tea

### Problem No. 8: "When I Feel Angry or Manipulated by a Co-Worker's Tears"

Even a wish to help a crying person is sometimes joined by a vague sense of irritation about the crying or by faint musings about manipulation. Sometimes people wonder, as did the news anchor Samuel, just why the crier "let" those tears fall.

Samuel felt some sense of concern for his colleague, Ruth, who shed the tears. But by far the greater part of his energy was allocated to figuring out what she wanted to get by letting those tears out. He grants that tears are sometimes shed innocently, even at work. But he assumes that there's usually something else going on underneath them.

Mary, the station executive, also felt some negative reactions to Ruth's tears. From the relative privacy of the control room, as she watched Ruth crying, Mary responded at first with amazement and then with no small amount of quiet outrage. Mary's assumptions about the meaning of tears at work ("People who cry at work aren't competent!"), the implicit challenge to her prior evaluation that Ruth *was* a highly competent professional, and her commitment to a political stance that values women who "make it playing by the rules" converged—after a brief pause for amazement—in anger. Laced throughout her anger were bits of other feelings as well: anxiety about her own ability to judge people (how had she judged Ruth to be so capable if Ruth could sit there and weep for all the world to see?) and fear that the progress of women at the station (and in the industry) might be set back by this obvious break from acceptable behavior.

#### SUGGESTIONS

For Samuel and for Mary—and for you, too, if you are one of those who feel a dose of anger entering the mix of their reactions when co-workers cry at work—there are specific things to be done.

• The first is to consider the most frequent causes of tears at work: strong feelings about something that's going on, something perceived by the crier to be a serious, work-related problem.

• Next, recognize that people who cry at work often report that they "can't help" the tears. Far from using tears to get their way in the modern work world, most people who cry at work spend significant time and energy trying to stop the tears or to hide them. In other words, more than likely the tears being shed in front of you on any given occasion are *not* coming from a wish to manipulate you or from willful self-expression.

• There are two concrete steps to take that should result in you and the crier achieving greater understanding of each other's feelings in the situation.

a) *Express your own feelings about the tears.* This is not the same thing as assuming you're right about the crier's reasons for crying. The point here is to present your own feelings of reaction to the tears, saying, for example, "I feel manipulated when you cry," or, "I really begin to wonder what you want when you cry because your tears violate my standards for office behavior." Your feelings are as legitimate as the crier's. If real problem solving is going to take place, the feelings that *both* of you have about the problem and its solutions will need to be addressed.

b) *Get to the bottom of the problem(s) underlying the tears.* For ideas on getting to the bottom of the problem, see Problem No. 7, page 272. If the tears came because the crier couldn't—or felt he or she couldn't—deal directly with the problem (i.e., if your suspicions about manipulation have some grounding in the crier's unwillingness or inability to deal directly with an issue), work together to develop alternative strategies for identifying and solving the problem involved.

### Problem No. 9: "When I'm Just Too Busy to Deal with Tears"

Tears usually fall at the most inopportune times: when there's work to get out, when you've got a deadline to meet, when a client has threatened to switch to a competitor if you're not there with the product now—times, in other words, when slowing down the flow of work is the very last thing you need.

Crying may occur when you don't think you have all the time in the world to spend on the problem-solving suggestions found on the previous pages. "They might work, I'll grant you," said one slowly believing manager, "but the crises around here never happen when I've got time for all that. So what do I do then?"

SUGGESTIONS

What she should do then—and what we'd suggest you do if you find yourself having to cope with co-workers' tears when there's no time to spare—is incorporated in these steps.

• Take another look at the issue of whether you really have "no time" to deal with tears. If the tears are being shed because serious problems are interfering with the smooth flow of work, it's just possible that dealing with the tears and the problems precipitating them will actually be cost-effective. The time spent on troubleshooting the problems pinpointed by the tears may increase, rather than decrease, your ability to get the job done.

• If you really can't stop things in order to deal with tears, develop ways of acknowledging the crier and the problems that probably underlie the tears. For example, "Look, I'm sorry things are this pushed. I know something's not right. I want to work with you on solving the problem[s] just as soon as we can. Tomorrow or whenever this project is finished, I want to sit down together and sort things out." Be alert, though, to cautions from the crier that current conditions might require immediate attention to the events that have precipitated the tearful response. You may need to assess again whether the underlying problems *do* need attention now if the job's going to get done, and done right.

• Follow through on the tearful episode as soon as there is a break in the action. Don't fall victim to the temptation of assuming that once the demands are over, the reason(s) for the tears have disappeared. Check it out. There may be problems involved that you can avoid during the next crisis if you review what went wrong this time.

## Making Anxiety Useful
### Problem No. 1: When Dealing with Anxiety Indirectly (Channeling) Provides Only a Partial Solution

A number of people commented that channeling anxiety into sports activities, aerobic conditioning efforts, hobbies, and productive work that is unrelated to the precipitating problems tended to help a lot—but usually only in the short run. In other words, these activities help make it possible to substitute more comfortable feelings for less comfortable ones, but they do not address the cause of the anxiety. For a while the physiological changes that accompany vigorous physical activity make it difficult to maintain anxious feelings. When one experiences significant feelings of accomplishment, it is similarly difficult to persist with apprehensive and worried feelings.

In an important sense these strategies provide quick fixes that act directly on the anxious emotions but do not act in any way on the *causes* of the uncomfortable feelings. Some people we talked with were aware that they use physical activities in this way. For example, one woman was clearly aware that she ran several miles at the end of almost every day when her anxieties had built up during that day at work. Since she experiences heavy doses of anxiety at work, she found herself running at least twice each week. In well over a year she had not gone running for any reason other than anxiety release. In other words, her aerobic activity was not incorporated into her life as a result of a decision to use running for reasons of cardiovascular fitness. Although she was undoubtedly gaining physical benefits, she had nonetheless begun to use running as a way of *eliminating* something from her life—anxious feelings—rather than of adding something to her life: regular fitness conditioning.

Similar experiences were reported by people who found themselves feverishly engaged in hobbies or other productive activities in an effort to substitute "good" feelings for "bad" ones. A marketing executive we talked with told us that her mother had modeled this trait for her throughout her childhood. Her mother, a homemaker, habitually cleaned house like Superwoman, or rearranged furniture, or made a gourmet meal each time she felt worried or apprehensive. Her daughter had incorporated this trait into her style of dealing with anxiety at the office.

For some the use of these strategies seems necessary. They believe that their work environments are rarely under their own control and that channeling their own anxieties elsewhere or covering them with a burst of work—i.e., controlling or eliminating them—is the best that they can do. Influencing or changing the precipitating situations seems impossible to them.

Other people find that they have more influence than that. Many people we talked with simply hadn't given much thought to developing styles of dealing with their own anxiety that orient them more directly toward the *causes* of the problems. Prior to thinking about these issues, they had simply assumed that anxious feelings are best eliminated. *How* they are eliminated seemed rather irrelevant. Their dominant goal was to get rid of these uncomfortable anxious feelings so that they didn't have negative effects on the quality of life.

SUGGESTIONS

Just realizing that one has been engaging in quick-fix activities is often useful in and of itself. We suggest the following steps:

• Decide why you have been using quick-fix activities. Has it been out of habit? Or have you concluded that direct impact on the troublesome situations is impossible?

• Identify for yourself those situations where using quick-fix activities will continue to be useful. Identify those where taking a more direct approach *might* be effective. Through this process you are likely to realize an important fact: You have a choice. Anxiety, like other emotional experiences, can be useful, and it can often be deliberately channeled in a direction of your own choosing.

• Take a few minutes to imagine the kinds of things you might do if you were to act directly upon the difficult situations that provoke your anxiety. As we pointed out in earlier chapters, visual imagery is a very useful tool for behavior change. It allows you to "see" yourself behaving in different ways. In a sense you provide your own model for yourself as you engage in imaging activities. As always, remember to be as specific as possible as you imagine situations in which you act on an anxiety-producing problem in a different way from the way you now typically do. For example, you may imagine asking a co-worker for an estimate of the time it will take to complete a project rather than just worry that a deadline might be missed.

• Identify a specific period of time for practice of the new, more direct strategy at work. Taking stock of your progress at the end of this period is always helpful. You may need to alter your decisions about which situations can be affected and which cannot. Or you may need to engage in more extended image rehearsal so that a second trial period can be even more successful.

### Problem No. 2: When It Seems Impossible to Think of Anxiety as Useful

There are quite a few people who cannot imagine that anxiety and worry have any useful functions at all at work. Most often these people have been working in very difficult situations for a long time, and their anxiety is chronic. In fact, they are no longer quickly able to associate their apprehensive feelings with specific causes. Anxiety has become generalized to everything that goes on in certain situations or with certain people at work. We have found that it's also often the case that people who think of anxiety as uniformly bad often grew up in homes where anxiety was treated almost as a disease. No one suggested to them any competing ideas about the role of anxiety in life. The individual's responsibility was to figure out how to eliminate anxiety as soon as possible.

Because anxiety seems to have no value for these individuals, they are unable to use it wisely to enhance the quality of their work and the environments in which they labor. They're almost at the mercy of their own anxiety.

People who attend to their apprehensive feelings and use them as guides for locating possible trouble spots often feel they have more control over routine activities at work. If you are interested in developing ways of using anxiety more beneficially, we suggest that you:

• Take some time to reflect on those occasions when your anxiety level tipped you off to an important set of dynamics operating at work. On such occasions it is likely that no one gave you any direct information about difficulties that were emerging. Nonetheless, your feelings of anxiety provided a warning. Such reflection can help you develop a greater appreciation for the benefits that anxiety can bring you on the job. In essence you can begin to use anxiety as an early-warning system.

• Set a specified period of time when you plan to pay closer attention to your feelings of anxiety and worry at work. Once you notice their presence, see how quickly you can make a connection between the feelings and their source. Ask yourself what *use* you can make of this information.

### Problem No. 3: When "Just Reacting" Is a Problem

People who cannot identify a dominant style (or two) that they employ when trying to manage work-related anxiety may well be experiencing the most troublesome aspects of this issue. Those who simply "react" and believe their reactions are not under their own control but largely under the control of the environments they work in are probably genuine victims of their own anxiety from time to time. Most often people who experience this problem just haven't really had the opportunity to *think* about anxiety, its various manifestations, and its functions at work.

For many people just thinking through some of the issues surrounding anxiety at work provides an effective impetus for change.

• Spend some private time reviewing occasions in your work history when your own anxiety provided an effective warning for emerging problems.

• Talk to friends and co-workers about their experiences with anxiety on the job. Find out how anxiety has worked for other people.

• Review the styles presented in this chapter. Design a set of strategies for dealing with personal anxiety that fits for you and the environment you work in.

• Identify a specific period of time during which you plan to practice your new methods of dealing with work-related worry and apprehension. At the end of that time review your progress toward the goal. Identify a second practice period if that seems necessary.


## A Concluding Remark

Anxiety has negative effects in work settings when people ignore it and don't act on it or when individuals pay a great deal of attention to the anxiety itself to the detriment of the work that needs to get done. People's anxious feelings can be distracting to others at the least, and sometimes they are even contagious. A feeling of generalized anxiety can ripple through a department or company, stopping the flow of productive work. Almost always these situations result when people are not using their work-based anxieties in ways that allow them effectively to diagnose problems.


## Changing Styles of Appreciation
### Problem No. 1: "When I Want to Increase Positive Comments and Feedback"

This problem emerges for many people whose styles are based on the assumption that little positive feedback to or from others is needed or warranted in the workplace. Such people may hold styles like Michael's or Troy's, but they may also be like Kim or Al, assuming erroneously that intended and adequate positive regard is simply "getting through" to their co-workers. If you are in this group but find yourself having developed an increased appreciation of the value of positive feedback, the following suggestions should be of some help.

• Your first step should involve an inventory of the ways in which the people around you—your employer, your colleagues, your bosses—enable you to be productive and efficient. What do specific people in your work environment do that increases your well-being on the job? Don't look here only for the extraordinary efforts. Focus in, too, on the everyday tasks that you perhaps take for granted (typing; word processing; getting the mail out; scheduling meetings; good self-expression; etc.). Identify those things that other people in your workplace do that cause you to be better off than you would be if you had to do it all yourself. Whom would you have a hard time replacing? What functions do they perform that enable you to do your job more effectively? Attend closely to your answers to these questions. Begin with one or two co-workers. Make a continuous inventory once or twice a week for a while. This should begin to give you a greater sense of the extent to which your own ability to work well and enjoy your work is dependent on the efforts and commitments of some of the people with whom you work.

• Select one person, preferably someone who is close to you in the work structure and who is not threatening to you for personal or professional reasons. Make note of the things that person does that you might overtly appreciate. Begin with one such thing, preferably a simple issue. Make a simple, direct comment to the person—e.g., "Thanks for getting this out so quickly for me"; "I really appreciate your attention to the chart detail in the report; it looks great." Make the comment directly and simply. In succeeding days continue the process by again giving a compliment on work or a note of appreciation. Keep your comments simplel, direct, and related to work at hand.

• Think about the kind of feedback that *you* like to get from others. What do others in your work environment say to you that increases your sense of being valued, of working well, of being considered a competent person? Is there anything in what you like to get from others that you can use as a model for giving positive, appreciative feedback?

• Think about the fact that others do not and cannot know what you're thinking unless you tell them. When your associates have to guess at your evaluations or reactions, they may impute meanings far from what you intended. You may be the only source of feedback for some of your associates about their performances. Think about the fact that it's very difficult to improve performance in the absence of specific, evaluative information about successes and shortcomings from a knowledgeable source.

• Consider increasing your time for informal interactions with associates (lunch, coffee break, etc.). Such times can provide easy and informal means of communicating compliments and small observations. (Obviously you need to limit your use of these times to those types of feedback that are appropriate for more public consumption. This would not be the forum for delivering a "You tried hard, but this section really needs reworking" message).

### Problem No. 2: "How Can I Show I Care Without Getting Overly Involved?"

A problem that some people have with beginning to express care and appreciation for others in their work environment is bound up in fear that people may not understand, may not respond appropriately. Like Gerald, they imagine that people may think the wrong thing or be embarrassed by positive statements. And for fear of creating an embarrassing situation, they hold back from any but the most perfunctory of positive comments. The problem, of course, is that the absence of positive comment is much more likely to be taken as lack of appreciation rather than as a sign of shyness or fear of embarrassment.

• Assess what your fear is in the situation. Do you fear that any compliment will be taken the "wrong way"? Are you concerned about loss of control of a situation? Do you fear that you and your colleague will be embarrassed if you say anything and so you say nothing? Try to understand the cause of your hesitation.

• Engage in some image rehearsal. Tell yourself that you can stay in control in a situation that opens to admit positive comments between co-workers. Use image rehearsal as a way of envisioning and of mentally practicing honest, direct, unembarrassing communication between you and one or more of your associates. Your images and efforts don't have to be elaborate. In fact, short and simple are often best.

• Try alternatives to face-to-face talking at first. Call an associate to give a quick compliment, or write a quick note at the top of a report. Use methods that will enable you to communicate positive regard and at the same time minimize the possibilities of embarrassment.

• Increase time for interacting informally as suggested in Problem No. 1. Positive comments may be less of a "big deal" if they come in casual interaction, and they may come more freely if more opportunities for interaction are present.

*Problem No. 3: "When I Want to Increase*
*Honest, Critical Feedback"*

As we saw with Claire's "Everything is wonderful!" style, and even in Al's polite-and-perfunctory style to some extent, many people have a hard time giving direct—especially negative—feedback. Often they fear that the interaction will become uncomfortable or that it will become more involved than they want it to be. And so they shy away from meaningful interaction, from communications that hold any possibility of getting "out of control." The problem, of course, is that co-workers who always get cheerful good news, as they do from Claire, or consistent, detached politeness, as they do from Al, often come to wonder, *What's really going on with her/him?* The positive feedback that they do receive may come to be viewed with suspicion, if not outright distrust.

There are several steps that may be taken by people wanting to improve the accuracy of their evaluative feedback and the authenticity of their positive interactions with associates.

• First, assess why you are holding back from giving other than cheerful or perfunctory feedback. Do you fear that criticism might be taken as personal negation or that more than perfunctory praise might open a Pandora's box of emotional response? Identify what's holding you back, and then begin to examine if the fear is well grounded.

• Choose a specific person, someone with whom you work fairly frequently and someone around whose work you have some specific concern. Commit to bringing *the* concern up with that person. The concern you choose should involve a specific action or incident. Focus explicitly on the event, not the person. Tell yourself that you *can* give warranted praise and criticism honestly and positively and that both are useful and can be appreciated. Remember that *no* feedback or the suspicion that someone won't tell you even if you do something extraordinary (either positive or negative!) can be far more damaging to another's self-esteem and efficient productivity than honest feedback, supportively given.

• Engage in image rehearsal. Imagine yourself complimenting the person *and* criticizing the aspect of performance that's lacking (e.g., "You got the report out in record time; I really appreciate that. I have concern with the graphics in the last section. They were difficult to read; they looked as if they might have been hurriedly done. Let's work on things next time so that we can get the graphics into the same great shape you achieved with the rest of the report").

## Changing Styles: Your Choice

One of the primary assumptions of this book is that personal satisfaction with our jobs and our job performances themselves will be enhanced to the extent that the workplace respects personal style. There is no doubt that getting the job done usually requires conformity to many workplace requirements (e.g., the responsibilities we must fulfill, the hours we are at work, the reasons for which we may take time off, etc.). But there is also no doubt that work performance for most of us has the potential for moving into the excellent range when we, as individuals, have significant room for exercising personal style, abilities, skills, and interests. When we exercise these at work we usually develop high levels of commitment—an emotional concern for the job and our job performance that usually underlies workplace success.

Part of personal style involves the ways in which we characteristically experience, express, and respond to human emotions. Most of us developed the core of our personal styles at home within the family as we grew up and then again as we began entering the adult world on our own terms.

People whose styles fit well with their work environments usually don't need to make many changes in personal style, if any. Others, however, find that they want to make major or minor adjustments—alterations that will bring personal behavior closer to personal values or personal behavior closer to their workplace culture's "way of doing things." Many such employees begin to make changes as they enter and gain experience on their jobs; many will find helpful the suggestions throughout this chapter focused on specific alterations they may have sought but found difficult.

A focus on personal styles of experiencing and expressing emotion at work runs at least two important risks.

One risk lies in assuming that the individual and his or her style can control the situation. This is simply not so. Individual attitudes and behaviors in any given situation are a function of the individual's *interaction with* the setting. The style that an individual brings to a work environment emerges from personality and personal history, but as it develops in the work setting, it responds—at least to some extent—to the demands, needs, and culture of the specific workplace. And in fact, almost all functional styles of emotional experience and expression that we have identified *do* merge individual style preferences with workplace needs and demands. Equally important is the other side of this coin: Just as the transaction between an individual and a given workplace influences the employee's "purely personal" style, so, too, does the individual influence workplace expectations. It is precisely because the development of style represents a transaction between a person and the work environment that so many of the people whose stories we used in the "styles" chapters found themselves adjusting and modifying their styles over the years. Their transactions also resulted in many modifications of the work cultures that dominated these people's work settings.

A second risk lies in a disbelieving query that we've heard from time to time: When you talk about individual styles, are you suggesting that people should run around yelling and crying whenever they want to at work? That question comes from a fear that any changes in commonly accepted workplace standards for individual behavior at work may cause emotions to run without restraint.

Freewheeling emotional expression, constrained only by an individual's personal sense of effectiveness and satisfaction is never appropriate at work. The development and acceptance of individual styles of emotional expression mean, rather, that individuals and workplaces should assume—more than many do now—that work-related emotions should be dealt with at work in ways that use the experience to increase personal effectiveness and workplace productivity.

Over the course of time that we spent collecting information about the variety of ways that people have of dealing with emotions at work in the workplace, we shared many of our developing strategies for change with the people we interviewed. In many cases people contacted us later to tell "just one more story" and to report on a given change strategy's success. As we culled through this information we came to the conclusion that the process of changing personal emotional style in the workplace does not have to be a particularly demanding nor difficult task—if certain basic principles are involved.

The people who reported the most significant and useful changes are the ones who had effectively identified their own styles, identified those work culture dynamics that evoked their emotional responses at work, had a clear idea of what styles they wished to adopt, and spent a little time on their personal change project each day or each week. When these basic elements were present, our respondents were able to use the strategies we had suggested with maximum effectiveness. And many of them were able to devise their own strategies, techniques that were uniquely suited to their particular work situations.

Change doesn't have to be painful, and it doesn't have to be difficult. It does require commitment and a fairly clear sense of where you are and where you want to go. And change that results in progress is always worth it. In fact, sometimes the experience of that kind of worthwhile personal change finds us getting a little emotional! We might even laugh or cry over it.

# Notes

1. Tavris, Carol, *Anger, the Misunderstood Emotion* (New York: Simon & Schuster, 1984), p. 23.
2. *Samuel Pepys' Diary, Cameo Classics,* ed. Willis L. Parker (New York: Grosset and Dunlap, 1933), p. 162.
3. Carnegie, Dale, *How to Win Friends and Influence People,* rev. ed. (New York: Pocket Books, 1941), pp. 60–61.
4. Ibid., p. 121.
5. Averill, James R., "Studies on Anger and Aggression: Implications for Theories of Emotion," *American Psychologist,* vol. 38, no. 11 (1983), p. 1150.
6. *The NIV Study Bible,* New International Version, Kenneth Barker, gen. ed. (Grand Rapids, Mich.: Zondervan Publishers, 1985), John 11:33–35.
7. Dostoyevsky, Fyodor, *The Brothers Karamazov,* tr. David Magarshack (New York: Penguin Books, 1958), p. 86.
8. Lewis, C. S., *The Last Battle* (New York: Collier Books, Macmillan, 1956), p. 158.
9. Cleaver, Eldridge, *Soul on Ice* (New York: McGraw-Hill Book Company, 1968) pp. 37–38.
10. *The NIV Study Bible,* loc. cit., Genesis 45:1–2, 14–15; Genesis 46:29.
11. Cousins, Norman, *Anatomy of an Illness as Perceived by the Patient* (New York: Norton, 1979), p. 76.
12. Yates, Richard, "The Best of Everything," in *New Sounds in American Fiction,* ed. Gordon Lish (Menlo Park, Calif.: Cummings Publishing Company, 1961), pp. 53, 56–58.
13. Stone, Irving, *The Agony and the Ecstasy: A Novel of Michaelangelo* (Garden City, N.Y.: Doubleday & Company, 1961), pp. 39–40.
14. The study involved a randomly selected sample of all employees in the organization. Of the 500 employees originally identified as members of the sample, 211 (41 percent) returned survey questionnaires. The final sample included employees in several occupational groups: professional personnel (50 percent); managers and administrators (20 percent); secretaries (20 percent); and technicians (10 percent). Respondents were asked if they had ever cried at work; they were also asked to describe reasons for their workplace tears and their responses to the tears of others on the job.
15. Iacocca, Lee, with William Novak, *Lee Iacocca: An Autobiography* (New York: Bantam Books, 1984), p. xiv.
16. Deal., Terrence E., and Allan A. Kennedy, *Corporate Cultures: The Rites and Rituals of Corporate Life* (Reading, Mass.: Addison-Wesley, 1982), p. 110.
17. Speech before the U.S. Conference of Mayors, reported in *The Tennesseean,* June 14, 1987, p. 41B.
18. Cosby, Bill, *Fatherhood* (New York: Berkley Books, 1986), pp. 76–77.

# References

Averill, James R. "Studies on Anger and Aggression: Implications for Theories of Emotion." *American Psychologist,* vol. 38, no. 11 (1983), pp. 1145–60.

Berger, Peter L., and Thomas Luckman. *The Social Construction of Reality: A Treatise in the Sociology of Knowledge.* Garden City, New York: Anchor Books, Doubleday and Company, 1967.

Becker, Ernest. *Revolution in Psychiatry.* New York: The Free Press, 1964.

Carnegie, Dale. *How to Win Friends and Influence People,* revised ed. New York: Pocket Books, 1941.

Cleaver, Eldridge. *Soul on Ice.* New York: McGraw-Hill Book Company, 1968.

Cosby, Bill. *Fatherhood.* New York: Berkley Books, 1986.

Cousins, Norman. *Anatomy of an Illness as Perceived by the Patient.* New York: Bantam Books, 1979.

Deal, Terrence E. and Allan A. Kennedy. *Corporate Cultures; The Rites and Rituals of Corporate Life.* Reading, Mass. Addison-Wesley, 1982.

Dostoyevsky, Fyodor. *The Brothers Karamazov* tr. David Magarshack. New York: Penguin Books, 1958. Originally published 1818.

Frey William H., II, with Muriel Langseth. *Crying: The Mystery of Tears.* Minneapolis: Winston Press, 1985.

Hoover-Dempsey, Kathleen V.; Jeanne M. Plas; and Barbara S. Wallston. "Tears and Weeping among Professional Women: In Search of New Understanding. *Psychology of Women Quarterly,* vol. 10 (1986) pp. 19–34.

Iacocca, Lee, with William Novak. *Iacocca: An Autobiography.* New York: Bantam Books, 1984.

Izard, Carroll E. *The Face of Emotion.* New York: Appleton-Century-Crofts, 1971.

James, William. *The Principles of Psychology.* New York: Dover, 1950. 2 vols.

Lazarus, Arnold A. *In the Mind's Eye: The Power of Imagery for Personal Enrichment.* New York: Guilford Publications, 1985.

Lewis, C. S. *The Last Battle.* New York: Collier Books, Macmillan Publishing Company, 1956.

Maccoby, Eleanor E. *Social Development.* New York: Harcourt Brace Jovanovich, Inc., 1980.

Miller, Alice. *The Drama of the Gifted Child.* New York: Basic Books, 1981.

*The NIV Study Bible.* New International Version, gen. ed. Kenneth Barker. Grand Rapids, Mich.: Zondervan Publishers, 1985.

Pepys, Samuel. *Samuel Pepys' Diary,* Cameo Classics, ed. Willis L. Parker. New York: Grosset and Dunlap, 1933.

Peters, Thomas J., and Robert H. Waterman, Jr. *In Search of Excellence: Lessons from America's Best-Run Companies.* New York: Warner Books, 1982.

Stearns, Carol Zisowitz, and Peter N. Stearns. *Anger: The Struggle for Emotional Control in America's History.* Chicago: The University of Chicago Press, 1986.

Stone, Irving. *The Agony and the Ecstasy: A Novel of Michaelangelo.* Garden City, N.Y.: Doubleday & Company, 1961.

Strongman, K.T. *The Psychology of Emotion.* New York: John Wiley and Sons, 1987.

Tavris, Carol. *Anger: The Misunderstood Emotion.* New York: Simon and Schuster, 1984.

Whyte, William Hollingsworth. *The Organzational Man.* New York: Simon and Schuster, 1956.

Wilson, Sloan. *The Man in the Gray Flannel Suit.* New York: Simon and Schuster, 1955.

Yates, Richard. "The Best of Everything." in *New Sounds in American Fiction,* ed. Gordon Lish. Originally published 1954, Copyright by Street and Smith Publications, Inc. Menlo Park: Cummings Publishing Company, 1969, pp. 47–60.

# Index